photographs by George Mott

# of Ireland

*Domestic architecture
from the medieval castle to the Edwardian villa*

BRIAN DE BREFFNY AND ROSEMARY FFOLLIOTT

A Studio Book
The Viking Press · New York

For Sita–Maria
and to the memory of
Eve

Title page: Leinster House, Dublin, now *Dail Eireann*

Copyright © 1975 by Thames and Hudson Ltd., London

Published in 1975 by The Viking Press, Inc.
625 Madison Avenue, New York, N.Y. 10022

SBN 670–38102–0

Library of Congress catalog card number: 74–7509

Printed and bound in Great Britain by
Jarrold and Sons Ltd., Norwich

Contents

FOREWORD   *page* 6

1   *Early domestic buildings* 1100–1600   7

2   *From the Plantations to Cromwell* 1585–1660   31

3   *From the Restoration to the Battle of the Boyne*
     1660–1690   57

4   *The sixty years of peace after Boyne* 1690–1750 83

5   *The lack of a master hand* 1750–1780   123

6   *Neo-Classicism comes to Ireland* 1780–1800   153

7   *From the Union to the Famine* 1801–1846   183

8   *Victorian and Edwardian building in Ireland*
     1846–1914   211

ACKNOWLEDGMENTS   232

FURTHER READING   233

NOTES ON THE TEXT   234

GLOSSARY   237

INDEX   238

Foreword

THIS book is neither an exhaustive encyclopedia of Irish domestic architecture nor a catalogue of Irish houses, and we wish to stress that the houses illustrated or mentioned in the text are our personal selection. The process of elimination, made in joint consultation, was often difficult, sometimes agonizing. We agreed that one of our main criteria in selecting houses to photograph for illustration must be, as far as possible, an unaltered appearance so that the reader would get the best possible idea of what the house originally looked like. This is the reason why we have not shown more interiors. So far as mentioning houses was concerned, we quickly realized that it would be easy to produce a book this size on each one of our eight chapter periods. Therefore we concentrated on houses still in existence and leave it to others to revive the many interesting, vanished buildings. Even so, some beautiful and even important houses have had to be omitted or only barely mentioned. Here our choice for inclusion has generally been in favour of houses that have not recently been documented in other publications. Together we have made an effort to reach a compromise, treating a fair cross-section that is representative of the development of domestic architecture in Ireland at all levels over several centuries. The history of a house should not be separated from that of the people who built and lived in it, and thus domestic architecture cannot be divorced from family history, social history or political events. Dates of marriage, of inheritance or of local troubles, for example, have a vital bearing on dates of building and rebuilding. Within the restrictions of our space we have tried to place the houses against their contemporary backgrounds.

BREFFNY
ROSEMARY FFOLLIOTT
GEORGE MOTT

Rome–Dublin

CHAPTER I

Early domestic buildings

1100—1600

THE VISITOR TO DUBLIN can hardly fail to be impressed by the high quality of the gold ornaments from the Irish Bronze Age now on display in the National Museum. They indicate a degree of civilization quite remarkable for western Europe, and in craftsmanship are comparable to work done in the Near East. Little is known of these early people, how they lived, or in what manner of houses, though it has been surmised that their dwellings were within the circular earthworks known as raths or ringforts, or (when formed of stone) cashels, whose remains can best be discerned by aerial photography.

Though Ireland never belonged to the Roman Empire, by the fifth century it had become an outpost of Christianity, and England was in part Christianized from Ireland. Ireland was earnestly Christian, and its highly developed and characteristic art seems to have been almost entirely directed towards religious objects, to the neglect of secular ones. Early Gaelic society was wholly pastoral. Though the first towns were founded by the Viking invaders during the ninth century, these remained largely outside the mainstream of Gaelic life, and it was only after the Anglo-Norman invasion of 1170 that towns and fortresses, with the economic needs they produced, began to impinge on the rural-minded population.

The rapid spread of the Cistercian monasteries introduced a new concept of ecclesiastical architecture which was able to develop during a period of comparative prosperity in the twelfth century. There are many beautiful remains from this time, such as the doorway of Clonfert Cathedral, Co. Galway; the monastery of Clonmacnoise, Co. Offaly; Boyle Abbey, Co. Roscommon, and Jerpoint Abbey, Co. Kilkenny. Although there are these substantial remains of great church buildings (and what survives is only a small proportion of what originally existed), there are very few remnants of domestic buildings, other than the castles introduced by the great Norman lords; and even the largest of the castles, though well designed and stoutly constructed, had scarcely any embellishments and few concessions to comfort.

In the remote Dingle Peninsula, Co. Kerry, where timber was scarce and loose stone plentiful, stand extensive remains of monastic settlements of the twelfth century and earlier. Some of these are beehive-shaped dwellings, known as *cloghauns*, which have neither window nor chimney and an entrance so low as to necessitate crawling. They are often grouped in clusters and enclosed by a wall, somewhat in the manner of the ancient cashels. They served as cells for the monks, and probably also for secular dwellings, and have continued to be built as animal shelters into the present century.

A doorway of St Brendan's House, parish of Kilmalkedar, Co. Kerry

A window of St Brendan's House

Near the twelfth-century Romanesque church at Kilmalkedar is a two-storey medieval structure, now known as St Brendan's House, which was probably the priest's residence. A few fields away, in the townland of Caherdorgan North, and the walls of another medieval house, now called the Chancellor's House, with two rooms and a baking-oven still in a good state of preservation. Both buildings have thick, unmortared walls, wider at the bottom and constructed on the same principles as the old stone hermitages, one stone overlapping the next with sufficient bearing to sustain the weight while advancing the arch. This technique has been in use for centuries, and still survives in the dry-stone walls which separate the fields in the west of Ireland. It is a construction that lends itself to easy demolition, which doubtless accounts for the fact that so few of these buildings remain, although some of the western chieftains and landowners must have had dry-stone dwellings of varying sizes and importance.

Early medieval Ireland was divided into a complex mesh of small kingdoms and principalities within a system of constantly changing vassaldom. The form of inheritance and succession practised under the Brehon Laws was an unique one: the heir, or tanist, was elected from within the sept, and the bulk of the estate enjoyed by the late chieftain passed to the newly elected successor rather than to the natural heirs. This may have been one reason, coupled with the deep religious convictions of the time, for the Gaelic princes' attention to the endowment of church foundations rather than to the adornment of their own residences. The native kings of Ireland were constantly at war among themselves and brutal forays, resulting in the sacking of the loser's property, were the regular order of the day. Livestock, being the most valuable asset of a pastoral people as well as the easiest prey, had to be protected. It was therefore essential to enclose the area round the dwelling so that the cattle might be driven in at night or in time of trouble. These enclosures were the direct descendants of the ringforts and cashels, and were known as bawns. The bawn and its wall survived in use for centuries, and some can still be seen attached to inhabited residences today, as for example at Springfield Castle.

The Norman invasion that began in 1170 ended in October 1175 when Henry II, King of England, was recognized as overlord of all Ireland, and Rory O'Connor was accepted as the *Ard Rí* (High King) of the as yet unconquered parts. The Anglo-Norman knights who proceeded to settle in Ireland frequently became embroiled in the endless internecine wars of the Gaelic chiefs, in addition to waging their own wars of conquest. By 1250, a mere eighty years after their arrival, they had over-run two-thirds of the island. Their first constructions were not stone strongholds but great motes of earth, sometimes as high as 40 feet, and surmounted by a battle-mented timber palisade with loopholes to emit arrows. Remains of these earth-works abound, the largest number being in Leinster.

Having occupied an area, the Normans imposed a certain peace and order where previously there had been only endless raids and counter-raids, and, in order to preserve their own supremacy, soon began to raise permanent structures. Both Carrickfergus Castle, Co. Antrim, and Trim Castle, Co. Meath are splendid examples of these early Norman fortresses. There is considerable speculation as to the exact date when Trim was built. The great sandstone castle replaced an earlier timber one, and seems to have been completed between 1212 and 1220, because in 1210 when King John stayed at Trim the then-existing castle was too small to accommodate his court. At its zenith the complex must have been a

8

spectacular sight. The keep stood in a bawn of over three acres, the perimeter of the bawn wall being 1,500 feet. The keep walls are 11 feet thick and contain only stairs, whereas English keeps of this period usually incorporated mural passages and chambers. Instead, Trim had four chambers projecting from the central block. Their walls were relatively thin, and the inclusion of so many vulnerable corners shows the architect's disregard for maximum defence, though this defect was mitigated by the castle's situation on the River Boyne and its extensive outer defences. An interesting reconstruction of Trim as it might have been about 1250 shows the curtain wall with its five projecting L-shaped turrets interspersed along the south and east sides, and two entrances with barbicans containing narrow walled passageways jutting outwards from the main gates.[1] These outer defences were built about 1250. Although the over-all effect of the castle was both massive and splendid, it is noteworthy that there was little or no attempt at decoration, except in the chapel.

Round and polygonal keeps within curtain walls were also built during the twelfth and thirteenth centuries. These were badly adapted for domestic purposes, precluding amenities such as a great hall which could be readily accommodated within a rectangular building. The meagre remnants of a polygonal keep and its curtain wall may be seen at Shanid, Co. Limerick; and at Dundrum, Co. Down, there are substantial remains of a round keep and part of its wall. A round keep that has been preserved and restored (for its upper part is modern) is the castle at Nenagh, Co. Tipperary. Here the four-storey keep itself formed part of the perimeter of the walled fortress instead of standing detached within the bawn. There were four smaller flanking towers along the curtain walls. Such a keep may have been somewhat vulnerable, but its walls are sixteen feet thick at the base and the entrance doorway on the first floor was approached by a removable ladder.

9

The Hook Lighthouse,
parish of Hook,
Co. Wexford

Of all the circular keeps, the one with the most romantic and unbroken history is that built by Raymond le Gros at The Hook, in the extreme south of Co. Wexford, between 1170 and 1184. It replaced the iron-basket fire-beacon established there by the Welsh saint Dubhan in the fifth century, and subsequently maintained by the Augustinian monks as a warning to sailors off this long, dangerous peninsula at the mouth of Waterford harbour. The plan illustrated shows its lay-out: one tower inside another with stairs filling the intervening space. The walls vary in thickness from nine to almost thirteen feet and have deep window-embrasures. There are three storeys of vaulted chambers, and for generations the ground level was used as a fuel-store, the first floor as the assistant lightkeeper's quarters and the upper floor as the head keeper's quarters. In 1657 the tower was described as 'white-limed for a Land mark', and as having 'a great fire kept on the Topp thereof'.[2] Two decades later the coal fire was replaced by a lamp. Today, fitted with a modern superstructure and the best twentieth-century lantern equipment, this otherwise virtually unchanged twelfth-century castle, with its stairs and three chambers, still serves the purpose for which it was built, though its staff now lives in the adjacent dwellings. It is the oldest station in the Irish lighthouse service, and older than any in Great Britain.

The oldest part of Granagh (sometimes called 'Granny') Castle, Co. Kilkenny, consists of three round turrets, part of the external fortifications, with their joining curtain wall rising from the River Suir. These date from the twelfth century. There are many later additions to this beautifully situated stronghold: the tall, square keep belongs to the fourteenth or fifteenth century, and the oriel-window in the south wall to the seventeenth century. Granagh had once a fine two-storey hall, whose surviving wall shows an example of vine-leaf carving and an interesting motif of St Michael the Archangel holding his scales on the Day of Judgment. Granagh was originally owned by the Le Poers or Powers, and then by the Butlers of Ormond who lost it to the Cromwellian troops in 1650. Its present state of preservation is largely due to the zeal of George Roch, who in 1827 repaired the ruins at his own expense and under the superintendence of Edward Rorke, a Waterford mason. The plaque he set into the wall mentions that while 'this Venerable Fabric was in part demolished during the Civil Wars of unhappy Ireland, the spoliating hands of the thoughtless neighbouring peasantry had nearly completed its destruction'.

All too many castles have been used as convenient quarries, a fate which probably befell the fine circular tower at Grantstown, Co. Leix, which, although evidently intact at the end of the eighteenth century[3] is now extremely ruinous.

The thirteenth-century Castleroche, Co. Louth, is an instance of a castle not wholly designed for defence. It was built, or fortified, by Roesia, daughter of Nicholas de Verdon. The legend is that she promised to marry the architect if she liked the completed building, but when he came to claim her, she had him flung out of a window instead. This is the only report of an architect in Ireland receiving

Granagh (or Granny) Castle, parish of Kilmacow, Co. Kilkenny: outer fortifications over the River Suir

Floor-plan of The Hook, Co. Wexford

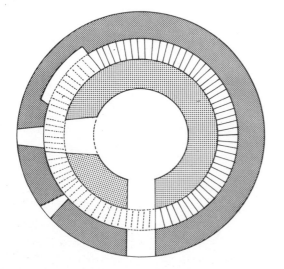

such retribution at the hands of a dissatisfied client, though it is said that Red
Mary meted out similar treatment to her Cromwellian husband at Leamaneh
Castle.

Defence at Castleroche concentrated on the single bawn entrance, a great
twin-towered gateway with a drawbridge, which more or less replaced the keep
as the main fortification. Inside the bawn, built against an angle in the south-
eastern walls and utilizing two of the exterior walls for two of its own sides, stood
a two-storey hall, its upper floor lit by three windows overlooking the valley
to the south. The stone window-seats are an indication of its domestic purpose.
The kitchen and other offices must have been separate buildings within the enclosure.

Architectural fashions changed little in the fourteenth century. Such Irish chiefs
as made treaties with the Anglo-Normans, or otherwise managed to achieve some
stability within their own territories, began to construct castles in emulation of the
invaders. Highly conscious of their rank as sovereign rulers, they did not wish to
be outdone by the alien lords; and they fully appreciated the practical value of a
good stronghold, both in defending their estate and in asserting superiority over
their own troublesome vassals. At Ballintober, Co. Roscommon, are the ruins of a
moated castle built about 1300 by the O'Connors of the Royal House of Connaught
for their main seat, and doubtless inspired by the Norman fortress at Roscommon.
O'Connor's large square castle had an open courtyard with a polygonal tower
at each corner. It was besieged many times, and at least part of the extant ruins
date from an early seventeenth-century restoration, according to an inscription on
a fireplace. This Irish royal residence, though one of the grandest of its time, was
a bleak abode, comparing unfavourably with the beautiful Augustinian Abbey at
Ballintober, Co. Mayo, founded in 1216 by Cathal Crowdearg O'Connor, which
has ribbed vaulting, fascinating carved capitals in the choir and fine carved window-
mouldings. The O'Connors seem to have been more concerned with the salvation
of their souls than with the grandeur of their residence.

Castles in the Norman style, especially of the rectangular type, continued to be
built throughout the fourteenth and into the fifteenth century, though with a
growing emphasis on residential accommodation. At Dunmoe, Co. Meath, there
remain two sides of a castle of about this date. The engraving shows it in 1792,
differing little from its present appearance when viewed from the same angle.
Sited above the Boyne, this fortress had some concern for domesticity as well as
defence.

The most popular castle-type proved a moated, rectangular enclosure with
high walls and round turrets at the corners. The quite considerable ruins of Kilbolane Castle, Co. Cork, demonstrate this plan clearly. Kilbolane was probably
built in the fifteenth century by the de Cogans, but is a continuation of the earlier
form, having stone-vaulted chambers with fireplaces in the turrets. There were
also rooms built against the inside of the curtain walls; and the parapet-walk
linking the towers was possibly originally roofed with timber. Here, too, are the
remains of an ogee-headed light, replacing the plain, round, pointed or segmented
windows of earlier times.

Some fifteenth-century castles had a high arch between two of the projecting
corner towers. Examples of this can be seen at Bunratty, Co. Clare, at Kilclief, Co.
Down, and at Donamon, Co. Galway, which is treated in a later chapter.

Gradually many castles came to include a detached hall standing within their
bawn. Stanyhurst writes:[4]

Banqueting-hall, Askeaton Castle, Co. Limerick: the west wall from across the River Deal. Right: interior showing blind arcade on south wall

So these chieftains . . . own castles, strongly constructed as regards fortification and mass of stone work, with which are united by a close connexion, fairly large and spacious halls, constructed of a compound of potter's earth and mud. These are not securely roofed either with quarried slates, or with rough-hewn stones or tiles, but are as a rule thatched with straw from the fields. In these halls they usually take their meals; they seldom, however, sleep except in the castles, because it is possible for their enemies with great ease to apply to the covering of the halls blazing torches inflamed by the fanning of the wind, since that kind of stuff takes fire very rapidly.

Though lesser halls were of earth and mud (all trace of which has, of course, long since disappeared), the banqueting-halls of the greater lords were spectacular stone buildings. That of the 7th Earl of Desmond, built between 1440 and 1459 beside his castle on the little island in the River Deal at Askeaton, Co. Limerick, is one of the greatest secular buildings of the Irish Middle Ages. The photographs show the great hall as it now appears; a drawing of about 1586 depicts it with what seems to be a slated roof,[5] and an engraving of 1779[6] shows it as roofless but with both gables intact. (In 1712 the Earl of Orrery, an indefatigable builder, had applied to the Government to refit the castle, but this was never done.) The vaulted ground floor contains five rooms or cellars, and has a door to the courtyard, a slit and several windows overlooking the river. The presence here of window-seats indicates that these rooms were intended not only for cellars and stores but also as servants' quarters, though there is no trace of a fireplace, and the kitchen itself may have been a separate construction in the bawn, possibly of mud or timber. A spiral stair of twenty steps leads to the banqueting floor (72 by 31 feet) which is lit by finely carved windows in three walls, some with cinquefoil- and some with quatrefoil-headed lights, and with boldly hollowed hood-mouldings and the remains of rich tracery – decorative details which resemble those in the near-by friary. There is an ambry in each wall at the north-west corner, but no trace anywhere of a fireplace. The south end of the hall was used as a chapel, but the partition has vanished; this south wall has a blind arcade whose arches end in moulded corbels, one of which is decorated with sprigs of roses.

14

The most disgracefully neglected secular medieval buildings in Ireland must be the once-glorious halls at Newcastle West, Co. Limerick. Even in their present sad state these retain clear evidence of their former splendour. A survey of 1583 describes this Desmond Castle as having many buildings within its curtain walls, in addition to a fish-pond, orchards and a three-acre garden. There was a 'great hall' and an 'excellent chamber'. The Great Hall, generally called the Desmond Banqueting-hall, is similar to that at Askeaton, being built over vaulted cellars, but differs in having a four-storey turret at the north-west corner. The main hall, again on the upper floor, is smaller than Askeaton ($52\frac{1}{2}$ by 21 feet), and has ambries and remarkable windows with stone seats in the recesses. There is a chimney, possibly a later addition, for the present chimney-piece with the inscription 'SH 16 (IHS) 38 EH' was brought from Kilmallock during the nineteenth century and will be mentioned again in the next chapter. The floor-level has been altered, but the original level can still be gauged from the joist holes. In the nineteenth century the hall was used by a Masonic Lodge. By 1909 it had become a fitting-shop although the Masonic Chair was still in place. In 1972 this great remnant of the Desmond affluence had sunk to being a bingo hall.

A window in the Desmond Banqueting-hall

The single-storey building, called the 'excellent chamber' in 1583, was used as a cinema in recent years. Then its roof was destroyed by fire and it now stands deserted, choked by weeds, the little garden wholly overgrown. This chamber measures $80\frac{1}{3}$ by 36 feet externally and was probably a reception-hall of the Earls. Its windows are of very superior workmanship and design; one of these, in the south wall and now much defaced, is illustrated.

Again not to be outdone by the Old English (as families of Norman descent like the Fitzgeralds of Desmond became known, to distinguish them from later arrivals), the Old Irish ruling families likewise proceeded to build themselves halls. One such was O'Rorke's hall at Dromahaire, Co. Leitrim, where the rulers of Breffny held court. This massive building was quarried by Sir William Villiers in 1630 to build Dromahaire Castle, but enough survived into the eighteenth century for Bigari to make a drawing of the ruins.[7]

A window in the 'excellent chamber', Newcastle West, Co. Limerick

The primitive manner of life of these Irish chieftains may be gleaned from Captain de Cuellar's account of his adventures in north-west Ireland after he had escaped from his wrecked Armada ship in 1588.[8] Doe, Co. Donegal, was one of the castles to offer help to such stranded Spaniards. It stands in a turreted square bawn on a commanding site in Sheephaven Bay. This stronghold had one of the most chequered histories in Ireland, being constantly taken and retaken between the MacSweeneys (who built it), their kinsmen the O'Donnells, other envious Irish chiefs and the forces of Cromwell and the Stuart kings. During the Williamite Wars a MacSweeney recaptured it, only to lose it again after a short time to the English.

Today the structure shows the extensive alterations and repairs made by the Harts who lived there in the eighteenth and nineteenth centuries; but despite these, its medieval aspect is still apparent.

Though no less hospitable to Armada sailors in distress, the businesslike and enterprising Sorley Boy McDonnell of Dunluce Castle, Co. Antrim, hired a Scots captain to salvage what he could from the wrecked galleass *Girona*, and the following year duly applied the proceeds to the rebuilding and modernizing of his castle.[9] De Cuellar was convinced the Irish had obtained 'great wealth in jewels and money' from the Armada.[10]

Decoration around a
window of
Ballynacarriga Castle,
parish of Ballymoney,
Co. Cork

Ballynacarriga Castle, Co. Cork, is of an unusually domestic nature. It consists of a large, strong tower with a good system of privies, wide stairs and spacious rooms with fine fireplaces. It is generally stated[11] to have been built by the O'Hurleys, but the initials inscribed on a window on the top floor are 'R▽MC▽C' which hardly seem to fit Randal Hurley and Catherine Cullinane, as is invariably claimed.[12] It is much more likely they are those of a McCarthy who held sway in the district, though admittedly pardons of 1601 do show O'Hurleys as of Ballynacarriga. The castle is generally considered older than 1585, which date is in a window-recess on the top floor. The window-carvings are an interesting feature and include emblems of the Passion, the Crucifixion and angels, as well as a heraldic bird and a selection of geometrical patterns. This top room is said to have been used as a church in Penal times.

Of course not everyone was an Irish chief or a Norman lord. The greater part of the population was engaged in humble agricultural pursuits, and most people lived in very simple dwellings of wattle and daub, wattle plastered with clay, or, at very best, in plain timber huts with the refinement of a chimney. The interiors were extremely primitive and there was seldom any furniture. It is easy to see why these dwellings have vanished without trace: their survival period must always have been brief, though longer than that of the seasonal huts or booleys built of branches on summer pasturing grounds.

Before the Norse invasion in the ninth century, towns had been unknown in Ireland, but the Vikings established a line of port-towns along the east and south coasts, with one town (Limerick) in the west. These settlements were composed of houses huddled tightly together within town walls, and all formed nuclei for later medieval towns. Like the rural dwellings, the earliest town-houses were of clay and wattle, but these were soon joined by stone houses; and as the extent of the town walls was gradually increased and town life and trade prospered under the Anglo-Normans, so old towns became larger and new small towns sprang up.

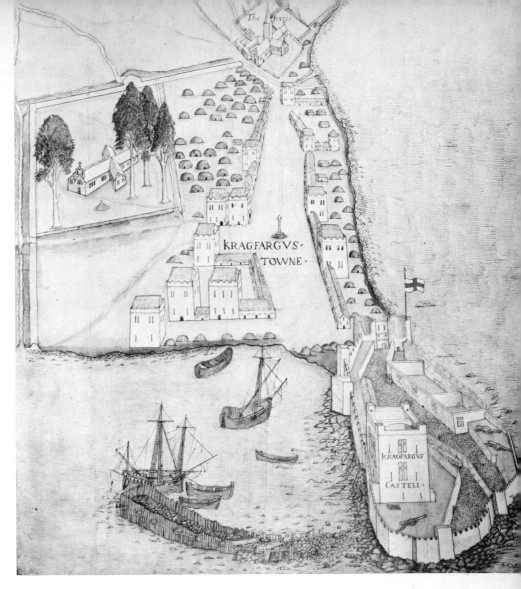

The Freres

KRAGFARGVS· TOWNE·

KRAGFARGVS· CASTELL·

By the fourteenth century quite substantial urban communities had developed, with prosperous merchants building themselves solid houses. Usually the town walls were adequate protection, but fortified town-houses also existed. A Letter Patent of 1310 allowed Geoffrey de Mortone to build towers and defensible embattled houses on the great bridge at Dublin.[13] Town tower-houses existed elsewhere, for example at Downpatrick, Co. Down, and there are interesting fifteenth- and sixteenth-century ones at Ardglass in the same county.

The view of Carrickfergus, Co. Antrim, dating from the late sixteenth century shows clearly the lay-out of a town of this period. It had a big fortified castle, church, friary, several tall tower-houses (apparently thatched), rows of single-storey thatched stone houses and a large number of windowless, one-room mud cabins.

A Statute of 1429 had offered a £10 subsidy to every 'liege-man of our Lord the King' within the area known as the Pale (Counties Dublin, Meath, Kildare and Louth) who chose to build a suitably embattled or fortified tower 20 by 16 feet, with a minimum height of 40 feet.[14]

Carrickfergus, Co. Antrim. A drawing made in the late sixteenth century

17

Carlingford, Co. Louth, on the northern edge of the Pale and magnificently situated between hill and sea overlooking a fine natural harbour, was a thriving medieval town. The imposing ruins of King John's castle still dominate it today, and there are also a few relics of the fifteenth-century town. The tower-house-type building now know as the Mint was presumably once used for such a purpose (although it is considered later than the Mint established in 1457).[15] It is almost square (29 by 27 feet), soundly built of rubble with granite quoins, and it is safe to assume that its external appearance is that of the better town-houses in Carlingford in the second half of the fifteenth century. It is three storeys high (each storey being about eight to nine feet) and was topped by a garret, partly in the roof. As was usual with such towers, it had a wall-walk at roof-level constructed of large flagstones, but there is little sign of fortification. The mullioned windows are decorated with fine Celtic motifs, evidence of the revival of the great native art of more than five centuries earlier. The interior is remarkably plain, its main features being a couple of stone window-seats and cupboard-recesses and a round-headed door on the first floor leading to a garderobe at the back of the house. Stair and floors were of timber, but as there are no fireplaces there must have been an open central hearth or brazier on the top floor, with a smoke-hole in the roof.

Tower-houses were built all through the countryside in ever-increasing numbers during the fifteenth century. Many factors contributed to their development. The gradual collapse of the old Gaelic order – steadily being undermined by Anglo-Norman domination – the emergence of towns and of external trade with the consequent more complex economic structure, the increase in population and the development of arable cultivation, all helped to produce an influx of people into hitherto hardly inhabited areas. Some of the largest Irish estates were broken up,

The Mint, Carlingford

and the freeholders on the new, smaller estates, as well as the leaseholders of the Norman lords, began to find it desirable to reside in their frontier areas to supervise their property. Life in such districts was even more precarious than elsewhere; apart from local and family feuds and endless political troubles, there was constant danger from marauding bands of robbers who burned, pillaged and sacked undefended houses of any substance. Villages clustered round the parish church and manor-house, like those of rural England, would have stood no chance in Ireland. The tower-house proved the answer. A mini-fortress, it retained the old idea of a bawn, where for centuries cattle had been sheltered with the great gates shut and guarded at night. The most fertile areas, like Limerick, Cork, Tipperary, Clare and Galway abound in these tower-houses; and indeed between them the five counties still contain about fifteen hundred castles.[16] From the fifteenth to the late seventeenth century the tower-house was the typical residence of the gentry. Some tower-houses even continue in use to the present day, usually integrated into later, more commodious buildings.

The tall, narrow buildings, while not as impregnable as the great strongholds, none the less were robust enough to withstand the ordinary perils of their time (which by the early sixteenth century included firearms and small cannon); indeed some tower-houses did manage to resist minor sieges. There were usually four, and sometimes five, floors. For safety under attack the residential quarters were almost always on the top storey. The illustration shows the floor-plans of Clara Castle, Co. Kilkenny, a typical tower-house. There were generally one or two rooms on each level and a stone stair, either winding within the walls in the old style as at Clara, or rising straight and built against an outer wall, as at Creagh Castle, Co. Cork.

19

The ceilings were either stone-vaulted or formed of timber carried on stone corbels. The ground-floor chamber, windowless for reasons of defence and thus very dark, must have been used for stores and possibly domestic animals, including several species now relegated to the farmyard. At Clara the first floor is divided into two rooms, the larger with wall-cupboards, the smaller with a 'murder-hole' covering the entrance below, and big enough to allow the use of spear, pike or gun on unwelcome callers. This floor was normally occupied by the stewards or guards. The second floor repeats the lay-out of two rooms, the smaller evidently a bedchamber and the larger having a fireplace and two mural passages leading to slits in the tower corners; one of the passages continues further to a mural garderobe. This floor was presumably for the use of the more important retainers, or possibly for an overflow of the family. The third floor contained the principal sleeping-chamber with a latrine in the wall, and a smaller chamber with separate entrance off the spiral stair. On this level at Clara there is an unusual feature: a long narrow secret chamber in the thickness of the walls, reached only through an opening disguised as the seat of a garderobe on the floor above. In time of danger valuables could be hidden here, and indeed also members of the family, should such need arise, confident that even the most rapacious robbers would not contemplate exploring the depths of a medieval privy. On the top floor was the most important room of all: a single, large apartment with a fireplace. This was the general living-room, where, with the safety afforded by height, the inhabitants could enjoy sizeable windows. It had four wall-cupboards, a slop-stone and a timber ceiling, above which was a loft, undoubtedly used as a sleeping-place. A narrow mural stair led by way of the turret to the roof-walk, which served for both gutters and a look-out. Tower-houses were roofed by timber rafters supporting slates, stone flags or, in rare instances, thatch. Very few now retain any roof; but Clara's floor-timbers do still remain in position. They are oak planks, about a foot wide,

Floor-plans of Clara
Castle, parish of Clara,
Co. Kilkenny

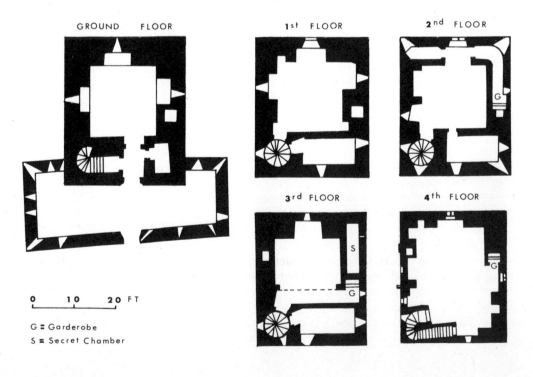

GROUND FLOOR   1st FLOOR   2nd FLOOR

3rd FLOOR   4th FLOOR

0   10   20 FT

G = Garderobe
S = Secret Chamber

20

resting on wall-plates which, in turn, are carried on stone corbels. Their survival
may be due to the fact that Clara was used as the residence of the Catholic curate
in the late nineteenth century. In most other tower-houses the floors have disappeared, though usually the corbels can be seen. At Clara, as in many other tower-
houses of this period, there is some attempt at simple decoration: the windows are
mostly square-headed with an ogee curve; most of the openings are chamfered on
the outside and there are also some round-headed windows.

Actually there is a surprising uniformity about these tower-houses; contemporary
accounts, such as the much-quoted one of Luke Gernon about 1620,[17] enable us
to form a clear idea of the standard domestic arrangements. As already stated,
the living-room was almost always on the top floor and here the guests, and also
some of the family and servants, slept after dining. Furniture was sparse; at most a
table with benches or stools, a chest or perhaps a settle; in the chamber, at best a
bed without hangings, at worst rushes or bracken on the floor.

Creagh Castle, Co. Cork, is another well-preserved tower-house. Its windows
are deeply recessed, and on the third floor the main room, entered through an
arched doorway, has the innovation of a gallery on two sides at half the height of the
room, and two small chambers beneath the gallery at one end. Here, too, are
internal garderobes and a fine pair of ogee-headed lights with square hood-mouldings. The house remained in occupation into the eighteenth century.

21

0   10   20 FT

Section of Belvelly
Castle, parish of Clonmel,
Co. Cork.

Above right: Springfield
Castle, parish of
Killagholehane, Co.
Limerick

Belvelly Castle, an eighty-foot-high tower, built by the Hodnets in the late fif-teenth century, commanded an important position in Cork Harbour (p. 49). A mortgage of 1573 refers to 'Edmundus Hodnet capitanus de castro de Bellvellie in magna insula'. [18] Eight years later Sir Walter Ralegh petitioned to have the castle bestowed upon himself, describing it as 'brokendown', no doubt to minimize its value. In 1636 Peter Courthorpe rented it at £60 per annum, but had apparently al-ready been resident there for some time, as his son, later Sir Peter Courthorpe, Member of Parliament for Cork, was born there in 1624.[19] The elder Peter was still living at Belvelly when he died about 1652.[20] In 1756 Smith noted a broken armorial escutcheon which he believed to be that of Hodnet, over the door.[21] In 1861 Gibson remarked on the beautiful vaulting of Belvelly, mentioning that the marks of the twigs on which the plaster arches had been turned looked as fresh as if the work had only recently been executed.[22] The section of Belvelly illustrated shows the in-ternal lay-out: it had latrines, large and small chambers and a slop-stone. Struc-turally it would have been easier to have continued the stairs unbroken up through the tower, but the break was designed to prevent the guards deserting their post, since they could not do so without crossing the main chamber in full view of its occupants. There is no trace of any fireplace, and the main chamber must have been like many that Gernon visited, where the hearth was in the middle of the hall. It can hardly have been a comfortable residence for the prosperous Courthorpes from Kent, even though there may have been additional outbuildings on the ground-level; a now-blocked doorway, north of the present door, could have given access to these.

Springfield Castle, Co. Limerick, is a well-preserved four-storey sixteenth-century tower-house of the Fitzgeralds, with crow-stepped gables, a mural stair and the usual stone vaulting on the ground floor. A later house was built within the bawn. The large eighteenth-century mansion of the Lords Muskerry, who inherited the property through a Fitzgerald heiress, was burned in the Civil War in 1923 and replaced by the house adjoining the tower, as shown in the illustration. This is now the private residence of the present Lord Muskerry and incorporates part of the old mansion. The aerial view shows how later building followed the line of the old bawn, of which the tower formed an outer corner. It has a good example of a deep firing-hole covering the approach to the doorway. Firing-holes were a regular feature; shorter ones also served as peep-holes, while the largest size permitted the dexterous use of a lance to prod undesirables.

Aerial view of Springfield Castle

Thoor Ballylee, parish of
Kiltartan, Co. Galway

The four-storey sixteenth-century tower-house, Ballylee, Co. Galway, now
famous as Thoor Ballylee, was restored as a residence in the 1920s by the poet
William Butler Yeats. His verse commemorating this event is carved on a tablet
in the wall:

> *I, the poet William Yeats,*
> *With old millboards and sea-green slates,*
> *And smithy work from the Gort forge,*
> *Restored this tower for my wife George;*
> *And may these characters remain*
> *When all is ruin once again.*

Thoor Ballylee is now a Yeats Museum and contains a collection of his works, but
its interior is so altered as to give little idea of its former appearance. Its external
aspect, too, has been altered by the windows inserted on the ground floor, as well
as by the shutters, though the romantic situation by the stream is much as the
Reverend D. A. Beaufort described it in 1789,[23] save that then the tower was almost
covered with ivy.

The discomfort endured by the Courthorpes at Belvelly has been mentioned. It
is noteworthy that the English settlers who arrived during the sixteenth century –
families like the Springs from Pakenham, Suffolk, who settled in Co. Kerry, or
the Daunts from Owlpen in Gloucestershire – did not import with them the fashion

24

in houses then current in England. The fact was that conditions in rural Ireland were such that they could not even contemplate living in the type of Tudor manor-house or yeoman farmstead that they had known in England: to paraphrase Cromwell, it was hell or the tower-house.

The great house built in 1568 and subsequent years by 'Black Tom', the anglophile Earl of Ormond, and protected by his defensible medieval castle at Carrick-on-Suir, Co. Tipperary, did copy the style of an English Tudor manor, but it was unique in Ireland. He decorated the long gallery-hall on the first floor with stucco medallions showing busts of his kinswoman, Queen Elizabeth, whom he hoped to entertain there. This gallery-hall was for Ireland an apartment of unprecedented size and magnificence. It had a splendid stucco ceiling and two stone chimney-pieces, the finer of which, dated 1565, states that it was made for Thomas Butler, Earl of Ormond and Ossory. The rest of the house followed the same pretensions to comfort and style: it was constructed of stone and brick, with brick gables and chimneys, and interior partition walls of lath and plaster. There were good stairs, large mullioned windows, a liberal supply of privies and extensive offices round a large cobbled court. Still, the firing-holes above and round the main door serve as a reminder that this was a house in Ireland, not England. It is clear that the household continued to occupy the castle as well as the manor, for in 1663 the Hearth Money Roll[24] lists 'My Lord Duke' at Carrick as having thirty hearths, nearly three times the number in the next-largest house in the county, the Archbishop's Palace at Cashel, which boasted only eleven.

The Castle and Great House, Carrick-on-Suir, Co. Tipperary. Above: detail of the chimney-piece in the Great Hall, dated 1565

25

In some towns, behind the comparative safety of the walls, the sixteenth-century citizens were able to build entirely unfortified houses. For example at Drogheda, Co. Louth, there were many picturesque timber cage-work houses similar to those still surviving at Chester in England, a town which traded with both Dublin and Drogheda. The illustration shows a drawing of the last wooden house of note in Drogheda, made shortly before its demolition in 1825. It stood on the corner of Shop and Laurence Streets, with its principal front towards Shop Street. It was mainly of Irish oak, said to have come from Mellifont Abbey (perhaps stolen at that abbey's dissolution) and the bressummer beam bore the inscription 'Made bi Nicholas Bathe in the ieare of ovr Lord God 1570 bi hiv Mor carpenter.'[25] Bathe's arms were also carved on one of the front timbers. As is usual with such cage-work houses each storey projected somewhat beyond that beneath: the parlour was on the first floor, with compartmented panelling decorated with carved foliage.

Throughout Ireland wooden houses have now totally vanished though they were once numerous; indeed sixteenth-century Dublin consisted mainly of cage-work houses. They suffered severely from the weather (Ireland being damper than England) and as they were seldom owner-occupied did not receive the regular maintenance they needed. In 1766 Harris[26] reported that most of the cage-work houses in Dublin had disappeared, including that reputed to be the oldest in that city, known as the Carbry and mentioned in 1532 as being the residence of the Earl of Kildare. It was in part of this building that Dick's Coffee House was long kept. He also reported on another house at the corner of Skipper's Lane and Cook Street which had been destroyed in 1745. It had a Latin inscription on its bressummer beam stating that it was built by John Lutrel and Joan his wife in the twenty-second year of Queen Elizabeth (1580). The adjoining house, described by Harris as an imposing cage-house, had an inscription over the door 'Robert Evstac an maning 1618'. Both Eustace and Lutrel had served as sheriffs of Dublin.

Cage-work house on corner of Shop Street and Laurence Street, Drogheda, Co. Louth. From a drawing made before 1825

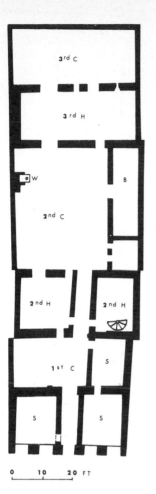

In 1787 the Glebe House at Maghera, Co. Derry, was said to be 'so antique as to be all built with and floored with oak but has had three or four different additions and is yet very ruinous and bad'.[27]

Kilkenny seems to have had virtually no cage-work houses,[28] but it still has examples of sixteenth-century stone houses. A fine one is Rothe House in Parliament Street, purchased by the Kilkenny Archaeological Society and restored by the National Monuments Branch of the Office of Public Works, and now open to the public. Its builder John Rothe, of Norman descent, was a prosperous Catholic merchant in the city and one of its first aldermen. On the façade he placed a handsome carving of his arms with his name in Latin, and at the top of the stone the date 1594. There are still shops in the front of the house where Rothe had his own shop. As his family grew (he and his wife Rose Archer had twelve children) he built another house across the courtyard behind the first one, making a second courtyard behind the new house, in which is a well dated 1604. Later he built yet a third house behind the second courtyard, with a third courtyard behind that, to which he referred in his will in 1619 as 'my new house'. His son Peter had married in 1610 and he and his family occupied one of the houses, all sharing the well and the brewhouse in the third building. John Rothe's will[29] gives explicit instructions as to what was to be common property and what his widow should enjoy. The will also

Rothe House, Parliament Street, Kilkenny. Left: ground plan.
B Brewhouse,
C Courtyard,
H House,
S Shop,
W Well

27

described some of the domestic furnishings which included 'all my drawing tables,[30] bedsteeds, cupboords, livery cupboords, virginalls, wainscott, ioynt-stools, chairs, my great cipresse chest and cipresse countor as they lye and stand in my said dwelling house . . . my pewter, brasse, batry, iron beddings of feathers and flocks . . .' and also mentioned the tapestry coverlet, 'sey greene hangings or curtyns of both my best bedsteeds', in addition to plate, diaper, holland and linen. Undoubtedly merchants like Rothe lived in greater comfort than most of the nobles in remote parts of the countryside. Indeed, in the sixteenth century the Irish Catholic merchants were the section of the population who had the most connection with the Continent, maintaining extensive trade links with France, Spain, Portugal and the Low Countries. In addition, most of them had at least one relation in Holy Orders who would have studied at such centres as Louvain, Salamanca or Rome. William Roche, a Cork merchant, was drowned on his voyage to Flanders in 1547, and his inventory mentions a cask of Spanish wine, while the 1567 inventory of another Cork merchant, William Verdon, lists his goods beyond the seas, which included 'fourscore banlays of white and black mantell frise' left in Rochelle, while the contents of his Cork house numbered several silver-gilt objects and even such refinements as 'nine napkins or servetty for a table', and his cellar was handsomely stocked with wines from Rochelle and Gascony.[31]

In consequence of these connections the merchant class became increasingly aware of the Renaissance ideas and styles which had swept across Europe from Italy during the previous century, and while it cannot be claimed that these influences were apparent in their rather stark stone houses, they can certainly be discerned in their furnishings. The wills of some of the Sarsfields in Cork city,[32] contemporaries of John Rothe's, mention such possessions as a pair of virginals, jugs of silver-gilt and a coral bracelet.

John Rothe's son Peter, who inherited his house, supported the Confederate cause in Kilkenny in 1642 and, like many others of his religion and standing, was sent with all his household to Connaught under the Cromwellian transplantation of 1653, where he died. The organized destruction of this educated and progressive class was a severe cultural setback to Ireland, severing as it did many valuable links with the Continent. Peter's grandson, Marcus Shee, regained the Kilkenny house and was its owner in 1690. In 1908 the second and third buildings were roofless ruins; the second has now been repaired. All the woodwork now to be seen in the first, or main, house is a restoration. The expert carpentry on the roof-beams shows what the original was like. All stonework, including the two fireplaces in the gallery-hall, is original, except for the oriel-window which only retains its old corbel. There is no decoration or carving except the armorial stone on the façade and several inscriptions.

Shee's Almshouse, Kilkenny, built in 1594 by Sir Richard Shee and endowed in 1604 with £40 per annum, is another plain stone house. It remained in the ownership of the O'Shees for more than three hundred years. A drawing of 1840 shows that it then had a bellcote and a slated hood over the door on the lane front, while the street front looked much as it does today. In 1870 the roof was re-slated and the exterior repaired; some further alterations were made later in the century when it was used by the Ladies' Charitable Association. Originally the ground-level had an earthen floor, and was divided into two rows of cells off a central passage that ran the length of the house. There was a large fireplace with cut-stone jambs and head. The upper floor was similarly arranged but there was no internal stair.[33]

Shee's Almshouse, Kilkenny, the street front. From a drawing made about 1840

Galway was another of the great walled trading towns. In the sixteenth century it had splendid stone houses that differed from those of any other Irish town, showing marked continental influence. Timber was scarce in the area, and this certainly encouraged extensive use of stone. The streets were straight and narrow with high stone houses roofed by heavy flags about an inch thick. Entrance was usually through a Gothic door or open stone archway, sometimes ornamented with pillars and sculpture, that led into a square courtyard round which were the domestic buildings. These houses have now all disappeared, but Beaufort gives a vivid description of them in 1787:

> On the right and left of the entry [within the courtyard] are stone stairs for one flight and there the apartments inhabited by gentlefolks . . . begin. . . . Some houses contain two or three families, no yards or gardens and it is said but three cloacinas in town. . . . The lower floors are mostly shops only in which not one in fifty live but shut them up and retire at night to other lodgings.[34]

He explained that the reason why so many of these houses had gone to ruin was that different floors of a house were the perpetual freehold of separate persons, who would not agree to the repair or sale of the premises.

The sixteenth-century house built by a mayor of Galway and now known as Lynch's Castle has undergone much restoration. In 1787 Beaufort reported that it was 'partly rebuilding, preserving all carvings'; and twenty-one years later, on another visit, he wrote: 'I observed an addition in making to Lynch's Castle in a similar stile preserving the carved mantler [sic], heads and arms that were in the old building. Most of the walls and all the gates have been pulled down.'[35] It was again altered in 1966 on conversion to its present use as a bank, but the exterior still preserves some gargoyles, as well as the arms of Henry VII and of the Lynch and Fitzgerald families.

Limerick too was an important town at this period. In addition to its stone and cage-work houses it had great houses of black marble in Elizabethan times (according to Father Wolfe, the Papal Legate). This black marble (or basalt) came from the quarries at Garryowen, and was used not only for house-building prior to the Siege of Limerick but also for paving the streets. Dineley reported on this unusual aspect of the city during his tour of 1681, and describing the houses as 'tall built and black and polished marble with partitions some five feet thick, with battlements on the top'. No trace of these buildings is now visible.

Thus we can form a picture of the island as a whole at the close of the sixteenth century. The merchants, artisans and their employees were living closely huddled together in the walled towns. The great Norman and Irish lords with their retainers lived in large fortified castle-compounds in their dominions (with perhaps a town residence for occasional use); the lesser landowners had cramped fortified tower-houses on their demesnes. The peasantry were in crude mud cabins, while in the wilder parts of the country, such as the unconquered north where the old Gaelic order was still supreme, the poorer members of the sept lived in impermanent huts clustered round their chief's castle. The general aspect was still distinctly medieval, rather than colonial as it was so soon to become. The seventeenth-century Plantations brought changes in varying degree to different parts of the country; semi-fortified and even unfortified houses began to be built in rural areas, and in time even small unwalled towns developed.

Houses and locations in Chapters 1 and 2

CHAPTER 2

From the Plantations to Cromwell

1585–1660

B Y THE SECOND HALF of Elizabeth I's reign the descendants of the Norman invaders had shown themselves no more amenable to the Government's efforts to
organize the country on an English pattern than were their intractable Irish neighbours. After four centuries the interests of the Norman families had become quite
divorced from those of the Crown. Many of them (like the majority of the Irish)
had refused to accept the Reformation, and they had formed alliances with the Irish,
either through marriage or on grounds of their common interest in resisting the
authorities. The Government, in turn, viewed such families as the Fitzgeralds of
Kildare and Desmond, the Burkes of Clanricarde, the Powers and the Eustaces as
scarcely more trustworthy than the O'Neills of Ulster, the O'Mores of Leix, the
O'Rorkes of Breffny, the McCarthys of Clancarty and the O'Sullivans of Bere. They
were all unreliable.

Even before Elizabeth's time an attempt had been made by means of official
Plantations to infiltrate Ireland with new settlers bound to the English interest.
Under the scheme in Leix and Offaly the towns of Maryborough and Philipstown
were laid out, named after the reigning sovereigns. However, as the settlers were
English Catholics who did not accept the Reformation they tended to marry and
form alliances with the local Irish population. Their newly granted properties were
confiscated in retaliation, and the Plantation had not much long-term effect, except that it showed the Government some things *not* to do.

The Fitzgeralds provoked and led three major rebellions, in 1534, 1568 and 1579.
When, after four years, the last of these risings was quelled, the vast Desmond
Palatinate was extinguished, and the 16th Earl forfeited the half-million acres
which he had ruled like an independent kingdom. The subsequent Plantation of
Munster, which began in 1586, was a serious scheme devised in London to colonize
these lands with 'loving subjects of good behaviour and account, none of the mere
Irish to be maintained in any family'. It was carefully organized; the lands were
surveyed and mapped, and as the properties of other rebels were sequestered so
they too were fitted into the scheme with ruthless disregard for their inhabitants.
The lands were allotted to prominent Englishmen, known as 'undertakers', on
condition that they should recruit and import loyal Protestant sub-tenant leasehold
farmers. This met with such success that in the first years eight thousand English
were established in Munster.

The Earl of Cork's
Almshouses, Main Street,
Youghal, Co. Cork

Although the new settlers did not have an easy time, the land–hungry younger
sons of English yeomen families were so pleased with the rich soil of Munster that
they faced their many difficulties with the zeal of true colonists, and soon most of
them were determined to remain. They hoped for better times, and were prepared
to cope with the native Irish, the wolves and the wild boars, much as their fellow
countrymen who left England for America in the seventeenth century dealt
with the Indians and the savage animals there.

The initial aim of the Plantation was to secure the countryside through a network
of English-held farms, and little heed was paid to the planning of towns. It was not
until the scheme had made some progress that towns were built up, either on the
ruins of older communities like Tralee, Co. Kerry, which was held by the adventurer
Sir Edward Denny, or on new sites like Bandonbridge, Co. Cork, which was skilfully laid out by another prominent adventurer, Richard Boyle, Earl of Cork. The
first houses in Bandon were built on the south side of the river in 1595–96, in
the simplest manner, of timber and plaster roofed with oak shingles. Remarkably,
this town was not walled until 1620.[1]

The will of this same Earl of Cork in 1642 mentions the almshouses at Youghal
which he endowed.[2] These early seventeenth-century houses still stand unaltered,
having been repaired in the nineteenth century retaining their original style.[3]
Similar houses with low Gothic doorways and sharp gables stand in the adjoining
Church Lane, and these suggest the aspect of the long main street of Youghal in the
seventeenth century, although it is known that some of its houses were built askew
to the street. Sir Walter Ralegh praised the quality of the local oak trees as worthy

Myrtle Grove, Youghal, Co. Cork

of use by the Elizabethan navy, and this oak was used for the joists, floors and doors of the houses.

There has been a persistent tradition in Youghal, cited in print as early as 1749, that the house now called Myrtle Grove was once Ralegh's residence. There is little reason to doubt its truth, since the tradition was in full swing locally only a century after the event, and such facts as are available in records give it support. The antiquarian T.J. Westropp found a resemblance between Myrtle Grove and Hayes' Farm in Devonshire where Ralegh was born, both houses having a projecting centre with a deep, open-arched porch under a triple window, as well as other similarities.[4] For many years the identity of Myrtle Grove was confused with that of the Old Warden's House, due to mis-statements in the *Dublin Penny Journal* of 1833[5] that were quoted and re-quoted by later writers. The certificate of the lands allotted to Ralegh in 1587 included 'four messuages or tofts in the town of Youghal'.[6] On 27 October 1602 William Jones, as trustee for Ralegh, acquired further Youghal property, being 'the New College of St Mary of Yoghall with all hereditaments spiritual and temporal thereto belonging', which had been granted to Sir Thomas Norreys of Mallow by the Warden for a term of sixty years on 28 September 1588. A mere six weeks later, on 7 December 1602, Ralegh's Irish estates were transferred to Sir Richard Boyle, later 1st Earl of Cork.[7] It is thus not clear whether the house known as Myrtle Grove was one of the four messuages obtained by Ralegh in 1587, or part of the New College property held briefly by him in 1602, but which he might well have occupied before that date, Sir Thomas Norreys having died in 1599.

33

Chimney-piece in first
floor drawing-room,
Myrtle Grove

Top: Mallow Castle,
Mallow, Co. Cork

Richard Boyle and his second wife settled at Youghal after their marriage. He effected considerable repairs and improvements to the College House and its garden, and there his eldest son Roger was born in 1606. In 1614 his nephew by a ruse acquired the seal, charter and records of the College, and in 1616 conveyed the entire College property to Sir Laurence Parsons 'for the use of his kinsman, the Earl of Cork'. Soon after, when the Earl made his chief seat at Lismore, he leased the College House to Parsons, although he continued to lie there on his visits to Youghal. In 1634, when he was charged with fraudulently obtaining the College property and with sacrilege for using the house as his own dwelling, he stated that it had previously been so occupied for several years by Sir Thomas Norreys, Sir George Carew and Mr Jones. In 1640 he paid a composition of £15,000 and the King made him a grant of 'his dwelling house the New College House in Youghall' with the surrounding gardens. It appears from the Lismore Papers that the building just inside the gate of Myrtle Grove, and for many years its stables, was originally an almshouse.

Whether Myrtle Grove was built for Norreys or for Ralegh, it is clearly dated prior to 1600, and despite some nineteenth-century alterations still retains its original character. The rooms are low, and those on the first floor have handsome dark oak panelling. In the main room (on the first floor) is an outstanding chimney-piece that reaches to the ceiling, elaborately carved in oak and possibly of continental origin. The house was acquired by the Haymans in the eighteenth century and in the nineteenth belonged first to Sir John Pope Hennessy and then to Sir Henry

Blake, whose grandson, Commander Bernard Arbuthnot, is the present owner.

Sir Thomas Norreys, the Lord President of Munster, who had held the New College of Youghal, was granted Desmond lands at Mallow, Co. Cork, in 1586, and there he built himself a 'goodly fair and sumptuous house upon the ruins of the old castle, with a bawn to it about 120 foot square and 18 foot in height and many convenient houses of office'.[8] The house was a single-pile with an entrance at the centre front, a small return at the centre back housing a garderobe, and two polygonal towers at the front corners. Later settler-houses on a smaller scale and not needing the defensive towers followed this ground-plan, having a central hall with a room at each side and the stair in the return.

The great Desmond stronghold at Newcastle West, Co. Limerick, with its fine castle and beautiful halls, fell to the undertaker, Sir William Courtney. The Poll Tax of about 1659 returned 154 adults in the town, 36 English and 118 Irish.[9] The seventeenth-century dwellings were sturdy, simple little houses with extremely thick walls and tiny windows. The illustration shows a row of these in The Coole below Maiden Street in 1971, prior to demolition by the Limerick County Council. In 1972, after the demolition, only one remained and was still inhabited; regrettably, since they were probably the oldest small dwellings in the country and, despite their primitive facilities, had both charm and interest. They could have been preserved as a showpiece, at least, when their occupants were rehoused. The cobbled street and open drain seen in the picture are much as they were in the seventeenth century, but the corrugated-iron roofs are a replacement for the original thatch.

35

Main Street,
Kilmallock, Co.
Limerick. Oil painting by
J. G. Mulvany, early
nineteenth century

Kilmallock, about thirty miles east of Newcastle West, was a larger town. Its unique beauty once earned it such glowing epithets as 'the Irish Balbeck',[10] and, after its decay, 'fallen princess'. That such comments were not unmerited can be seen from Mulvany's painting of what was left of this remarkable town in about 1820. Today one may pass through without seeing any vestige of its former glory, since one has to search carefully for remnants of the stately stone houses. The ruins still to be seen a hundred years ago were those of houses built in the beginning of the seventeenth or, at earliest, at the end of the sixteenth century. After the important and wealthy town had been burned by James Fitzmaurice's men – who first seized a handsome booty in the form of ornamental silver goblets and other valuables – Sir John Perrot, Lord President of Munster, had it rebuilt and fortified; but it seems likely this was done in the elaborate manner of the former town, since its appearance was so unusual. The newly rebuilt town had a chequered existence. It was severely damaged in the Cromwellian Wars, when the defences were dismantled, and in 1690 it was finally destroyed by the Irish forces, after which its importance never revived.

The Civil Survey of 1654–56 shows that the town belonged at that time almost exclusively to 'Irish Papists', there being only one English proprietor within the walls (a non-resident, who held only thatched houses). Three other proprietors are described as 'English interest', but from their names they must have been Irish collaborators. Of this trio, Ann Cassye of Dublin and Cathiline Coyne of Kilmallock each had a stone house. The other stone houses within the walls consisted of thirty-one with three storeys and three with two storeys, the largest of which belonged to Patrick Kearny, and had no less than twenty-six rooms, eight on the ground floor, thirteen on the second floor, and five on the top floor. Seven other houses had ten rooms or more each. The largest number of rooms was invariably on the second floor, and the top floor seems to have been a big dormitory. Indeed, two of the houses had but a single room on the third floor corresponding with five or six on the floors below. These houses and the six buildings described as 'castles' (four having three storeys and the other two having two) were all in the hands of the Irish.

The remainder of the town within the walls was composed of thatched houses, of which four were two-storey and eighty-one single-storey structures, nineteen of the latter being one-roomed cabins and twenty-nine two-roomed. These last undoubtedly resembled the houses in The Coole.

Signs of the recent troubles are evident in the numerous ruined thatch houses and even stone houses listed by the Survey. Kilmallock saw rapid changes in Cromwellian times: by 1659 when the Poll Tax was compiled it contained 610 adults of whom 537 were Irish and 73 English, and 15 new English proprietors had established themselves.[11] This late influx of English indicates that the original appearance of Kilmallock was that of an Irish town, and not one of planter inspiration.

In 1775 Dr Campbell wrote of the ruined town that 'it preserves a greater share of magnificence than anything I have yet seen in Ireland. There is but one street now standing entire.'[12] In 1778 Beaufort observed that the ruined houses were 'all of cut stone to the middle floor with a singular facia over it'.[13] Thomas Crofton Croker, seeing the place about the time Mulvany painted it, noted that the three-storey houses were 'ornamented with an embattlement and a tasteful stone moulding on the outside. . . . The square window frames and large chimney-pieces are well carved in a bold and massive style and such is the durability of the limestone, though exposed to the weather and casual injuries, that it retains the sharpness of the chisel as if only yesterday from the hands of the sculptor.'[14] In 1889 some inhabitants could still recall a then-demolished house which had had traces of gilding on the ornamental stonework, but by that time such old houses as survived had been submerged in new buildings.[15]

A fine chimney-piece from one of the houses still exists. Beaufort and Croker both saw it at Kilmallock, but in the nineteenth century it was moved, first to Ballingarry and then to the Desmond Banqueting Hall (now the bingo hall) at Newcastle West, where it can still be seen, bearing its original inscription: 'SH 16 (IHS) 38 EH'. Beaufort and Croker were told these were the initials of Simon Hely. There were Halys at Kilmallock, but it seems more likely that the initials are those of Symon Hurly (who appears in the Civil Survey) and his wife. The exotic appearance of the houses in Galway has already been noticed in Chapter 1, and Mahony's drawing (overleaf) shows a handsome early seventeenth-century window above a doorway there, much in the style of the Kilmallock fireplace.[16]

Doorway in Galway. A
drawing by Mahony,
about 1850

Right: entrance doorway,
Kanturk Castle, parish of
Clonfert, Co. Cork

A few of the pre-Plantation landowners in Munster managed to retain their
possessions by a system of tenuous treaties. One who did so was the fierce Donough
McCarthy, who started to build himself a splendid castle at Kanturk, Co. Cork,
in 1600, introducing elements of Tudor style and a fine Renaissance doorway on
the first floor. The plan of Kanturk, with its four flanking towers at the corners,
is reminiscent of Rathfarnham Castle, Co. Dublin, built in 1585 for Archbishop
Loftus. McCarthy's English-settler neighbours were perturbed by the size of his
new structure and complained to the Privy Council that it was much too large for
a subject. Jealous they certainly were, but their fears may also have been well
founded, for McCarthy was ambitious, and determined that his castle should
surpass all others in the vicinity. Moreover, he was an unpopular man. Two hundred years later tales were still current locally of how he had halted all travellers,
compelling them to labour on his building site as slaves until they died of hunger
or exhaustion, and that the seven masons who built the castle were forced to do
so without wages. Be this as it may, the settlers' complaints bore fruit, and McCarthy
was ordered to stop work just as the battlements were about to be raised. Tradition
says that in his furious disappointment he had the 'glass roof', which was nearly
ready, smashed to atoms. The almost-finished castle – never roofed or inhabited –
still stands, four storeys high, of dressed limestone. It is composed of a central
rectangular block with a square tower at each corner. In each tower is a stair with
a communicating doorway into the main block on every floor. Each storey is
marked by a string-course, but only the corbels of the machicolations exist, showing clearly the point at which construction ended. There are many two- and three-
mullioned windows. As usual, the kitchen was on the ground floor and the main
chamber on the third floor. The latter has a particularly handsome chimney-piece
in the same style as the great doorway. There were also numerous other chimney-
pieces, in keeping with McCarthy's ideas of grandeur.

Another of the old Munster proprietors who managed to retain his family lands was Sir Walter Coppinger, who lived in Carbery in West Cork. The Coppingers had been in Ireland since before the Norman invasion. In 1616 Sir Walter surrendered his estates to James I and had them re-granted next day. He was on better terms with his neighbours than McCarthy, and succeeded in completing his fine house, Coppinger's Court, and occupying it peacefully. Here the lay-out is a rectangle with three projecting rectangular towers, one at each front corner and the third at the centre back. This was a very practical design, since the two front towers protected the entrance. Although there are numerous machicolations (now much concealed by ivy) the house does not present a very fortified appearance with its mullioned windows and elegant tall chimney-stacks (p. 67).

Tickincor, Co. Waterford, on the banks of the Suir, is another example of a fortified house built by an old inhabitant. It has been attributed to Sir Richard Osborne,[17] but was in fact built by Alexander Power during the reign of James I. His son, Richard Power, 'Irish Papist', still held it in 1654–56, when the Civil Survey described it as 'a faire stone house'.[18]

Tickincor, parish of Killaloan, Co. Waterford

The tall, gabled ruin still exhibits some Tudor features, though several of its mullioned windows have been blocked up. It is generally less refined than Coppinger's Court. The plan is a rectangle, with a central return at the back which must have contained the stair, since there are communicating doorways on each floor. The kitchen with its huge fireplace was at ground-level; the residential apartments were on the first and second floors, where now only fireplace-recesses remain; there were garrets on the top floor.

By 1659 the Powers had been supplanted by Sir Thomas Stanley. A letter from Charles Alcock to Sir John Percival in 1663[19] casts further light on the situation:

> Sir Thomas Stanley being returned home informed me concerning my interest in the lands I possess which formerly belonged to Alexander Power of Teigener which is the house Sir Thomas now lieth in and was laid out to him as part of his lot. The said Power and his father have been sufficiently notorious in rebellion but the said estate is claimed by the Duke [of Ormonde] under the clause in the Act which gives him the forfeiture of all lands in which he had any chiefery. My fear is that the Duke's favour is intended for this Power and may be fixed on my interest which would also be my ruin. I request that you will acquaint the Duke of me and of the condition of my adventure it being of the best qualification of adventurers.

Soon afterwards the house passed to Nicholas Osborne; his son, Sir Thomas, the 4th Baronet, lived there until his death in 1713, as did his grandson, Sir John, the 6th Baronet, until he moved to Newton Anner between 1740 and 1743.

The quarrels over Tickincor between the old chief (Ormonde), his vassal, the old landlord (Power), the new Crown adventurer (Alcock) and his new leasehold tenant (Stanley) aptly demonstrate the problems of land tenure under the Munster Plantations, quite apart from Cromwell's and Charles II's need for land wherewith to pay off their officers when ready cash was short – which was always.

It may have been the difficulties experienced by the Munster planters in holding rural areas quietly that inspired the authors of the Ulster Plantation to vary the scheme. In 1595 Hugh O'Neill, Earl of Tyrone, launched a rebellion which ended in disaster at Kinsale in 1601. In 1607 O'Neill and his ally O'Donnell, with over ninety of the leading men of Ulster, went into exile on the Continent. The Plantation of Ulster began the year after the Flight of the Earls: from its start the establishment of new towns and villages was envisaged as an integral feature of the project. Hitherto most of the province had been held by the Gaelic lords, who had displayed remarkable independence of the Crown and adherence to their own customs. Now their former territories were organized into counties like the English shires, and Scottish and English settlers were invited to colonize them. The chief undertakers were divided into three classes: those who received two thousand acres and had to erect a strong castle and bawn; those who got fifteen hundred acres and had to build a stone or brick house with bawn, and those who got a thousand acres and need only put up a bawn within two years of their settlement. Presumably at first many in the last category built only simple wooden houses, while the poorest adopted the Irish form of wattled cabins. They chopped trees, made a frame of the trunks or large branches and wove undergrowth through the beams; sods were then placed over the whole, including the roof.

Before the Plantation there were only two real towns in Ulster besides the small port communities, namely Carrickfergus, Co. Antrim and Newry, Co. Down. Now twenty-three new walled towns were laid out, all on a grid pattern with a central square for public buildings. Of these, Londonderry, Belfast and Enniskillen became the most important. The O'Neill lands in what is now Co. Derry were allocated to various London Companies as adventurers, and Sir Thomas Phillips's Survey of 1622 includes pictorial plans by Thomas Raven[20] of the houses built on the Companies' Plantations by their agents and tenants. These drawings, together with Pynnar's Survey of 1618[21] give a fair idea of what was being built. Not unexpectedly, the houses strongly resembled English domestic building; as for example those with tall bays erected by the Goldsmiths' Company at Clondermot, the Clothworkers at Killowen and the Haberdashers at Ballycastle. Being in Ireland, they were surrounded by the ubiquitous bawn walls with flanking towers, and some even had castellated features, like the house of the Mercers at Movanagher, or the Merchant Taylors' at Macosquin, which was actually battlemented. At Magherafelt the Salters began typically English cage-work houses with exposed beams and tall triangular gables. On the Skinners' allotment at Dungiven, where there was already a sixteenth-century tower-house with a hall attached, Captain Edward Doddington added a gabled house to the tower and used the entire complex.

All the Companies' houses have vanished, but an interesting isometric reconstruction and floor-plan has been made, based on the remains of another house of the same period at White House, Co. Antrim.[22] This house was a long rectangle with round towers at the front corners and a rounded projection at the centre back with the stair, a lay-out strongly resembling that of Mallow Castle. Similar round towers still exist at the corners of the building known as Dalway's Bawn, on the Bellahill Road, north-east of Carrickfergus, built by John Dallowaye in 1609.[23]

In marked contrast was the tall mansion called Joymount, built at Carrickfergus by Sir Arthur Chichester about 1610. As shown in a drawing made by Thomas Phillips in 1885 it had projecting bays, mullioned windows and Jacobean turrets. No trace of it now exists.

In 1622–24 Sir Toby Caulfield erected a similar house at Charlemont, Co. Tyrone. It was burned in 1921 and later demolished, but photographs taken before the fire show it much as it appears in Raven's drawing of 1624 (and again in a watercolour made at the end of the seventeenth century), with tall projecting bays. Pynnar, viewing the nearly completed house, described it as the 'fairest building that I have seen'. Yet at the very same period traditional tower-houses were still being built within fortified bawns. A surviving example of such a castle is Kirkistown, Co. Down, still in good condition due to some eighteenth-century restoration.

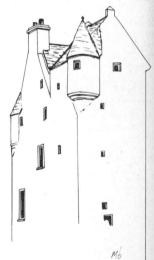

Ballygalley Castle, parish of Carncastle, Co. Antrim

James I had been James VI of Scotland, and hence there was encouragement for Scots settlers to cross the narrow sea to the new Plantation in Ulster. They brought with them the distinctive, defensive building-styles prevalent in the Scottish Lowlands and border country, which had always been subject to wild forays. Hill asserts that the Scottish craftsmen had a poor reputation,[24] and that this may have been the reason Scots taste was less widespread in seventeenth-century Ulster than it might have been. None the less, skilled Scottish workmanship survives at Ballygalley Castle, Co. Antrim, built by James Shaw of Greenock in 1625. It is a tall, rectangular building with a projecting tower containing the entrance and spiral stair, and has an essentially Scottish feature in the small round turret at the upper angle of the tower, carried on solid rows of strongly moulded corbel-courses and capped by a conical roof. This construction was not used in Ireland outside Ulster, though there are several other examples in that province. These may well have been the inspiration of the architects who popularized the Scottish Baronial style in Ulster in succeeding centuries.

41

Sir James Hamilton from Ayrshire built his castle at Killyleagh, Co. Down, on the site of an earlier fortress. Not surprisingly this too was in the Scottish style. A drawing made in 1625 shows it shortly after completion with a conically roofed turret supported on moulded corbels. Though the castle was much enlarged about 1660 and extensively altered and repaired by Sir Charles Lanyon in the nineteenth century, the 1625 drawing proves that the front of the present castle (p. 212), to the left of the main door and including the entrance and machicolation above it, dates from the original building.

In 1611 the Plantation Commissioners had reported that the indefatigable Sir James Hamilton was preparing to build a house at Holywood, Co. Down, and had 'two hundred thowsand of brickes with other materialles ready at the place, where are some twenty houses inhabited with English Scottes'. They also reported that he had already built a 'fayre stone house' (60 by 22 feet) in the town of Bangor, which then consisted of eighteen new houses entirely inhabited by Scots and English, and that he had brought from England 'twenty artificers who are makinge materialles of tymber brickes and stones' for another house there.[25]

Following the general success of the Ulster Plantation, settlers were established in Longford, Leitrim, Offaly and Wexford. With them came not only imported livestock for breeding, but the English plough and other agricultural implements. Those who failed to get a sequestered tower-house built farmsteads, of which few traces survive, or else made do with simple log-houses until they could achieve something more substantial.

In the 1630s a certain false aura of peace surrounded Ireland. Disgruntled settlers, or those who had not been able to hold their new lands, had returned to England. The second generation of those who remained had been born in Ireland and felt established there. Some of the previously dispossessed landlords had contrived to recover at least part of their estates by one means or another, and both groups were lulled into an illusion of security, not realizing the seething discontent of the masses, who would shortly find ready leadership among the embittered sons of those landlords who had not managed to regain their estates, or who were too proud to attempt it. This delusion even extended in part to the Government. The Lord Deputy, Thomas Wentworth, Earl of Strafford, embarked on the erection of an ambitious brick palace at Jigginstown, Co. Kildare, with a frontage of 380 feet and no fortification at all. The surviving ruins are still impressive, and the stone-faced basement, expertly vaulted in brick, is intact. Jigginstown was as much outside the mainstream of Irish seventeenth-century building as had been Carrick-on-Suir in the preceding century, and it, too, was built to entertain a monarch (Charles I) who never came. Strafford was executed in 1639 and his vast house – which appears never to have been occupied – soon fell into decay. Almost a century later Sir Edward Lovett Pearce drew a somewhat inaccurate reconstruction from the ruins.[26]

Another house built in the Pale during this period of calm was Oldbawn, near Tallaght. First built about 1635 by Archdeacon William Bulkeley, son of the Archbishop of Dublin, it was burned by the O'Byrnes and O'Tooles in 1641, only to be repaired again before 1664, when it was assessed as having twelve hearths.[27] This typical Late Tudor house, which would already have been old-fashioned in England, was of a style that was still current in Wales, from whence the Bulkeleys came. It was bulldozed in 1970 and now little remains but one wall of the house and the bawn walls. The lay-out was an elongated **H**, with the hall

Loughmoe Castle, parish of Loughmoe West, Co. Tipperary. Left: ground plan

in the central part, the kitchen and offices to one side and the parlour and private apartments to the other. There were small twin gables over the central block and on the inner walls of the wings. The elaborate chimney-piece from the parlour, with its plaster representation of the rebuilding of the walls of Jerusalem modelled in high relief, is now in the National Museum in Dublin. It is thought to have come from Wales where similar stucco-work of the period is known.

During this brief span of peace a number of landowners made adaptations and additions to their existing tower-houses so as to transform them into substantial mansions. A good example of this is Loughmoe, Co. Tipperary, which belonged to the Purcells, an old Norman family. Thomas Purcell, Baron of Loughmoe, had died there in 1601, and his widow, Joanna Fitzpatrick, made her will there in 1611. They must have lived in the fifteenth- or sixteenth-century tower-house with rounded corners that was to become the projecting south-east wing of the new house, built either by their son Richard, who died in 1624, or by his son Theobald, born in 1595. The plan shows the arrangement, with the projecting wing at the north-west corner to give an effect of symmetry on the garden front. There are no string-courses round the old tower to match those on the seventeenth-century addition, so the complete unity of the building is broken. The only remaining stair is in the old tower, which has a doorway communicating with the new house on each of the four floors. There is a particularly fine chimney-piece on the first floor of the old tower, and it is clear that the tower continued to be used for residential purposes, and probably also as a refuge in time of trouble.

43

Donegal Castle, Co.
Donegal

Above right: Leamaneh
Castle, parish of
Killinaboy, Co. Clare

This chimney-piece has a moulded stone frame with leaf-work carving and two
shields at each end. The armorials on two of these are defaced, but the other two
appear to be the arms of Butler (who several times intermarried with Purcell),
and there are the initials – so far as they can be read – of JFP and TP, which may be
those of Joanna Fitzpatrick and Thomas Purcell. Below the shields are other
decorations, one being the Star of David and the other six rings interlaced with a
star.

The new house was a handsome one: its second and third storeys were lit by
numerous mullioned windows and had small cut-stone chimney-pieces. The main
rooms were on the second floor. The attics had no windows, and must have been
lit by dormers or skylights. It is noteworthy that the new house has no sign of
fortification at all, which was evidently its undoing. In 1654 Theobald Purcell,
'Irish Papist', still held Loughmoe, but he obviously had had trouble with Cromwell, since his castle is then described as 'destroyed', and 'out of all manner of
repayre'.[28] In 1665 Colonel John Fitzpatrick (who had married the widow of
Theobald's son) was living there and paying tax on five hearths. Since the ruins
show signs of far more fireplaces, it may be that only part of the premises (perhaps
the old tower-house itself) had been again rendered habitable. Unlike many other
such families the Purcells remained at Loughmoe into the mid-eighteenth century.

Another seventeenth-century mansion attached to a fifteenth-century tower-
house is Sir Basil Brooke's residence, added at right angles to the massive O'Donnell tower in the town of Donegal. Hugh Roe O'Donnell, chief of Tir Connell,
fled to Spain after his defeat at Kinsale in 1601 and died there. His property was
leased to Sir Basil who – on receiving a permanent grant of it in 1623 – proceeded
to erect the new house. It is a three-storey building with a gable over each of its

five bays, and has a variety of two-, three- and four-mullioned windows. There is a fine round-headed Renaissance-style doorway on the first floor, whose steps have now disappeared. Here, as at Loughmoe, the old tower was incorporated into the new mansion to form part of the residential accommodation. In the fireplace on the first floor of the old tower Brooke inserted an enormous, ornate Jacobean chimney-piece, quite out of proportion with the height of the room (p. 50). It is elaborately decorated with swags, chains, rosettes, masks and two finely executed armorial escutcheons, one showing his own arms (Brooke of Norton Priory, Cheshire) impaling those of his wife (Leicester of Tabley, Cheshire), and the other bearing the Brooke arms alone. In 1665 his son, Sir Henry, also Governor of Donegal, was living in the house and was taxed for ten hearths, it being then one of the only two large houses in the whole county.

Leamaneh, Co. Clare, is another interesting example of a seventeenth-century mansion built on to a fifteenth-century tower. In this instance the width of the mansion exactly fits that of the old tower. The gateway which stood in front of the hall door bears the date 1643 and has a finely moulded arch and sculptured armorial decoration. It has been taken down and re-erected at Dromoland Castle. The house was probably begun in 1639 when its owner, Conor O'Brien, married the famous Maire Ruadh, 'Red Mary', daughter of Sir Tirlogh McMahon. A contemporary portrait of this redoubtable lady shows her to have been no beauty, although magnificently dressed in a rich gown with a broad lace collar and adorned with many jewels.[29] Despite her appearance and masterful character (or perhaps because of the latter) she managed to acquire three husbands, of whom Conor O'Brien was the second. It is told that in 1651, when he was killed by the Cromwellian troops on their way to besiege Leamaneh, and his body was brought home by his retainers, the indomitable Mary refused to admit the party, declaring 'We need no dead men here.' Next day she went off to Limerick, having decided that the best means of preserving the property for her infant son would be to marry one of the enemy officers. This she promptly did, a Cornet John Cooper filling the role. Many other stories are told of her, including that she hanged her men-servants by the neck and her maids by the hair on the corbels at Leamaneh; that she kept a famous blind stallion there, so fierce that when the grooms let him out from his stall they had to stand in specially constructed niches while opening his door; and not least that when her third husband, Cooper, made a disparaging remark about his predecessor, Conor O'Brien, she threw him out of an upstairs window to his death.

The O'Briens' house at Leamaneh has four storeys and many mullioned windows, and although its aspect is now somewhat stark, in its time it had pretensions to gracious living. The elegant gateway has already been mentioned, and the house was set in walled gardens, with a fish-pond fed by a stream, and graced by a brick summer-house and two turrets.[30]

Where new mansions were not attached to an existing castle, their builders still usually incorporated some fortified features, if only as protection against local bands of armed robbers. One such defensible house is Monkstown Castle, Co. Cork, built by John Archdeacon. He and his wife, Anastasia Goold, were both of old Catholic stock, long established in the county. They were a prosperous couple: in 1634 he had sold his paternal estate of Dromdowney to Philip Percival for £1,000,[31] and her wealthy father, Alderman Thomas Goold, a Cork merchant, had died in the same year. Tradition tells that John Archdeacon was serving in the

Monkstown Castle,
parish of Monkstown,
Co. Cork

King of Spain's Army in 1636 when the house was built under his wife's supervision, and that on his return he liked neither it nor its situation, despite the fact
that his wife, by deducting the *per diem* board and lodging of the masons from the
wages due to them at the completion of the work, had contrived to bring her
total outlay down to twopence, or, according to other versions, fourpence. If this
tale is true the masons were certainly extremely badly treated, for they had done
an excellent job. The same masons, or at least the same architect, must have been
responsible for Monkstown's twin, Mount Long Castle, near Oysterhaven, built
in 1631 and now a total ruin; the Archdeacons may have seen it and asked for a
replica. Tristram Whetcombe wrote of Mount Long in 1642 that 'it is a very stately
building and the like cannot be built for £2,000'.[32]

Monkstown consists of a three-storey single-bay gabled central block, flanked
at each corner by adjoining 27-foot-square four-storey gabled towers, each with
garrets and one room on each floor.

The garrets, which have loophole-windows, give access to the machicolations
which project on corbels at the outermost corners of each tower. The floor-levels,
except the garrets, are marked by string-courses, and tall chimney-stacks rise above
the gables.

The interior arrangements are interesting. The towers each have a simple
wooden stair and communicate with the body of the house on the ground and
first floors. A great galleried hall on the first floor occupied all the central block,
rising to its roof above the first storey. Its stone chimney-piece bears the date

1636 and is decorated with a Celtic motif identical with that on the front doorway
at Burncourt, which was built at the same period. The chimney-piece has been
added to, and also bears the inscription B.S. 1804 (for Bernard Shaw, who did some
restorations) and marble columns of the Tuscan order. Finally, an ugly brick
interior was inserted during this century, which completely wrecks its appearance.

The newly built house would have been well furnished. When its twin, Mount
Long was besieged in 1642, Whetcombe reported that 'the people were all run
away . . . [with their best things] . . . only a few chests, stools, Bedsteads . . . remain.'[33]
Some idea of its probable contents can be deduced from the inventory of a contemporary Cork alderman of the same class as Anastasia's father. Besides the usual
household items and kitchen equipment, bedsteads and cupboards there were six
'stooles covered with Turkey cusions', two presses, two round tables, one 'Turkey
Carpett' and other carpets, three drawing-boards (extendable tables), a silver-
gilt salt, silver wine-bowls, a silver beer-bowl and other objects in silver, brass
and pewter.[34]

The Archdeacons did not enjoy their new house for long. By 1647 they had
been removed and Lord Inchiquin, commanding the forces, gave it to Captain
Thomas Plunkett of the Parliamentary Navy.[35] Soon afterwards the Plunketts
were out and Cromwell gave it to Colonel Huncks, an associate of the Regicides
of Charles I; with the Restoration in 1660, Huncks, of course, was out in turn.
The Reverend Michael Boyle, then Dean of Cloyne, wrote to Sir John Percival[36]
that he had heard that Huncks's estates had been sequestered and asked Sir John

to use his influence to obtain him the tenancy of Monkstown. Apparently this application was successful and in 1685 – by which time he had become Archbishop of Armagh and Lord Chancellor – he received a full grant of the property.[37] In the eighteenth century it remained in the hands of his descendants, who let it to tenants until it was acquired by the Shaw family at the end of the century. Bernard Shaw made some repairs and re-roofed the castle, replacing some of the tie-beams. He also made a large carriage entrance on the ground floor, with a Tudor-type doorway and hood-moulding. During the Peninsular War some four hundred soldiers are said to have been billeted at Monkstown. The Shaws lived there until 1869 when Bernard Robert Shaw moved to England. (George Bernard Shaw, the playwright, was descended of another branch of this same family.) The last private residents at Monkstown were the Misses Newman who were there until 1908, when it became the property of the Monkstown Golf Club. The Club maintained the castle in good order without spoiling the exterior, but it now belongs to a property development company and its future seems uncertain.

Estate agents proudly proclaim that Ballea Castle, near Carrigaline, is 'the oldest inhabited house in Co. Cork', but it has undergone so many alterations that it is hard to decide how much of it is original. It was built by the McCarthys, who inevitably lost it in Cromwellian times, and no owner is shown in 1659, when there were twenty-two Irish and no English on the townland. The McCarthys did recover possession, for Charles McCarthy of Ballea was Member of Parliament for Bandonbridge in 1689; but they lost it again for their support of James II. It then belonged to the Hodders, an English settler family, who kept it into the present century, since when it has changed hands several times. The castle is an L-shaped gabled building, with tall chimneys, and its 4-foot-thick walls denote considerable antiquity. In 1837 Tuckey mentioned that it has rude machicolations at the corners, two of which remain'.[38] The Tudor-style hood-mouldings over the windows (which have been modernized and deprived of their mullions) give the house a very bogus effect: they were already in position when Colonel Lunham visited Ballea in 1883.[39]

The Everards were a distinguished Catholic family, long resident at Ballyboy, Co. Tipperary, which commanded the road over the Gap in the Knockmealdowns between Tipperary and Waterford. The 1st Baronet, Sir Richard Everard, obtained his title in 1622, inherited a large patrimony from his father in 1624 and in 1627 married Catherine Tobin. Twelve years later Charles I granted him a vast area in Co. Tipperary, which the Letters Patent constituted into the Manor of Everard's Castle.[40] In 1641 Sir Richard completed Everard's Castle, known at the time as Clogheen, whose 1641 date-stone is now inserted into a wall at the entrance to the near-by farmyard. That year he and his family left Ballyboy to take up residence at their new home, six miles away, but which they were fated not to enjoy for long. When Cromwell appeared on the scene Sir Richard defeated the Parliamentary forces near Mitchelstown, but the Protector soon overcame this temporary reverse, and on 31 January 1650 attacked what he called 'the strong house of Sir Richard Everard' (p. 47). The house was burned. It is disputed whether this was done by the Cromwellian troops or by Lady Everard in order to prevent them taking it. Burned however it was, and in an Inquisition held at Clonmel in 1693 it is referred to as 'Burnt-Clogheen'. Locally it became known as 'Cuirt-doigte', translated into English as Burncourt, which has now long been its official name. Sir Richard was hanged in 1651; and although his son was restored to the estate by Charles II,

he did not repair Burncourt but lived at Fethard. Later in the century the Chearnleys built a house in the large bawn under the shadow of the ruins (p. 76).

II Left: Chimney-piece, Donegal Castle, Co. Donegal (pp. 44–45)

Burncourt follows the same plan as Kanturk, having a long rectangular body flanked by four projecting square towers, one at each corner. It has a gracious aspect, with twenty-six gables, seven hexagonal chimney-stacks and a great number of mullioned windows with hood-mouldings. All the windows, except those in the kitchen part, are in embrasures, and those on the ground floor were above eye-level. The front and side doors not only have firing-holes themselves but are covered by others in the towers. On the back and front of the house are corbels which carried a timber guard-walk between the towers; this walk must also have served as a machicolation. The front door has a well-cut hood-moulding, and the carved Celtic motifs round it are identical to those on the great chimney-piece at Monkstown.

General Sir Hardress Waller was a staunch Cromwellian who lived at Castletown, Co. Limerick. He was an energetic planter who had built a considerable number of stone houses on his estate. There is no real description of his residence in the parish of Kilcornan, but it is referred to as his 'castle and manor house', which suggests a house attached to an old tower. This establishment was sacked in the Irish Rising of January 1641, which started in Ulster, where many settlers were murdered, and spread like wildfire throughout the country, with much plundering and sacking of settler property. Sir Hardress duly lodged a claim for his losses, and even allowing that he exaggerated both the contents of his lost house and their value (to secure maximum compensation), the list is most impressive.[41] It includes dining-room hangings, two chambers of tapestry, and a great quantity of other curtains, hangings, counterpanes and valances, couches, 'great chayres', 'turkey work chayres' and turkey cushions, 'very rich cushions', 'richly ymbroydered sattin cussions', down, feather and flock beds, carpets, pewter, brass, iron and white earthenware vessels and a 'great chest of Bookes'. There were several imported items such as a 'greate Iron Jacke being hard to bee gott in this Kingdome', a 'clocke brought out of England', and a barrel and a box 'lately brought out of England of Venice glasses'. Although so little is known of the house itself the claim does mention its outbuildings – a dairy, wash-house, brewhouse, malthouse, turf-house, kennels and a pigeon-house well stocked with pigeons – which indicate a high degree of domestic comfort for this period in Ireland. Finally, Sir Hardress added a demand for £500 for his losses in 'planting trees, ditching and quicke setting, levelling of an over yard and garden about the lands of Castletown'. Needless to say, his total claim ran into several thousands. In 1653 his property at Castletown was described as 'a ruinous castle, sixteene cottages, a pigeon house, one orchard and one weare seat on the river of Shanen'. Like the ruin of Burncourt, it was a sad end to so much effort and magnificence.

The substantial castle-house of Ightermurragh, Co. Cork, built at the time of the 1641 Rising, is well fortified. Its form is again a rectangle with projecting square towers at the centre, front and back. It has fine string-courses, mullioned windows, external chimneys topped by tall stacks, and machicolations borne on corbels over the front door. No signs of decorative work remain, though the mutilated chimney-piece on the first floor has a Latin inscription with the names of its builders, Edmond Supple and his wife Margaret Fitzgerald, whom God joined in love: EDMUNDUS SUPPELDOMINUS MARGRITA QVEGERALD HANC STRUXERE DOMUM QVO LIGATVNVS AMOR 1641. The house now stands isolated in the fields, but the old high road from

Ightermurragh Castle,
parish of Ightermurragh,
Co. Cork

Right: Derryhivenny
Castle, parish of
Kilmalinoge, Co. Galway

Cork to Youghal used to run close to it. In 1756 Charles Smith described it as 'one of the most modern structures of this kind in the county'.[42] It is, in fact, one of the last of the castle-type houses to have been built. The Supples presently moved to Droumada, or Supple's Court, a handsome seat near by, and Ightermurragh became the property of a younger branch of the Smyths of Rathcoursey. Percy Smyth made his will there in 1714, and it passed to his nephew Beverley Smyth. This unfortunate man was barbarously burned there in 1772, being roasted on a gridiron over his own fire by a band of robbers from Cloyne in an attempt to force him to tell where his money was hidden. His will is dated from Ightermurragh but he died in his nephew's house at Rathcoursey on 7 August 1772. It is not clear whether Ightermurragh was subsequently occupied – probably not, because after this time most families of the Smyths' standing expected to live in a neat Georgian house.

Derryhivenny Castle, Co. Galway, may be the last of the true fortified tower-houses built: in any event it is the last dated surviving example. It was erected by Daniel O'Madden in 1643, and the inscription D OM ME FIERI FECIT 1643 is carved on a corbel of one of the bawn turrets. Perhaps because it was only two years after the Rising, O'Madden took the precaution of building himself a four-storey tower which was highly defensible, standing on the edge of a small L-shaped bawn; it had projecting turrets at its south-west and north-west angles as its main defences. The chief apartments were on the third floor, faithful to tower-house tradition, although all the upper floors are lit with two- and three-mullioned windows.

Portumna Castle, in the same county, is a few years earlier than Derryhivenny, and some observers have suggested that O'Madden may have copied his mullioned windows from those in the great Burke house, with which family he was connected by marriage. This splendid Jacobean mansion was visited by Beaufort in 1808, who noted that the arms over the hall chimney-piece were those of James I or Charles I.[43] The house is a six-bay double-pile with three floors above an overground basement. The central block is a large rectangle with a square projecting tower at each corner, again following the plan of Kanturk. There are hardly any signs of fortification – no machicolations or loopholes – except the firing-holes that can still be seen beside both doorways. At the front of the house a short flight of steps leads up to the fine Renaissance doorway which gave access to a Great Hall extending the full length of the central block. Originally all the principal chambers were on the floor above, but when Beaufort was there in 1808 the 'eating room' was on the garden front on the hall floor, though the big drawing room was still upstairs, and ran the full length of the house above the hall.[44] All the staircases were of timber, the main ones being of dark oak. In the eighteenth century some decorative changes were made to the inside, and these will be discussed in a later chapter; but with the exception of a curved porch added on the garden front, little or no alteration was made to the exterior. A fire in 1826 destroyed the interior of the building, but the romantic shell standing today on the verge of Lough Derg corresponds exactly with a painting of 1819.[45]

The garden front, Portumna Castle, Portumna, Co. Galway, and below: the entrance doorway

The old Bishop's Palace, Raphoe, Co. Donegal

The house of Bishop Robert Leslie at Raphoe, Co. Donegal, built about 1661, is now also a shell. It has five bays, and follows the same lay-out of a rectangular block with four square flanking towers at the corners and an overground basement. Although later than Portumna, it has a more fortified, less gracious aspect. When Beaufort visited it in 1787 he noticed loopholes in the towers, and indeed loop-windows can still be seen in the wall of the garden front. The battlements may be an eighteenth-century addition, as is, of course, the Gibbsian front door. John Oswald, who was Bishop of Raphoe from 1763 to 1780, walled in fifty acres, which he planted with oak, ash and laburnum, as well as making some improvements to the house, adding a new kitchen and offices – for which he charged £4,000.[46] It was still used as the Bishop's Palace in the 1830s.

There were only two big houses in Co. Donegal in the mid-seventeenth century; the Bishop's Palace and Donegal Castle, both taxed for ten hearths in 1665.[47] The next two largest houses had only four hearths, followed by three houses with three hearths. This makes a remarkable contrast with the situation in Co. Tipperary.

Donegal's area is slightly larger than Tipperary's, although only half the land was cultivable, compared with eighty per cent of Tipperary. Even so, the difference is very marked.

Much of Tipperary had been included in the old Ormond Palatinate over which the Butlers had rights of chiefery. The Ormondes, wily politicians and usually in favour with the Crown, were able to assist their numerous Catholic relations to hold on to some of their property, at the same time desisting from open attack on the newcomers. An analysis of the 1665 Hearth Money Roll[48] shows that, as previously stated, the Duke of Ormonde, in his castle and manor-house at Carrick,

was taxed for no less than thirty hearths; the next largest establishment was the Archbishop's Palace at Cashel, which had eleven. Below this came three houses each with ten hearths, two with nine, four with eight, three with seven, ten with six, fifteen with five and twenty-nine with four.

John Godfrey, who was taxed for five hearths at Knockgraffon, Co. Tipperary, in 1665 and for six hearths there in 1666–67, was an English officer who had been rewarded for his services in the 1641 Rising by a grant of this old Butler property, on which was a tower-house in poor repair. The chimney-piece still to be seen on its top floor is dated 1603. Godfrey and his family must have lived in the tower until he built the two-storey double-pile house with high gables and chimneys now in ruins across the road, where his widow made her will in 1686 and their son made his in 1696. If the change from five to six hearths is an accurate indication, it may provide the date of their move. The new house had a privy – still to be seen – jutting out on corbels from one of the back corners.

This rare seventeenth-century concession to comfort appears on another not dissimilar house of the same period, Reenadisert, Co. Cork, near the road from Bantry to Glengariff, overlooking the sea.

Sir Owen O'Sullivan Bere's castle at Reenadisert was taken by Ireton in the Parliamentary War, and demolished by his orders.[49] The gabled ruins now standing appear to be those of a succeeding house, rebuilt with the old material and probably incorporating part of the previous castle. This house had two twin-seat privies on the first floor, jutting out from the corners on corbels and with external drainage. Rather curiously, one of these remained in use in that part of the house which was inhabited until very recently.

55

The first half of the seventeenth century brought little change to the towns, although building in sixteenth-century styles in both stone and cage-work continued briskly. For instance, at Athlone, Co. Westmeath, a considerable number of houses were put up at this period, among them Court Devenish (built about 1620) described in the Civil Survey as a 'great stone house', and in 1682 as the best and finest house in Athlone 'exceeding all others in politeness of architecture'.[50] By 1890 most of the early seventeenth-century houses in Mardyke Street had been modernized in front, although the ancient structures could still be discerned at the back from the riverside; earlier in the century a house in Victoria Place, with a date-stone of 1626, still retained its original form.[51]

The Civil Survey of 1654–56 gives a good picture of many provincial centres. That for the small town of New Ross, Co. Wexford, is particularly detailed, and shows it was composed of: 1 castle-house, 84 slated houses, 127 thatched ('chaffe') houses, 1 slate house with a thatched kitchen and backside, and numerous thatched cabins. In Waterford most houses are shown as stone with slate roofs, but there are a few instances of part stone and part cage-work, also slated. Kilkenny is listed as consisting entirely of stone houses without any cage-work, in contrast to Limerick which still had an exceedingly high proportion of cage-work houses. Cork had a fair mixture of stone and cage-work, and there was still a great deal of cage-work in Dublin, where vast changes and expansion were so soon to take place.

CHAPTER 3

From the Restoration to the Battle of the Boyne

1660–1690

FOLLOWING THE DEATH OF CROMWELL and the Restoration of King Charles II, Ireland enjoyed another decade of punishments and rewards. The restored King – who was chronically short of ready money – needed to gratify the supporters of the Royalist cause and repay them for their loyalty, long service and many losses. The most rabid Cromwellians were therefore dispossessed, although most of the lesser fry contrived to retain what they had acquired. The Commissioners of Settlement had the unenviable task of distinguishing between pardonable and unpardonable Cromwellians, rebellious Irish and that choice group defined as 'Innocent Papists' – and fine lines of distinction they were indeed. Some had turned their coats so often that they themselves hardly knew which side they were on, and the most wily preserved the reversible coats in their closets for further turning later in the century.

Some of the Catholics who had been banished to the remoter parts of Connaught under Cromwell's Transplantation Scheme of 1654–58 returned and regained at least part of their property. By that scheme the Protector had reduced almost two thousand heads of families – representatives of the old aristocracy, gentry, merchants and physicians – to a dreary state of degradation. At the Restoration the Crown had to steer a careful course between recompensing these unfortunates and other dispossessed Catholics, and alienating too many of the settlers who, even though they might have supported Cromwell, belonged after all to the 'English interest'. Without their help the Government feared it would be impossible to control the country, since if the 'Innocent Papists' were to achieve a position of power they might readily ally themselves with the 'Rebellious Irish'. Indeed, an Act of 1657 mentioned that the 'children, grandchildren, nephews, uncles, next pretended heirs' and other kindred of the transplanted Catholics were then living idly (with the aid of their ex-tenants) and 'waiting an opportunity as may be justly supposed to massacre and destroy the English who, as Adventurers and Soldiers or their tenants are set down to plant upon the several lands and estates of the persons attainted.'[1]

The Commissioners of Settlement meted out their attribution, retribution and distribution from Dublin. Working with them in the capital and under the new Viceroy, the Duke of Ormonde, was a rapidly expanding administration with all its many ramifications. Ormonde personally promoted the growth of the city of Dublin, which, at the time of the Restoration, still had only one bridge over the Liffey, the old medieval structure at the foot of Bridge Street near the present Four Courts. The houses were concentrated on the south of the river in the area of the old Viking city round Christchurch Cathedral, chiefly in the parishes of St John, St Michael, St Audoen and St Werburgh. In 1660 most of them were old cage-work houses, forming a maze of narrow, twisting streets. Alderman John Desminicres, a Dublin merchant, writing to his landlord in 1684, mentioned that in 1636 his house in Bridge Street had been bought 'as a very old house' for £227 by Sir John Percival's grandfather, adding, 'I have laid out some money on it to keep it up but now there is a great part of it which must be pulled down to the ground and rebuilt.'[2]

Under Ormonde, Dublin began to expand in two directions. New houses were built across the river in St Michan's parish, where Oxmantown Green was partly enclosed in 1665 and all the ground leased out in ninety-nine lots. The Corporation intended this to be a selective development, and granted the Viceroy seven acres in the hope that he too would build there – which he did not. However, the Lords Dungannon and Massareene and other prominent men were among the original leaseholders. New buildings also went up to the south-east of the old city, where the Corporation leased eighty-nine lots round the periphery of the twenty-seven acres that was to become Stephen's Green. The ninety-nine-year leases for these lots (60 feet wide, sufficient for the erection of two houses) were distributed by ballot. The lessees were not obliged to build, but should they do so they had to covenant to construct houses of 'brick, stone and timber to be covered with tiles or slates with at least two floores or loftes and a cellar if they please to dig it'.[3] Houses were first built on the two sides nearest the old town, but by the end of the century they were extending along the southern and eastern sides of the Green.

Alderman Desminieres's letter of 1684 continued, 'there is no encouragement for laying out in this part of the city [in St Audoen's parish] the trade being all gone to the new parts of the city by reason of the Markets being removed thither so that all rents hereabouts are mighty fallen, for Sir William Parsons's house that was set formerly for £110 p.a. is now set but for £45 p.a. . . .' and, 'I am offered houses in several places in the new city as also ground to build on at very easy terms.'[4]

The new houses were of stone or brick, and the cage-work houses in the now-depressed old part of the city quickly decayed, so that by 1782 there were only ten wooden houses left in Dublin.[5]

By the last quarter of the century four-storey houses were being built with their roof-ridge at right angles to the street and its gable masked by quadrants sweeping up to curved or triangular pediments, in the style then flourishing in Holland. This fashion may have been imported by Flemish and Huguenot immigrants, some of whom had come to Ireland long before the Revocation of the Edict of Nantes.[6] But there were also Dutch settlers in Ireland many years before those who arrived in the train of William III,[7] and one such gable was built in Co. Limerick as early as 1683. In due course Dublin acquired several streets of houses in this style.[8]

As Dublin prospered it attracted people from the countryside. Younger sons of both settlers and old families, dispossessed Irish landlords, their tenants and unemployed labourers, ambitious provincial merchants and artisans all flocked to the capital to seek their fortunes, or at least in the hope of bettering their circumstances. The city grew so rapidly that the number of houses built in the new areas before the end of the century was considerable. An account in 1695[9] gives the total population as 40,508; and of the 28,263 adults, no less than 6,881 were male or female servants. The new district north of the river in St Michan's parish had 793 houses tenanted by 'people of some condition', and 119 more with those 'not only who receive alms but also those unable to pay'. The average density per house over the whole city was 7·75 persons, but in the oldest area in St Audeon and St Michael's parishes the figure reached an average of 13 persons per house. Here the houses had an average of six to seven hearths, and this suggests multiple family dwellings. In the other old parishes, too, the density was high: ten persons to a house in St John's and eleven in St Nicholas Within, with six to seven hearths per house, indicating a similar situation. In the parish of St Nicholas Without (outside the old walls) there were just over a thousand houses, 858 of which were occupied by people of condition; and as there was an average of four hearths per house, with an average density of four occupants, this suggests spacious though not grand houses.

By the end of the century the Corporation had achieved its desire and most of the aristocracy had their town-houses in St Michan's parish, in the north suburbs. Although the south suburbs did have a number of large houses (in 1664 Lord Killooney's had twelve hearths, and there were four residences with ten hearths and one with nine), it is clear that a great quantity of smaller houses had been built there. In 1664 over one-third of all the two-hearth houses in the county (96 out of 265) and almost half of the three-hearth houses (43 out of 95) were in the Liberties of Donore and of St Patrick's, principally in the Coombe, New Row and New Street. It is also abundantly clear that the native Irish were in humble circumstances. The great majority of householders with two or more hearths had non-Gaelic names, and examination of some common Leinster surnames shows that of the sixty-nine Kellys, sixty-eight had only one hearth; of the sixty-three Byrnes, sixty had one hearth; of the forty-nine Doyles, forty-eight had one hearth; and of the thirty Connors, all had one hearth. These figures speak for themselves.

Ormonde, who had never liked Dublin Castle, fixed his own residence first at Phoenix Lodge and later at Chapelizod, thereby doubtless giving a fillip to house-building in the county, where there were already many sizeable houses. The Co. Dublin Hearth Money Roll of 1664[10] returned 4,000 houses (excluding those in the city) of which 3,500 had only one hearth and were presumably cabins. Twenty establishments had nine or more hearths: the largest was Rathfarnham Castle, where Lady Dorothy Loftus had eighteen, followed by Mr Richard Phillips at Finglas with fourteen, Archdeacon Bulkeley at Oldbawn, the Lord Baron of Howth at Howth, Thomas Luttrell at Luttrelstown, Sir Theophilus Jones at Lucan and the Lord of Killooney in the south suburbs all with twelve apiece. Colonel Edward Vernon at Clontarf, Thomas Vincent at Palmerstown, Sir John Stephens at Santry and John Talbot at Malahide were all taxed for eleven hearths.

Of these great houses, Malahide and Howth (which was rebuilt in 1738 but retains some original features[11]) are still inhabited by descendants of their 1664 owners. Rathfarnham and Clontarf both still exist but have been subjected to many alterations and additions; Luttrelstown is 'cloaked in an elaborate mantle of early nineteenth-century Gothic'[12] and Lucan has been entirely rebuilt.

A surviving house which does appear in the 1664 list is Rathbeale Hall. Sir Walter Plunkett is shown as taxed for eight hearths at 'Rabell, Swords'. This may be significant in dating the seventeenth-century interior of the present house, whose façade was given a Palladian dress by Hamilton Gorges in the mid-eighteenth

century. John Cornforth[13] has discussed at length the probable stylistic origin and date of the seventeenth-century panelled rooms and staircase, but the hitherto unnoted fact that Sir Walter had eight hearths at Rathbeale in 1664 proves that a substantial house then existed, and this would allow panelling and stair to be earlier than previously supposed.

Further north, at Beaulieu, Co. Louth, Sir Henry Tichbourne was building himself a beautiful house, the earliest example of a wholly unfortified gentleman's residence now existing in Ireland. Before 1650 he had obtained the lands of Beaulieu from Oliver Plunkett, who forfeited them for his part in the 1641 Rising. At the Restoration Sir Henry became Marshal of the Army in Ireland and the lands were confirmed to him under the Act of Settlement in 1662. The Grant states that he had already expended £450 on buildings and improvements,[14] which fits the dates

traditionally given for the erection of the house, 1660–66. Beaulieu is still in the possesion of his descendants, and possibly the only exterior alteration is the substitution of the windows, which may originally have been of the mullioned casement kind. It is built of rubble-stone, plastered over, and with brick dressing. It is wainscoted throughout and much of the original interior decoration has been preserved, including the old stair; a second and grander staircase and elaborate wood-carvings in the arched niches over the doors in the hall were added in the early eighteenth century. Beaulieu's cantilevered eaves are carried on carved consoles very similar to those at Eyrecourt, Co. Galway, another house built soon after 1660, which also has a hipped roof in the so-called artisan style. Eyrecourt is now derelict and beyond repair: its very ornate double staircase with finely carved newels and finials was dismantled, and is now in the Institute of Arts, Detroit.

Adjoining the Catholic church in the village of Eyrecourt is a curious house, now the presbytery, which displays some ridiculous features. It is said to have belonged to an eccentric named Martin,[15] who, after spending many years on the Continent, returned to Eyrecourt where he transformed his house into a folly. At what is now the back of the house he made an ornamental garden, referred to locally as 'the Spanish Garden', with tall arcades and some extraordinary outbuildings. The fine seventeenth-century doorway may have been his hall door, and was apparently brought from some other house, as it bears no relation to the rest of the premises.

Doorway on garden front, Roman Catholic presbytery, Eyrecourt, Co. Galway

Left: entrance doorway, Beaulieu

61

Swiftsheath, Co. Kilkenny, is another puzzling house. The porch is, of course, an addition, and the white-painted plaster gives the whole house a deceptively late and somewhat crude appearance. However, at the left side and back of the house it can be seen that it is built of rubble-stone, and that the giant pilasters, with Corinthian capitals, are of pink brick. Four Swift brothers came to Ireland in the seventeenth century: one was the father of the celebrated Dean of St Patrick's, while Godwin, the eldest, became Attorney-General to the Duke of Ormonde for the County Palatine of Tipperary. Under the aegis of this Duke and his Duchess, building-work flourished in Co. Kilkenny after the Insurrection and throughout the reign of Charles II. The Duchess built a great brick house at Dunmore, about three miles north of Kilkenny, and also had work done on Kilkenny Castle, whose great seventeenth-century gateway has giant Corinthian pilasters. Since this decoration occurs at Swiftsheath, it is interesting to find that it was in use by the seventeenth-century builders in the Ormond Palatinate.

In view of the stylistic elements, and the early brickwork, Swiftsheath must be basically a Carolean house, begun by Godwin Swift in the first phase of building just before the Restoration, but possibly not finished until some years later. On the front cornice of the house is a date-stone inscribed 1656. According to the Admission Registers of Trinity College, Dublin, Godwin's eldest son Thomas was born in London in 1658, but the family undoubtedly moved back and forth, like the Percivals of Burton Hall. The arms on the pediment (Sable an anchor in pale or, stock azure, the stem entwined by a dolphin or swift descending argent) are the fanciful ones – a pun on his own name – that Godwin Swift assumed for himself; they are quartered with the proper arms of Swift (Or, a chevron vair between three bucks in full course proper). As none of the four Miss Swifts, brides of their cousins, the heads of the family in the succeeding generations, was an heiress, it is difficult to assign these arms according to the laws of heraldry. They are certainly a late addition to the building, purporting to refer to the first Godwin.

The Warings had been in Ireland since the early years of the Plantation of Ulster, and in 1658 William Waring purchased Donaghcloney, Co. Down, from John Barrett, a Cromwellian Captain of Horse who had received lands confiscated from the Magenis family, the original Irish owners, as debentures. An interesting, if pathetic, correspondence survives, showing that Waring was on good terms with the Magenises, who remained in their old dominions in reduced circumstances, and that he made an allowance to them.[16] Immediately after the purchase Waring lived in a log house on Holden's Hill in true pioneer fashion until he had built Waringstown House in 1667.[17] This house was originally only two storeys high, with walls of stone and mud and a thatched roof. Something of its former appearance can be deduced from the sides, where dormers with shaped pedimented gables can be seen, similar to those at Rich Hill, but the façade has undergone much alteration. In the same year Waring established the weaving village of Waringstown, whose core retains some of its early character, although in this century many of the interesting, single-storey thatched and gabled houses have been demolished.

Colonel William Meade, born in 1612, was a Royalist and friend of the Duke of Ormonde. At the Act of Settlement he acted as one of the trustees for the 'Forty Nine Officers'. Though of old Cork Catholic stock, he himself was a Protestant, his father having conformed to the Established Church. His maternal uncle, the 2nd Viscount Kilmallock, was a Catholic, and his first cousin, the 4th Viscount, was

a staunch Jacobite who died in exile in Spain. Even in his own immediate family
the Colonel had religious differences: two of his daughters married Catholic
Jacobites while two of his sons were Protestant clergymen. On his paternal estate
at Ballintober, Co. Cork, he built a three-storey eleven-bay gabled house with
dormers on the top storey of the central block, and two oblong multi-bay parallel
wings set forward in echelon at the front. These wings ended rather strangely,
having external chimneys on their front walls between windows on either side on
every floor. The house has been demolished, but a print made in the late seventeenth or early eighteenth century[18] depicts it in some detail. It was set in extensive
formal gardens and had large outbuildings.

Considerably smaller than Ballintober, but following the same idea of a rectangular block (85 by 28 feet) with two square wings (28 by 28 feet) set forward in
echelon at the front, is Rich Hill, Co. Armagh, built about 1670–80. Edward
Richardson paid Poll Tax there in 1659, but as no Hearth Tax was paid in 1664
it may be inferred that the house was not then built. The roof-ridges of the wings
are masked by Dutch gables, as are those of the four dormers at the front, and that
of the return (which contains the stair) at the back. There is no basement; unless
the kitchen was an outbuilding, it must have been the room to the right of the
entrance where there is a great fireplace, 10 feet wide. The room to the left of the

entrance has a small fireplace and may have been a hall or dining-hall. There is also a fireplace in the room in each wing. The drawing-room would have been on the first floor over the hall. This room has an extra fireplace, whose external chimney is corbelled out at the back above a ground-floor window. The chimneys at the ends of the main body of the house are also external, with tall panelled stacks in brick. Beaufort remarked of the house in 1808, 'it seems a very antient fabrick'.[19]

Another Ulster house with Dutch gables was Echlinville, Co. Down, where each bay of the centre front rose to a gable crowned by an ogee-shaped pediment, with similar gables on the dormers at the side. The house has now been rebuilt, but a print made before 1848 shows its former appearance.[20]

The Turret, Ballingarry, Co. Limerick provides an unusual instance of the use of a Dutch gable to mask a roof-ridge at right angles to the ridge on the main block. Careful examination of the interior shows that the gabled wing, which has thick walls and floors at different levels from those in the rest of the house, was originally a tower. According to tradition The Turret gained its name from having been integrated with a turret of an old Hospitaller habitation.[21] The house was built and the bastion incorporated by Major John Odell, whose arms and the date 1683 are upon the gable. Above them is now a cross with the date 1890, which is when the house was repaired for a presbytery. The story goes that the parish priest, mistaking the crescents in the Odell arms for Islamic emblems – perhaps through association with Hospitallers, Crusaders and hence Saracen infidels – insisted that the cross should be placed above it for safety. At the same time the regrettable porch and plate-glass sash-windows were added, and also the wing at the back, which contains a kitchen beneath a first-floor extension to the reception-rooms. The house of 1683 is long and narrow, one room thick, with a small return at the centre back containing the original wooden stair. Excavations made near the house in 1880 revealed a large quantity of kitchen refuse, which included boars' tusks.[22]

John Odell's antecedents and career are not without interest for they are representative of many others of his class and time. Indeed, in his affairs and those of his descendants one has almost a microcosm of three centuries of Irish history. If he had any right to the arms he set on The Turret in 1683, his ancestors had been prominent gentry in Northamptonshire, but as his immediate family do not appear in the Visitation they must have been a younger branch – of which there were several – living as yeomen. His father, and probably his grandfather, came to Ireland in the late sixteenth century, among the first settlers in the Munster Plantation. His father died young and his mother later married Richard Bettesworth, a widower whose first wife was a niece of Sir John Jephson of Mallow Castle. Their combined families, with about a dozen children, lived in primitive conditions at Pallas in the parish of Corcomohide, Co. Limerick, which John Odell's father had obtained by mortgage from the adventurer Courtney. It was a far cry from Fynings Manor House, Rogate, Sussex, Richard Bettesworth's old home. The Pallas property was sacked by the Irish in 1641; John Odell's mother claimed and received £2,240 compensation on his behalf. Bettesworth was a Royalist officer before 1649, but both his stepsons, John and Charles Odell, served as officers in the Cromwellian army. Many families changed sides due to feelings of having been left without sufficient support and protection from the Crown, which was heavily engaged in England with its own struggles against the Parliamentary forces. Indeed, Lord Inchiquin himself, having commanded the Royalist troops, switched his allegiance from King to Cromwell, taking most of his army with him.

In 1659 John Odell still held Pallas, and his brother had managed to obtain the castle and lands of Castletown (now Castletown Conyers), sequestered from Simon McEnery, an Irish Catholic. In 1660 and 1661 John was a Commissioner for Poll Tax in Co. Limerick; in 1662 he presented silver to Trinity College, Dublin, possibly to enhance his repute with the Commissioners of the Act of Settlement, who granted him 1,679 acres in Co. Limerick. In 1671 he purchased from London Adventurers a thousand-year lease of Ballingarry with its fairs and markets. (This had been confiscated from the De Lacys, Catholics of Norman origin, whose much-reduced heirs remained on fragments of their old estate, protected by the Odells. In time some of them escaped the indignity of this situation and left Ireland to rise to extremely high positions in Spain and Russia.)

John Odell served as High Sheriff of Co. Limerick in 1678–79, in which year the Earl of Orrery reported that 'Captain Odell, High Sheriff of Limerick had his sub-sheriff (though a Paptist) murdered by some Irish while doing his duty'. He was then living in the De Lacy Castle at Ballingarry, and had applied – unsuccessfully – for leave to fit it out and fortify it. In 1681 he and his wife presented Communion plate to Ballingarry Church, dedicated to 'ye Service of god'. Thwarted in his plans to refurbish the old castle, and anxious for a residence befitting his status, he built The Turret in 1683. He may have seen such Dutch pediments in Limerick city or Dublin and considered them the height of fashion – though as he had only one gable to mask, it produces a curiously lopsided effect. In 1692 he became Member of Parliament for Askeaton, and proceeded on his ambitious upward path by marrying his eldest son to a daughter of the 20th Lord Kerry. The Fitzmaurices were old Norman stock who had become Protestants, made their peace with the Government, and thereby kept their title and lands. The bride was as tough and cunning as any of them, and this illustrious alliance proved John Odell's undoing. The lady sued him for non-completion of her marriage settlement, with the result that he spent several years in prison, during which time his estates were badly mismanaged; he died in 1700, according to his outraged daughters (who had been left dowerless) due 'to his imprisonment and other severe treatment' by his son's wife.[23]

There were professional architects in Co. Limerick before The Turret was built; one of these, Captain William Kenn of Cahernarry (possibly John Odell's father-in-law) was building Burton Hall near Liscarrol, Co. Cork, for Sir John Percival in 1665. On 3 August he wrote to his employer from Liscarrol concerning 'an estimate of what the mason, bricklayer, carpenter, carver and sawyers work will amount to to erect such a pile'. Bricks had been prepared locally (according to Kenn, 'overdone') but he advised Sir John to import from Bristol 'freestone' sheet lead, square-bar iron for the cellar windows, elm and elm plank for stairs which are to be through cut in leaves and antics, as I believe your worship has often seen them in balconies in London . . . linseed oil colours for all the work . . . glass and piglead'.[24] Sir John's premature death on 1 November 1665 probably interrupted the work, for his children were still infants; their uncle, Robert Southwell, was their guardian and administered the Percival Irish estates.

In May 1669 Kenn submitted to Southwell details of designs for a house to be built in the park at Burton,[25] and on 27 September 1670 they signed the agreement for its construction.[26] The specifications are given: it was to be 76 feet long by 57 feet wide; the height from the upper part of the hall floor to the wall-plate $30\frac{1}{2}$ feet; the walls to be of stone, lime and sand, the outside $3\frac{1}{2}$ feet thick and 3 feet on

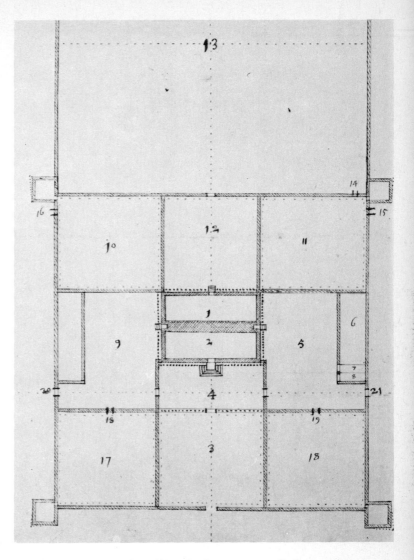

Thomas Smith's draft for the courts and gardens of Burton Hall, parish of Churchtown, Co. Cork: 1 and 2 main house; 3 forecourt (84 by 78 feet); 4 a gravelled court; 5 a stable court; 6 stables (60 by 20 feet); 7 and 8 coach-houses; 9 court with buildings (60 by 74 feet) for brew-house, bakehouse and wash-house; 10 court to lay firing in; 11 court to serve a stable; 12 back court entering garden; 13 the pleasure garden (248 feet square); 14 side-gate for labourers to enter and dung for the garden; 15 gate for hay-yard; 16 gate for fire-yard; 17 and 18 waste courts; 20 and 21 side-gates for front door

IV Left: stucco decoration on ceiling and walls of the dining-room, Riverstown, parish of Templeusque, Co. Cork (pp. 112–13)

the upper storeys. The middle wall of the double-pile was to be 7 feet thick and 3 feet on the upper storeys, and to have twelve chimneys with brick shafts rising 7 feet above the top of the roof, four on the hall storey, four on the dining-room storey and four in the garret.[27]

Less than five months later one Thomas Smith submitted another proposed plan for Burton.[28] Kenn died before the house was finished and his son Benjamin continued work with Smith, so that by July 1674 stone had been brought in and beds of mortar made up containing 2,500 barrels of lime. In July 1676 young Sir Philip was at Burton; and by 1678, when he came of age, the house appears to have been finished. An inventory he prepared of his late father's goods lists twelve family and two other portraits, in addition to a religious subject and a 'little picture of a woman making sausages' which were 'left out to air in the dining room at Burton'. Five other family portraits, with furnishings and two paintings entitled *The Judgement of Paris* and *Ulysses' Companions Turned into Swine*, were still stored in his mother's house in Kinsale.[29]

Sir Philip died when he was twenty-four and was succeeded by his twenty-year-old brother, Sir John, who was born near Burton in 1660. His letters show an intense and intelligent interest in building and design. In 1682 he wrote to Thomas Smith, 'contriver at Burton', requesting measurements, plans and details of the proposed alterations to the interior there.[30] Smith sent these within a month. They state that the house had 'twelve principall rooms on four floors'. He proposed inserting windows at both ends of the great cellar, which had no light, with an assurance that this would neither weaken the house nor spoil its uniformity. The stairs were to be moved, and rearrangements made on other floors. As to the outbuildings, he wrote:

> this I would do were it my own . . . set window frames in ye dead walls against ye adjoining Cloyster and Herbhouse in ye south and against ye turf house, otherwise it will look very un-uniform, which windows may be made open through ye walls as other and be usefull should those rooms be ever converted to other uses, in the meantime fild up with dry wall and plaistered over within, and windows glassed without.

He advised Sir John to obtain in London 'patterns of the newest fashion wainscott and of cullering . . . and also patterns of ye best ornaments about doors and chimneys'.[31] Within a month Sir John sent a long and detailed reply, approving most of the suggestions and desiring other changes. He had ascertained what was most fashionable in London and wanted the same interior styles at Burton. He also notified Smith that he had sent 'a ton of sheet lead' from London, and promised to order a copper ball of the size required, fifteen pounds of block tin for soldering and two gallons of linseed oil.[32] In the autumn of the same year his agent in Cork wrote that 'iron brick' for chimneys could be procured there, and the following March Lord Shannon wrote recommending a potter who 'serves all Cork and the county about it; he has made pipes for me to save leaden ones that hold very well, as also flower pots for the garden'.[33] In November 1683 John Barbor signed a contract to level the garden, so work on the house was probably almost completed.[34] Sir John had expressed his intention of sending over a gardener from England, and in addition to the gardens beside the house there was to be a walled kitchen garden.

In 1687 Sir Richard Cox, the Lord Chancellor, passing Burton Hall, remarked that it was 'a stately new house in a large noble park'.[35] It was not surprising he was impressed; such a house in the height of fashion was indeed rare in rural Ireland. Under the dome which crowned the centre of the building was a timber spiral stair which Smith had moved slightly southwards, thereby disposing of a little stool-room on the garret floor in order to accommodate the stair-shaft which he lit through a leaded glass 'lanthorn' in the roof. There was also a back stair at the north end of the house. The drawing-room and dining-room communicated, and both had doors on to the gallery. On the dining-room floor were a pantry and other useful offices and at least one small bedroom. The main bedrooms were on the floor above the dining-room, Sir John and his lady's chamber being over the hall. Their bedroom was handsomely furnished with embroidered mohair cushions and a Persian carpet, and among its other fittings were a cabinet, a chest of drawers and tinned copper sconces. Off the room was Lady Percival's closet, which contained an escritoire and a close-stool and pan. The Mohair Closet, which also communicated with the main bedroom, had another bed, a small table and a looking-glass in a tortoise-shell frame. The other big bedrooms were the Velvet Room (with crimson velvet hangings embroidered in white silk), the Blue Room and the Red Room; among the smaller bedrooms on the top floor were a Yellow

Room and a Blue Drugget Room, as well as five servants' rooms which opened off a corridor where there was a fireplace for their use, the servants' hall being 'below stairs'. In the nursery there were four canopy-bedsteads and two 'twig cradles'. The parlour and hall were furnished with three dozen cane-bottomed chairs (some with cushions), four tables, a black ebony cabinet inlaid with tortoise-shell and ivory, and a clock and case. In his study Sir John had an escritoire, a slate table, a pair of organs, a bass-viol, a suit of armour, three swords, five hundred 'books of all sorts', tables, a folding-bed, curtains and a green rug.[36]

The numerous outbuildings at Burton included an aviary, herb-house, turf-house, laundry, dairy, brew-house, coach-house and stables with sleeping accommodation above, arranged in two of the courtyards. The illustration shows Smith's draft for the whole compound. The four turrets were to be 16 feet square, and Smith specified that one of the front ones might be a porter's lodge with recourse from it to the gate, since a gatehouse would blind the house.

Sir John had sent strict instructions that the dairy was not to be too near the wash-house lest 'ye constant fire will spoyle what is in ye Dayry'. Nor was the dairy to have a chimney, though there was to be one in the little room next to the wash-house for boiling milk, and another room adjoining it, without a chimney, for the milk to stand in. This large household is said to have consumed weekly two bullocks, twenty sheep and the milk from thirty cows.

That enthusiastic builder, Sir John, did not long enjoy the fruit of his expenditure, for he died in April 1686, leaving debts of £11,000.[37] The heir was his three-year-old son, but he was not to enjoy it either, for in 1690 lovely Burton Hall, its contents and about fifty substantial houses and other smaller dwellings on the estate, were burned by the routed forces of James II retreating from their defeat at the Boyne.[38] The total losses were assessed at £40,000, and no trace of the house now remains.

A great house built in the same decade whose walls are still standing is Ballymacward (or Wardtown), Co. Donegal. Henry Folliott, who was created 1st Baron Folliot of Ballyshannon in 1619, acquired extensive estates in that part of the county, and his son, the 2nd Baron, purchased the lands of Ballymacward from Trinity College, Dublin, after 1657. He promptly leased them to his first cousin, Major John Folliott of Ballyshannon, who built a small house there with only three hearths,[39] his main place of residence being Ballyshannon, where he died in 1682. Ballymacward was inherited by his son, Colonel John, an ambitious, prosperous man, who was Member of Parliament for Ballyshannon in 1692. He resided at Ballymacward, but deeming the three-hearth house out of keeping with his position, he built a large establishment on this glorious site about the time of his marriage to Lucy Wynne in the late 1680s. He died at Ballymacward in 1697, and his widow remained there until her death in 1730. Later in the eighteenth century their descendants abandoned Ballymacward with its spectacular views of sea and mountain, for Hollybrook, Co. Sligo, a ponderous block, much more in keeping with Georgian taste, but in an extremely dull situation.

Ballymacward is a three-storey, five-bay house with basement and garrets, built of brick and stone, its centre and end bays having curved projecting fronts. The narrow windows have either round or elliptical heads: in 1938 some of the sashes and glazing bars were still in position, but now only the shell remains. Above the windows on the third storey is a ridged cornice, similar to that on the Garden House at the Royal Hospital, Kilmainham, which also has curved wings. Unlike most Irish houses of this period it has tall chimneys that rise from the wall which divides each bay vertically, rather than from the one which divides the two piles, or from the end gables. At each end of the ground floor at the front are matching circular rooms with domed ceilings, the cupolas and frieze decorated with floral motifs in plaster. A stone-walled ditch like a moat – some ten feet deep in front – surrounds the front and sides of the house, access to the front door being across a little bridge. This channel cannot have been filled with water since it communicates with the basement. The large subterranean passages in the outer walls are said to have led to the shore: their purpose is unknown.

On the other side of Ulster, the Act of Settlement bestowed the estate of Gill Hall in Co. Down, upon Alderman Hawkins, who had raised £75,000 for the distressed in Ireland during the Cromwellian Wars, and procured food, lodging and clothing for five thousand Protestant refugees who had fled to London to escape the furious Irish.[40] The body of the present house has seventeenth-century panelling, and this must be the part in which John Magill of Gill Hall was living when he made his will in 1677, leaving as his heir his grandson, Sir John, the 1st Baronet. It was in a bedroom of this house that Sir John's sister-in-law, Lady Beresford, when staying there in October 1693, claimed to have received the visitation of the ghost of Lord Tyrone who came (as he had promised to do) to relate his own recent death and tell her whether God existed or not. His report was in the affirmative. After Sir John's death in 1699 the house passed to his sister's son, John Hawkins of Rathfryland, who assumed the name Magill. It was probably he who added the early eighteenth-century wings which, although giving a balanced appearance, actually have asymmetrical fenestration on the ground floor. At this time an attempt was made to marry the new decoration to the older house by adding similar architraves to the windows of the central bay. The door is encased in a Gibbs surround, a style flourishing in England about 1725. This surround is within another formed by two Tuscan columns separated from a segmental pediment by a sculptured frieze.

Not all great houses were built anew like Ballymacward and Gill Hall. Some were built on long-used sites, like Curraghmore, Co. Waterford, where the keep of the old Poer castle was incorporated into a great house, first in the seventeenth and again in the eighteenth century, although the form of the ancient fortress remains clearly evident on the façade.

Dromana, in the same county, the stronghold of the Fitzgeralds of the Decies, is perched on a crag overhanging the Blackwater and commands one of the most glorious views in Ireland – the broad river flows darkly below and in the distance, beyond the luxuriant woods, are the blue peaks of the Knockmealdown and Galtee mountains. At sunset its beauty is breath-taking, and the view has barely changed since Gerald, second son of the 7th Earl of Desmond, built or improved a castle there early in the fifteenth century, when his father gave him the lordship of the Decies. His grand-daughter, who was born at Dromana, was the famous Katherine, wife of the 16th Earl of Desmond, about whom many tall tales have been told. Sir Walter Ralegh, who had met her in 1589, started the ball rolling by saying that she lived for many years thereafter, and had been married in the reign of Edward IV.[41] Others seized on the story, and soon the old Countess was credited with having danced with Richard III[42] and survived to see James I on the throne! She died in 1604, so in order to accommodate all her adventures it has been alleged that she was 120, 147 or even 160 years of age at her death, which is supposed to have resulted from a fall when climbing either a nut tree or one of the cherries planted by Ralegh in the Blackwater Valley. The best-known feat attributed to her – the

visit, on foot to London in 1587, pushing her daughter in a cart from Bristol – actually refers not to her but to Eleanor, widow of the Rebel Earl.[43] Possibly the old Countess herself told Ralegh that she was 125 at the time of their meeting. He had become her landlord,[44] and this could have been a means of attracting his benevolent interest. In fact her husband, had he been alive, would have been this age, but she was his second wife,[45] a daughter of his first cousin and thus of a younger generation. Judging by the age of her brother, Gerald, Lord of the Decies, who lived at Dromana, she must have been about ninety when she met Ralegh and well over a hundred when she died.

Dromana was surrendered to the Irish rebels in 1642 and not retaken by the Government forces until 1647, when the old castle was severely damaged. Building on to it probably began at the Restoration, for in 1675 Richard Francklin, uncle of Katherine Fitzgerald, the heiress-owner, was living there. After her marriage in 1676, Katherine and her husband, Edward Villiers, made their home there until his death in 1693. This suggests two series of building operations after the destructions of the Civil War, the earlier house being further enlarged and embellished to accommodate the bridal pair. After a period when its owners lived mainly in England, a large Georgian mansion was added to the earlier constructions. This has now been demolished, but the seventeenth-century building remains, still owned and inhabited by a descendant of the fifteenth-century Lord of the Decies. It is now almost impossible to tell where the old castle ends and the two seventeenth-century houses begin: many rooms have thick castle walls, and the ancient dungeons form the cellars of the present house. The low building to the east may perhaps be the earlier seventeenth-century house, and the portion at right angles to it, looking straight across the river and built into the castle foundations, may be the addition.

Burton Hall, Ballymacward, Gill Hall and Dromana all had one factor in common – money. The Percivals and Villiers were extremely rich, with extensive

Kilbline Castle, parish of Tullaherin, Co. Kilkenny

English as well as Irish estates. The Folliotts and Magills, though not as rich, were still wealthy by the standards of their time. These families, however, were exceptional: most of the newcomers to Ireland had little means beyond what they could squeeze out of their estates, and most of the estates, having been cruelly ravaged in the late wars, were at a low productive level. Thus those who could afford large or extravagant houses were in a small minority.

Many of those who had lived in a tower-house until the Restoration contrived to make their quarters more comfortable and less cramped by the economical addition of a communicating house. This was usually a low, two-storey building, with access to the tower either at the side or back. Indeed, judging by Dineley's sketches made during his tour of the south of Ireland in 1681,[46] by this time most of the country gentry were living in houses attached to a tower-house and surrounded by stout bawn walls enclosing outbuildings. The bawn itself seems sometimes to have become a garden, and was often entered through solid timber gates hung on handsome pillars, some of which are shown as being capped with ornaments such as balls or urns. An elaborate example of this kind was Ballyclogh, Co. Clare, which had, in addition, a turret at each corner of the front wall. Many of these houses were subsequently levelled to make way for Georgian residences, but a few still survive in good condition, such as Kilbline, Co. Kilkenny, which is an excellent instance of the integration of house with castle. The castle had originally belonged to the Comerfords, who were there before 1556,[47] and on its first floor it has a chimney-piece dated 1580. From the Comerfords it passed in 1586 to the Shortalls, who remained there until at least 1668. It may have been Thomas Shortall who added on the house. Later Kilbline became the property of Ralph Gore, and by the mid-eighteenth century was occupied by the Candlers. For over a hundred years now it has been in the hands of the Ryans, who still employ two floors of the tower as store-rooms, and until recently used a panelled room in the tower as a sitting-room.

74

A somewhat similar situation may be seen at Castle Salem, Co. Cork. William Morris was a Baptist elder from Wales who served as a captain in the Parliamentary Army, but became a convinced Quaker and thus fell foul of General Cromwell and was discharged. Under the Act of Settlement he was granted the fifteenth-century castle of Benduff in West Carbery, which had been confiscated from the rebellious Irish chief, Florence McCarthy. The good Quaker and his family lived in the old fortress until his death in 1681. The following year his son Fortunatus married, and the L-shaped two-storey five-bay house with garrets abutting on the castle was built for his bride, the whole property being renamed Castle Salem. Fortunatus's will, made, on 8 February 1686/7, bequeathed 'the new building that I built since my father deceased' to his wife, and the old castle to his infant son.[48] House and castle still communicate at the turn of the house stair, and until recently the old twin-seat privy in the castle was the only sanitary fitting in the entire premises. Presumably the widow Morris and her son were intended to share it. Little Castle Salem, which in the eighteenth century boasted ornamental gardens with ponds, islets and clipped yews, is still inhabited. The yellow-washed house, nestling under the stump of the old fortress on the rock outcrop among the rugged hills, is most enchanting at evening light, virtually unchanged since it was built, except that in the last twenty years the timber door-frame – two Tuscan pilasters surmounted by a pediment – has been removed, as has the seven-pane fanlight, of the same long narrow type to be seen at Moyvanine, Co. Limerick. The banisters of the Castle Salem stair are identical to those at Moyvanine – simple, turned columns; in both houses a pair of these are used instead of a newel at the bottom and top of the stair, with a single column in place of a newel at each bend, an arrangement also found at Castletown Conyers.

William Morris is said to have taken off the top of the Benduff tower-house: at Assolas, also in Co. Cork, a small tower-house was obviously truncated to make a more acceptable dwelling. Its front is still to be seen, sandwiched between two bow-ended wings, one of which forms the front of the new house. The rooms of the tower still have seventeenth-century panelling in the deep window-embrasures of the thick walls.

Assolas, parish of Castlemagner, Co. Cork. The centre part is the seventeenth-century house

75

Anthony Chearnley's house in the bawn of Burncourt, parish of Shanrahan, Co. Tipperary. An engraving of 1792

Above, right: Moyvanine, parish of Robertstown, Co. Limerick, and below: floor-plan of Moyvanine

A more ambitious venture was undertaken at Trim, Co. Meath, where seventeenth-century (and later) additions were made to the early fifteenth-century castle of Sir John Talbot, 1st Earl of Shrewsbury, afterwards Lord-Lieutenant of Ireland. At the front of the present building, where the old tower is still clearly visible, there is an oblong stone bearing the arms of the 1st Earl (Talbot quartered with Furnivall) supported by two talbots. On the garden front can be seen the seventeenth-century gables, though the Gothic dressing and the long house to the left are later embellishments.

An engraving of 1792 shows the three-storey, five-bay double-pile in the bawn of Burncourt, Co. Tipperary (p. 47). This was built by Anthony Chearnley, whose daughter married a grandson of Colonel John Godfrey of Knockgraffon, an earlier but not dissimilar house. The remains of Chearnley's once-smart residence are now cowsheds, and, although the bawn wall survives, the only trace that can be observed of its elegant formal garden is the fact that the ground has been levelled. These stylistically unpretentious stone houses became very popular towards the end of the century, being inexpensive to erect, sturdy, warm and very comfortable compared with a tower-house or a log-house, the main alternatives.

About 1680 one type of stone house became increasingly favoured in Munster and Leinster. This was a two-storey, single-pile with garrets, a stair in the return at the centre back and external chimneys with panelled stacks on the gable-ends. The lay-out is illustrated by the floor-plan of Moyvanine, Co. Limerick. The Moyvanine banisters are indentical to those at Castle Salem, and the two houses were undoubtedly built about the same time, 1682. Moyvanine belonged to a younger branch of the O'Briens of Ara, Catholics who kept quiet and thereby managed to retain it. One of them is said to have ridden his horse upstairs to the garrets – it is hard to imagine why. Helena O'Bryen made her will there in 1784;

thirty years later the house was in the hands of Stephen Roche of Limerick. Its last resident owner in this century was Mr Clery (who claimed kinship with Desirée Cléry, Queen of Sweden). Now used as a barn, it is fast becoming ruinous. The drawing made in 1972 shows the central round-headed window beneath the pediment and the general effect of symmetry.

An almost identical house stands on the townland of Sheephouse in the parish of Donore, Co. Meath, and is now divided between two families. This is the structure depicted in an illustration of 1840 as the farmhouse briefly defended by James II's troops during the Battle of the Boyne.[49] Though the 1654 Civil Survey does list a stone house on these lands,[50] in view of the evidence of Moyvanine and Castle Salem, the existing house was almost certainly built about twenty-five years later.

Mount Odell (formerly Kilcrump), Co. Waterford, is a variant of this type; its floor-plan is the same as Moyvanine's, but its height is considerably greater, having an additional storey. It was built by Charles Odell after he married a daughter of Sir Richard Osborne of Ballintaylor in 1678. His son and grandson, both High Sheriffs of Co. Waterford, lived in the house, which the Odells did not leave for a more elegant residence until 1740. Comparing their social and financial position with the simplicity of their house this might seem strange, were it not that the Osbornes, the principal landlords of the district and baronets to boot, did not move from Tickincor until the same time. Mount Odell long remained Odell property, and was leased to a series of tenant farmers. The illustration of the back of the house with its return shows clearly the original weather-slating.

Mount Odell, parish of Whitechurch, Co. Waterford

Some time after his move to Waterford, in 1697, Charles Odell sold his former property at Castletown McEnery, Co. Limerick, to Captain Charles Conyers, who may already have been living there as a tenant. Mrs Conyers was a daughter of John Odell; she was born in the De Lacy castle at Ballingarry and spent her youth at The Turret (p. 65), built by her father. The home of her married life shows another stage in the progress of domestic taste. It is practical, comfortable and though simple does not lack a certain elegance. At the back, where there is the usual return containing the stair, and where two dormer-windows still survive, the other windows have no architraves; the architraves on the front were probably added when changes were being made to the fenestration. The gardens were landscaped at an early date. The ornamental pond has a central lead-figure of Neptune placed on an axis with the hall door. The building to the left of the house is the stable block. Another single-storey wing, with three windows on a curved bay front, once added to the right of the house, has now been demolished. In a photograph taken before this demolition, Castletown Conyers bears a marked resemblance to Springhill, Co. Derry.

The exact date when the present house at Springhill was built has never been determined. The end wings were added in 1765, but there can be no doubt that the central block is the house referred to in William Conyngham's will in 1720 as his 'dwelling house, barn, stable, brew house, Turf house, cow house . . . old orchard, new orchard, cherry garden, washing green, Pond garden, stackyard and Green garden'.[51] A likely date for building is 1680, when this William, of Scots Presbyterian descent, married. Family tradition has it that the gardens were laid out about this time, which agrees with the mention of new and old orchards in the will; the shaped gables on the outbuildings also point to such a date. Springhill, which is now in the care of the National Trust and open to the public, has a particularly fine panelled oak staircase, with banisters composed of alternate turned and twist-turned columns and plain newels. There are several other panelled rooms, and some of the top chambers have sloping alcoves for the accommodation of beds.[52]

It should be noted that quite a number of seventeenth-century buildings can be discovered at the backs of later houses. A perfect example of this is the old gabled house with dormers and tall chimneys concealed behind the Georgian front of Newhall, Co. Clare. It was converted into a kitchen, servants' and nursery wing for the mid-eighteenth-century house.

The two distinctive rows of almshouses endowed by Sir Robert Southwell at Kinsale, and dated 1682, are built of rubble-stone. They have garrets with dormers above the ground floor, and all the windows have small diamond panes. The two-storey house between the rows is also of rubble-stone with a brick porch. The almshouses have recently been restored.

By the end of the seventeenth century building in most of the towns was in stone or sometimes in brick. Limerick city was an exception, for there as late as 1692 to 1700 a number of new cage-work houses were being erected. The city must have had a strangely heterogeneous appearance, for simultaneously on the same lots were going up part-stone and part-cage-work houses, thatched cabins, slated cabins, slate houses, slated stone houses and low, small pantile houses.[53] The street frontage of most of these premises was narrow (some are specified as being only 16 feet wide) but the plots were long, and often one house was built behind another, with access from the street down a narrow alleyway. The tenants of the front,

Castletown Conyers,
parish of Corcomohide,
Co. Limerick

Springhill, parish of
Templemore, Co. Derry

Morgans, parish of
Morgans, Co. Limerick

middle and back houses all had right to the water coming from the spouts to the gutters, and the whole arrangement was not unlike that of the Rothes in Kilkenny a hundred years previously (p. 27).

Thomas Rose, who was Sheriff of Limerick city in 1674 and Mayor in 1695, built Morgans on his estate in the county. His son George built a more stylish house near by at Mount Long, and removed there as the family fortunes soared. George's son, Henry Rose, MP, was a Privy Councillor and Lord Chief Justice of the King's Bench, and married the sister of a peer. He may have spent his youth at Morgans, and continued to own it, though he lived at Mount Pleasant. The mason who built Morgans built solidly but apparently without following designs: the effect is naïve, with the upper windows dwarfing those below, which are placed unevenly. Inside, the arrangement is rambling: the kitchen and offices are on the ground floor, with the dining-room, drawing-room and bedrooms upstairs opening off each other without any corridor. The ghost of the benevolent Madam Rose is said to haunt the house. In the nineteenth century it belonged to a branch of the ubiquitous Odells, and it is still inhabited. The building with a panelled chimney-stack, seen to the left in the illustration, seems to be an even earlier house, and in the gardens are the ruins of the inevitable castle.

A house in the same vein as Morgans is Berwick Hall, near Moira, Co. Down. It is, however, more symmetrical, having its larger windows downstairs and squat ones just under its steeply pitched thatched roof. This house, also still inhabited, is of a type known in Ulster as a 'settler's house' or 'yeoman's house', terms not applied elsewhere in Ireland.

Ballinaha, Ballingarry, Co. Limerick, is an even simpler two-storey four-bay stone house, one room thick, with end gables and brick chimney-stacks. The only immediate indication that it was not always just a farmhouse is the huge walled

and partly cobbled stable-yard at its back, quite out of proportion to the house itself.[54] Until late in the nineteenth century it was the home of the Scanlans; but in 1793–94 the then head of the family built Ballyknockane, a fashionable house, near by; he went to live there, keeping Ballinaha for future use by a younger son. Several years before his enhanced status was demonstrated by the move, his eldest sister had married a peer's son, but of course even then Ireland had some fairly dim peers. Well born did not necessarily mean well breeched, even though a title always commanded respect.

House in Fiddown parish, Co. Kilkenny

The traditional small dwellings in the countryside changed little during the century, as is amply proved by many drawings. The lowest category could only be described as hovels – windowless, chimneyless, built of any available materials, mud, scrap-timber, rough stones gathered from the fields or quarried from tumble-down buildings, and roofed with twigs or rushes weighted with stones. An improvement on this was the stone cabin, still windowless, with a chimney-hole in the thatched roof. These were the homes of the poorest labourers. A more prosperous labourer or small farmer might have a thatched cabin, built of stone or rubble, plastered over and with a smoke-hole or simple chimney. Such houses had windows, either one beside the door or one on each side. A more substantial farmer had a house of similar type, but usually longer to include an extra room, and also outbuildings, which were often a continuation of the walls of the house. The house near Fiddown, Co. Kilkenny, is one of these, built of rubble coated with a wash of lime and plaster. Apart from the room to the right with the slated roof, which is an addition, and the chimney-stack, which has been renovated, this house looks just as it did when it was built, and as many such houses looked when James II and his son-in-law William of Orange faced each other at the Battle of the Boyne.

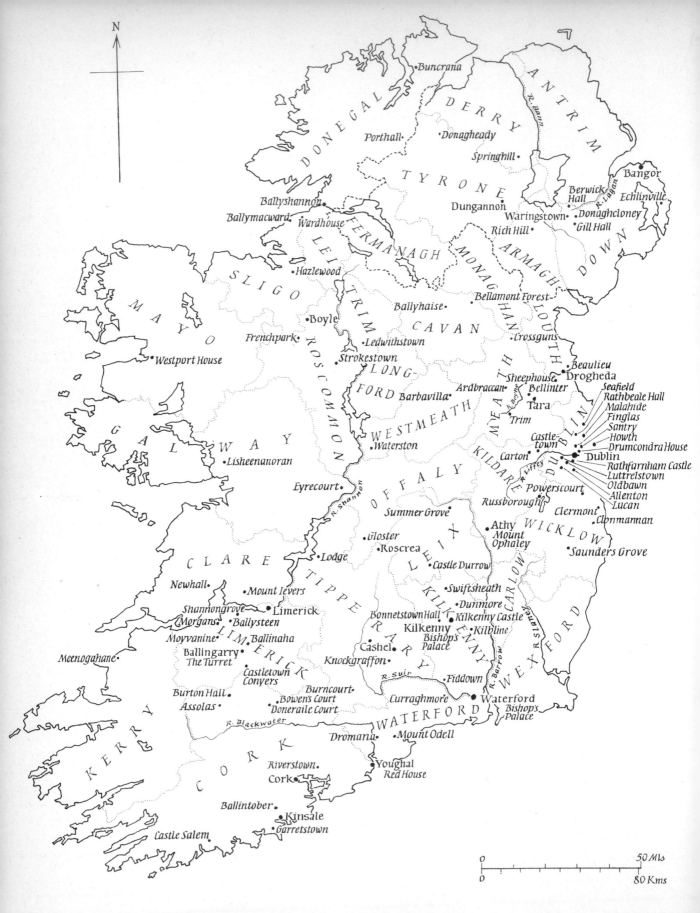

Houses and locations in Chapters 3 and 4

CHAPTER 4

The sixty years of peace after Boyne

1690–1750

THE DEFEAT OF James II's forces, first at the Boyne in 1690 and finally at Aughrim and Limerick in 1691, sounded the death-knell of the old Irish aristocracy. The exiled King set up a court in France as a guest of Louis XIV, and the Catholic nobility and gentry, who had rallied to the Jacobite cause, flocked after him to the Continent. Soon there were Irish colonies in France, in Spain, in Portugal, in Austria and even in Russia. America attracted very few of the Wild Geese, still being essentially Protestant. Hardly any of the *émigrés* returned to Ireland: there was nothing there for them.

Determined to forestall another Irish rebellion, William III's government devised methods of reducing the native population (which was still mostly Catholic) to a position which would effectively prevent the mounting of further revolts. While the rank and file may have been persuaded that in opposing one another they were engaged in a spiritual struggle of Christ versus Antichrist, the Government was cynically exploiting religious differences for a political purpose. Thus the Penal Laws were enacted, forbidding the holding of public office or of commissions in the armed forces by Catholics or Dissenters, who were also prevented from attending the University, buying land or bequeathing an estate intact to an eldest son. Should one son conform to the Established Church he was entitled to claim the entire estate. Worst of all, the Penal Laws promoted the iniquitous system of Protestant Discovery, whereby the so-called 'Discoverers' could report Catholics whom they found breaking these laws, and claim their property in reward. At first all Catholic clerics were officially banished, but soon amendments were made to permit a limited number to remain under licence. It was, of course, impossible fully to implement all these harsh laws. Unlicensed priests and friars, disguised as laymen, travelled the countryside, celebrating Mass in the hedgerows and barns. A few Catholic families contrived to hold on to their property, either with help from a relative who had nominally conformed, or with the co-operation of Protestant friends, but they had to be very careful not to attract the attention of the Discoverers or of the authorities, limitations which precluded any but the most discreet building efforts. An interesting case of this was the Pierse family of Meenogahane, Co. Kerry, who succeeded in keeping their two-storey eight-bay thatched house, built in the very late seventeenth century, and little altered until its demolition in 1972.

Front doorway, Damer
House, Roscrea, Co.
Tipperary

The staircase, Damer
House

v Right above:
Shannongrove, Co.
Limerick (p. 90)

vi Right below:
Bonnetstown, parish of
St Canice, Co. Kilkenny
(pp. 108–9)

The departure of the Wild Geese – the cream of the Catholic majority – and the laws which put the descendants of settlers and the few converted Irish into a privileged position, laid ample foundations for a new Protestant aristocracy. The rising men were eager to display visible signs of gentility – a fine house, a neatly laid-out demesne, fashionable furnishings and elegant clothes. Since many of them never crossed the sea, trends in Ireland inevitably lagged behind those in England, and by degrees distinctive Irish fashions evolved. Most gentlemen who built a house either selected one from a book of patterns or copied from a neighbour. Some were inventive enough to copy from more than one neighbour, or to combine several patterns, and this amalgamation produced some strange results. They tried to obtain maximum effect at a reasonable cost: they wanted a gentleman's residence that could not possibly be mistaken for a farmhouse, although, for practical reasons, they usually needed their farm-buildings close at hand. Various solutions to this problem were essayed. One such solution was seen at Garretstown, Co. Cork, a house built for the Kearneys in the 1720s, where the stable block was placed directly opposite the front door across a small forecourt, and was pedimented and decorated so as to be a virtual replica of the house itself. Some years elapsed before a wholly acceptable answer was found. This was achieved by the adoption of a style which had originated with Palladio, who had had to cater for a similar requirement for his Venetian clients who wanted their farms to bear the aspect of pleasure villas. The adaptation has been called 'Irish Palladianism'.

Most of the smaller houses of the early eighteenth century have vanished, either swept away in the building boom of a hundred years later or so submerged under additions and alterations as to be unrecognizable. Their owners were the subjects of those anonymous family portraits, long unprized and relegated to the attic until eagerly sought out again by interior decorators. Examples of their furniture and table silver abound, but their houses survive mainly as names in deeds and documents. Most of the new houses were given the old Irish townland names, sometimes in an English translation like Hare Hill, Ashgrove, Bushfield or Elmvale. Other houses received more grandiloquent names which were not necessarily a measure of their grandeur. These could result either from mistranslation or corruption (like Castle Matrix which all too quickly turned into Castle Matress), or from their owners' flights of fancy: Saffron Hill, Fairy Hill, Pencil Hill, Bachelors Lodge, Jockey Hall, Racecourse Hall, Harmony Hall, Mount Venus, Mount Music, Castle Comfort and Jerico [*sic*]. The Henn family even went so far as to select Paradise. Some owners gave their house the name of their wife, hence Bessbrook, Barbavilla, Doraville, Annesgrove, Catherine's Grove, Elizavilla, Castle Mary, Castle Jane, Castle Constance and Mount Juliet. Many thought the best effect was obtained by bestowing their own surname on the house, making it Drewscourt, Anketell's Grove, Knoxville, Castle Cooke, Castle Fogarty, Frenchpark, Moore Park, Loftus Hall, Mount Plummer, Mount Leader or Mount Uniacke.

It was a Uniacke of the Mount Uniacke family who, between 1706 and 1715, built himself a town-house in the long main street of Youghal, now known as the Red House or the Dean's House. It has long been attributed to a mysterious Dutch architect named Leuventhen,[1] but as one writer has blindly copied another in making this assertion its origin is now obscure. The house is a fine example of Dutch domestic architecture with a handsome eaves cornice and contemporary Memel pinewood panelling in the interior.

VII Left above: Bellinter, parish of Assey, Co. Meath (pp. 106–7)

VIII Left below: Ardbraccan, parish of Ardbraccan, Co. Meath (pp. 106, 160)

The Dean's House (The Red House), Main Street, Youghal, Co. Cork

A few elegant, though not Dutch-inspired, houses from this period survive in other small provincial towns. That of the Damers in Roscrea, Co. Tipperary, is generally stated to have been built in 1718, but this date is unlikely. It was not until 1722[2] that John Damer of Tipperary obtained the town and lordship of Roscrea. He married in 1724, and it was probably about this time that he built the house which stands within the bawn walls of the old castle in the centre of the town. In 1730[3] the lease was renewed to him and his brother Joseph, and the will of Joseph Damer of Roscrea was proved in 1736. Their nine-bay three-storey house over basement is no longer inhabited, and seems doomed to decay unless a rapid and efficient rescue operation should save it. The front door has an open pediment like that at Buncrana, Co. Donegal, built in 1716. The fine staircase leading to the first floor has reeded Corinthian column newels; its handrail and the ends of the risers are finely carved and there is a carved frieze beneath the first-floor landing.

The red-brick house in Laurence Street, Drogheda, Co. Louth, now the Grammar School, was built during the first quarter of the eighteenth century and belonged to the Singletons, prominent merchants in the town. It was the residence of Henry Singleton (1682–1759), Chief Justice of the Common Pleas and Master of the Rolls. It too has three storeys over basement, but is larger than the Damers' house. Some alterations were made later in the century, including the insertion of the round-headed window lighting the staircase. In general the interior has been remarkably preserved and retains much of its original aspect, including panelling in the entrance-hall, in a room off it and in some upstairs rooms; as is usual in residences of this period all the windows are fitted with panelled window-seats.

87

Two factors have contributed to the decay and disappearance of the town-houses of this period, of which there were once fine examples in Cork, Limerick, Waterford and Athlone. After a couple of generations the descendants of their builders were either out of trade, or had delegated their commercial interests to others, deeming it more fitting to live as country gentlemen. Their town-houses degenerated into use as warehouses or tenements and hence into decay; the value of the sites, the growth of towns and finally the exigencies of town-planning completed the work and most of them have now vanished. One survivor, though in a sad state, is the great town-mansion of the King family in the small town of Boyle, Co. Roscommon, the residence of Sir Henry King, MP,[4] who died in 1740. The house, which is attributed to Sir Edward Lovett Pearce,[5] was probably built at the time of, or soon after, King's marriage in 1722, and many of its features, such as the handsome windows, show the work of a skilful architect. When the Reverend Daniel Augustus Beaufort dined there in 1787, Sir Henry's son, the 1st Earl of Kingston, was still in residence, though already in process of laying-out and embellishing a country seat near by. Beaufort remarked on the great number of rooms and on the gallery which served for a hall (13⅓ feet wide and 118¼ feet long), but considered the house 'not well contrived'. It is vaulted throughout, which Beaufort was told was to avoid fire, an earlier house on the site having been burned; but soon after his visit it did suffer badly in a conflagration. The Kings moved out to the country and by 1837 their old mansion had been converted into an infantry barracks, housing 12 officers, 260 soldiers and a hospital for 30 invalids.

In Ulster the finest surviving town-house of this period is the handsome, three-storey five-bay building in Ann Street, Dungannon, Co. Tyrone. For a time it was used as the Technical Institute, but it is now empty and derelict. The centre bay of the façade has, on the ground floor, a door with a pilastered and pedimented surround, on the first floor a Venetian window and on the top floor a Diocletian window.

Henrietta Street, on the north side of Dublin, was part of the development promoted by Luke Gardiner in the 1720s. Nos 9 and 10 were designed by Sir Edward Lovett Pearce.[6] No. 9 (Mountjoy House) was Gardiner's own residence. It has a splendid interior, including a remarkable hall with an elaborate coffered stucco ceiling, and was inspired by a London house designed by the architect Lord Burlington. No. 10 (Blessington House) has undergone alterations but nevertheless retains some fine interior features; it has become offices of King's Inns. A century later the other great houses were inhabited by prosperous attorneys, proctors, judges and officials of King's Inns; but by the beginning of this present century they had become slums, occupied by the exuberant tenement-dwelling families so brilliantly portrayed by Sean O'Casey in *The Plough and the Stars*.

The early eighteenth-century private houses near the elegant Church of St Anne Shandon in the city of Cork have vanished, but the attractive group of almshouses built round an L-shaped arcade behind the church is still standing. One plaque on the building states that it was begun by the city of Cork 3 July 1718 and finished 21 September 1719, and another plaque states, 'This part of the Almshouse belongs to the Foundation of Mr Clement Skiddy alias Scudamore who about the year of our Lord God MDCXX settled a perpetual annuity of twenty four pounds paid by the vintners company of the city of London for the benefit of twelve aged widdows of this city. The end of the commandments is charity. Ist Tim. 1st.' This unique complex, with its Italianate arcade (described in the contemporary Corporation Minutes as 'piazza work'), has now been bought by the Cork Preservation Society in order to save it from destruction.

Skiddy's Almshouses, parish of St Anne Shandon, Cork

89

Front and back elevations, Shannongrove, parish of Ardcanny, Co. Limerick

In the early years of the eighteenth century Dutch influence was still to be found not only in towns such as Youghal and Limerick but also in the rural areas, as for example at Shannongrove, Co. Limerick, built in 1709, which date is carved over the front door. The elevations illustrated show the main house built for John Bury, allegedly by a mason named John O'Brien, and the flanking wings added by his son William Bury about 1723. In that same year William married the Hon. Jane Moore, daughter of the 1st Lord Tullamore, and their arms – Bury impaling Moore – appear over the door which he placed on the garden front. The present owner, Mr John Griffith, has noted the similarity between the ornamental stone frame of the cartouche bearing these arms and the memorial in Adare Church to John Bury (who died in 1722) and which is inscribed 'Rothery fecit'. It seems reasonable to conclude that this Rothery was responsible for the additions to the house. The Rothery family was in the building business in a big way: a recently published list gives nine Rothery craftsmen, beginning with Nathaniel, a pewterer and Freeman of Dublin in 1674, and ending with George, a mason and Freeman in 1756.[7] To these can be added Thomas of Dublin, mason, working in 1718[8] and Nathaniel of Dublin, glazier, whose will was proved in 1731[9] and who left a son William, alive in 1735.[10] John Rothery was the architect-builder of Mount Ievers, Co. Clare, and when he died in 1736 work there was completed by his son Isaac.[11] Shannongrove has fancy red-brick chimney-stacks with decoration in the panels (p. 85). There is an elegant staircase which may be compared with those in the Damers' house at Roscrea and at Mount Ievers. There is also good-quality panelling in the hall and in several of the rooms.

The well-built house now known as Kildrought House, at Celbridge, Co. Kildare, the property of Mr Gerard Whyte, has all the appearance of being by one

Kildrought House,
Celbridge, Co. Kildare

Left: the staircase,
Shannongrove, Co.
Limerick

of the Rotherys, and could well be the house on the main street of Celbridge described in 1724 as 'lately held and enjoyed by Joseph Rothery'. The garden front,
of stone with brick dressings, markedly resembles Mount Ievers, Co. Clare.

The St Legers acquired their property at Doneraile, Co. Cork, from the son of
the poet Edmund Spenser in 1627, but their first house there was burned. It had
been rebuilt before 1687 when Sir Richard Cox, the Lord Chancellor, remarked
on the house and park.[12] The present building (p. 94), designed by John or Isaac
Rothery,[13] has the date 1725 cut on a stone above one of the windows and may have
incorporated part of the second seventeenth-century house including the vaulted
basement. The projecting porch was added later but contains the original windows
and door. Before the addition of this porch and the curved bays on the sides of the
house, Doneraile Court must have borne a marked resemblance to another house
of Rothery's: Bowen's Court, seven miles away, once the home of the writer
Elizabeth Bowen, and recently demolished. The Viscounts Doneraile remained at
Doneraile Court until the death of the 7th Viscount in 1956. Unfortunately the
heir from California was unable, for some technical reason, to establish his claim
to the property, and the demesne has now been acquired by the Land Commission,
the contents of the Court have been removed and sold and the historic house stands
empty. It was here that the only recorded initiation of a woman into the rites of
Freemasonry took place. Elizabeth, daughter of the 1st Viscount (and later wife of
Richard Aldworth, and mother of St Leger Aldworth, 1st Viscount Doneraile of
the second creation) hid in the library to spy on a Masonic meeting. When she
was discovered, the outraged Masons decided that the only means of ensuring her
silence was to make her take their vows and become one of them. There was a
portrait of her at Doneraile in her Masonic garb.

The little Awbeg River, overhung by willows, meanders through the Doneraile demesne, and in the park are bamboo groves, a lime walk, fish-ponds and lily-ponds, now choked and desolate. For centuries red deer have been kept there, and it was said that when the doctor came out of the house after attending the deathbed of the 7th Viscount, the herd was waiting, gathered into a great half-circle, close to the house and facing the door, as if mourning the end of an epoch at the Court, and as if they had sensed the despair that would presently come upon all those who tried hard – and apparently in vain – to save it from needless destruction. Today, shut up and decaying, Doneraile is probably the saddest house to be seen in Ireland.

The Reverend Francis Gore (1683–1748) was born of a prosperous Co. Clare family, and in 1714 was appointed to the livings of Ballyclough and Castlemagner, Co. Cork, and about the same time acquired the lands of Assolas with its little converted tower-house mentioned in Chapter 3 (p. 75). On the west side of the tower he built a two-storey single-pile with bow ends and made this the front of his new house: between this and the tower, and communicating with each, was built the new staircase-hall, rising the full height of the house. In order to achieve symmetry on the old front a bow-ended kitchen was added to the other side of the tower. The principal rooms have early eighteenth-century panelling, the chair-rails are carved with dentils and the bow-ended dining-room has timber Ionic pilasters. In 1749 the house was inhabited by Philip Oliver; it was later acquired by the Wrixons and remained with the Wrixon-Bechers for many years. It is now the property of Mrs Bourke who runs a guest-house there.

Colonel William Flower, MP, spent many years on building and improving his house, the present Castle Durrow in Co. Leix, which has the date 1716 above its door. The Flowers had been at Durrow for two generations, living in an old tower-house, which was apparently quarried when the new building was done, as a bricklayer was paid for 'brakeing the lumps at ye old castle for making the shore in the cow house'. In 1712 Colonel Flower purchased a large quantity of timber, and in September of that year and the following March the carpenter was paid for making and setting windows and lintels, partitions in the garret and partitions and shelves in the second storey; so presumably the walls of the new house had already been raised. The Colonel had engaged Benjamin Crawley (or Crowley) to supervise the building-work, and the contract stipulated that he was to attend four hours of every working day in winter and six hours a day between 25 March and Michaelmas. Crawley's specifications for the house exist, but are undated. In April 1714 the glazier was paid for glazing 'Madam Flower's closet', and in November a large glazing bill was settled for the upstairs rooms, the hall, nursery, dining-room, etc. At the same time new outbuildings were going up, for in March 1714/15 a slater from Ballyragget, Co. Kilkenny, was engaged to roof a new barn, stable, cow-house and hen-house then being built. His work proved unsatisfactory, for in April 1722 it was reported that the 'slating work of the stables done about four years ago by Andrew Moore of Balliraggit is very much out of repair and absolutely requires to be stript'. In September 1715 the carpenters were paid for their work on the outhouses, and in December two masons were paid for the new haggard, pig-house and pig-yard. In March 1715/16 two other masons – who had already been engaged to build the new barn, cow-house, stables and hen-house – contracted for further extensive work on stables and offices and to make walls in the cellars of the dwelling-house. In May 1716 John Robinson of Mountmellick was employed to sink a well and erect a pump near the new buildings.

Front doorway, Castle Durrow

The big order for panelling was given to John Rudd, joiner, in November 1716, who contracted to finish it within two years, flooring the hall with oak boards. The panelling in the dining-room, drawing-room and best bedchamber was to be 'framed work with a full oge stuck on the framing and a small oge stuck on the margent of the pannels'. In the same month agreement was made with the carpenters to dress and fit the shingles for the new house, and to make the roof completely watertight – for £20. In December the sashes, doors and windows of the offices were painted, and in February following the plumber received £106 for work on the cisterns, and agreement was made with Isaac Tuck of Durrow to flag the lower part of the new house. In December 1718 he was paid £211 6s 9d for flagging other parts of the premises. In March 1716/17 a contract was made with a mason to arch over the lower passage, and by June a considerable amount of painting and plastering had been completed, including the modillion cornice in the hall (which cost £5). In October Thomas Lett was paid for painting and plastering in the new dwelling-house, his labours having included two large 'street doors', three back doors, other doors, nine large and four small 'transum' windows and six 'dormond' windows. Next month the carpenter was paid for turning 5 posts for the gallery and back stairs, $16\frac{1}{2}$ dozen balusters for the stairs (which cost £1 13s 0d) and $8\frac{1}{4}$ dozen balusters for the gallery (which cost £1 1s 3d). The next April a bill was settled for the plastering and tiling of the hall chimney and steward's hall and for bricking the still-room. But work was not over. In November 1726 John Rudd – who had done the more important panelling-work – was paid £21 0s 9d for $229\frac{1}{2}$ yards of oak wainscot in the dining-room, $10\frac{1}{4}$ square feet of flooring for the same room, and 14 feet of sash about the dining-room door; he had also taken down, mended and replaced the closet window in the 'Blew Room'.

After Colonel Flower's elevation to the peerage in 1733 (when he house-proudly took the title Lord Castle Durrow) he made more improvements. In 1734 Richard

Front doorway, Castle Durrow

Left: Castle Durrow, parish of Durrow, Co. Leix. An old photograph taken before removal of the dormers

Entrance porch,
Doneraile Court, parish
of Doneraile, Co. Cork
(see p. 91)

Comerford was paid for work on the stairs, two sets of architraves and a quantity of furniture; Thady Ryan, carpenter, was paid for windows and doors, a pantry table and a table for the pleasure-garden. In 1737 Frank Trumbull, the glazier who had been working on the house since 1714, was still busy glazing. Apart from a few men of obviously Gaelic stock like Ryan, Kinsela, Wholohan and Phelan, most of the artisans seem to have been of settler stock – Hall, Coltman, Tuck, Robinson, Lett, Woods, Rudd and Trumbull.[14]

Little change has been made to the outside of the house, which is faced in an attractive pinkish-grey cut stone. The Flowers, who eventually became Viscounts Ashbrook, lived there until 1922 when the Bank foreclosed one morning at breakfast-time.

The house is now owned by the Presentation Sisters, who keep a school there. To prevent leaking they removed the dormer-windows when the roof was repaired a few years ago. The protruding porch was added in the nineteenth century, but includes the original front door. The old panelling is still intact in one small room, probably a gun-room, on the ground floor and also in the adjoining room to the right of the hall. The large room to the left of the hall with three windows has good plaster-work on the ceiling, which matches the window-panels of the drawing-room, both having the same rosette and shell motifs.

Contemporary with Castle Durrow, but in poor condition, is Buncrana, Co. Donegal, a nine-bay, two-storey house over basement, built for George Vaughan in 1716. The family had already been there for a century: Captain Henry Vaughan held Buncrana Castle (an earlier building) in 1622; his son made his will there in 1671,[15] and *his* son, George senior, who renewed the lease from the Earl of Donegal in 1698, was tenant in possession in 1721, when his son in turn, George junior, again renewed the lease.[16] Like most houses of its period and quality, Buncrana has fine interior panelling.

William Conolly (1662–1729) was also a Donegal man, but of less exalted origin, being the son of a prosperous innkeeper. Beginning as an attorney, he was elected Member of Parliament for Donegal Town in 1692, was Commissioner of the Revenue in 1709 and Speaker of the Irish House of Commons in 1715. From a modest beginning, through astuteness, diligence and clever dealing in forfeited estates after the Jacobite defeat in 1690, he rose to being generally considered the wealthiest man in Ireland. To design his magnificent seat at Castletown, Co. Kildare, he employed the Italian architect Alessandro Galilei (1691–1737). Galilei visited England in 1714, but was back in Italy before actual work began at Castletown in 1719. Several masons were employed there in 1722,[17] but it is not clear who was supervising them, apart from Mr Conolly himself. Edward Lovett Pearce was in Italy, and did not return until 1724, after when he was associated with the work, and some of his drawings relating to Castletown exist.[18]

Castletown, with its centre block linked on either side by colonnaded curtain walls to twin pavilions, was a complete innovation in Ireland, and became the prototype and source of inspiration for many houses throughout the country, though none would rival its pristine elegance. Many of the Speaker's associates in Parliament, fellow lawyers and country gentlemen in general must have come to stare at the rich man's wonderful house.

The Speaker died at his town residence in Capel Street, Dublin, in 1729, but his widow retired to Castletown where she lived until her death in 1752, lavishly entertaining a wide and varied circle of friends. She built the corkscrew barn, the Obelisk and other features in the grounds, but it was the Speaker's grand-nephew, Thomas Conolly, who completed and remodelled the interior of the house, mainly between 1759 and 1765, commissioning the great staircase by Vierpyl and the stucco-work by Francini.[19] The house remained in the family until 1965 when it was sold by Lord Carew (whose mother was a Conolly). Two years later the Hon.

95

Drumcondra House,
parish of Clonturk, Co.
Dublin

Desmond Guinness, with amazing courage, purchased the house and 120 acres for
£93,000, as a headquarters for the Irish Georgian Society and to preserve it for
posterity. Thanks to his public-spirited action, his enthusiasm and perseverance,
it has now regained some of its original furnishings as well as other handsome pieces
donated or loaned by friends and benefactors of the Society, and is open to the
public.

In the early eighteenth century few could hope to emulate Castletown in size or
splendour, but the principle of the linked pavilions quickly proved attractive, since
it allowed the owners either to accommodate or to mask the needed outhouses and
farm premises behind a gracious façade. Among the first to adopt the idea was
William Bury, who added the wings to his father's house at Shannongrove shortly
after 1723, and Henry Ingoldsby, MP for Limerick City, the owner of Carton, Co.
Kildare. A view of his Carton, painted by Van der Hagen before 1738, depicts a
nine-bay building, two storeys over basement and with dormers in the attics: on
each side are twin eight-bay pavilions with dormers in their mansards above the
single floor, and linked to the house by curved curtain walls. These walls were removed when alterations were made to the house about 1739.

Sir Edward Lovett Pearce (c. 1699–1733), who was associated with the building
of Castletown, was the foremost exponent of Palladianism in Ireland. It is not
known where he received his architectural training, but his father was a first cousin
of the great Vanbrugh, and as a young man Pearce travelled in Italy, becoming
well acquainted with the works of Palladio and returning home with a copy of the
Master's *The Four Books of Architecture*. By 1730 he was Surveyor-General for
Ireland. His greatest achievement is held to be the Parliament House in Dublin,
built during Speaker Conolly's time, and now the Bank of Ireland. Despite his
early death, there exist a number of fine examples of his work in private practice:

the town-mansion at Boyle built for Sir Henry King and the houses in Henrietta Street, Dublin, have already been mentioned. More notable still is Bellamont Forest, Co. Cavan, built in the late 1720s, still excellently preserved and occupied as a private house. This has been described as one of the purest examples of a Palladian villa in England or Ireland.[20] Pearce designed it for his uncle, Thomas Coote, and his original designs[21] show that instead of the projecting entrance portico, he intended the principal architectural feature to be a recessed portico, reminiscent of the one by Palladio on the garden front of the Villa Pisani in Italy. The house, whose proportions conform to the standards of the Burlington School and which has an elaborate interior, is illustrated in *Irish Houses and Castles*.[22]

Another elegant example of Pearce's virtuosity is in Cashel, Co. Tipperary. Now a hotel, it was built as a Palace for the Archbishops of Cashel in the late 1720s, and bears similarities to Pearce's houses in Henrietta Street. His designs show it without the dormers which it now has.[23] The symmetry of the entrance front, facing the street and executed in red brick, is very pleasing. The garden front, looking towards the Rock of Cashel, is entirely faced in cut stone. The hall retains original panelling of high quality and has fluted Corinthian columns and pilasters, then so fashionable.

Drumcondra House, Co. Dublin, just outside the city, was built in 1727 for Marmaduke Coghill, Chancellor of the Exchequer, who died in 1738. Above the door on the south front are the arms as certified to his father, Sir John Coghill, and the Coghill crest, a cockerel. The south front is certainly Pearce's work. The east front has giant Corinthian pilasters. There is some plain panelling in rooms on the ground floor and on the stairs, and some fine panelling in rooms on the first floor. The house is now All Hallows College, and well maintained. In the grounds, apparently erected as a folly, stands a ruined temple. This charming Italianate building has been attributed to Galilei, but could also have been an essay of Pearce's.

Temple folly in the garden of Drumcondra House

The architect of Seafield, near Donabate, Co. Dublin, to the north of Drumcondra, has not been identified. The house stands on the townland of Ballymadrought and in the early eighteenth century was known as 'Ballymadrought alias Newport'. There may have been a house there as early as 1659, when Andrew Delahoyd, Gent., is listed as the titulado, though he does not appear in the Hearth Tax in 1664. Prior to 1735 the property was acquired by Benedict Arthur of Cabra and Dublin, who served as High Sheriff in 1729. The garden front of the present house was previously the entrance front of a late seventeenth-century brick house, not dissimilar to Rathbeale in the same vicinity. The old front door at ground-level opened into a flagged entrance-hall with rooms on either side, and this was the house referred to in a deed of 1735[24] as Benedict Arthur's 'dwelling house with stables, coach house, brew house, pigeon house, gardens and offices'. To this house he made considerable alterations, probably between 1737 and 1741, only after which latter date is he consistently described as 'of Seafield'. The old ground floor was treated as a basement, and above it the centre of the house was gutted to create a lofty well-lit central saloon, two storeys high, splendidly decorated with two tiers of Ionic pilasters separating the panels which now contain grisaille paintings of classical figures. The paintings were probably added later in the eighteenth century. A railed gallery, perhaps inspired by that at Castletown, crosses the saloon, linking the two sides of the house on the first floor. The panelling of the rooms on the hall floor was also refurbished: the dining-room, to the left of the new front door, is especially remarkable for its exquisitely carved cornice, frieze and fluted Corinthian pilasters. A flight of steps and a prostyle Doric portico, whose pediment reaches above the first-floor windows, were placed on the old garden front, making it into the new entrance front, with the door leading directly into the saloon and giving an immediate impression of grandeur on a small scale. While the façade is not nearly as delicately executed as the interior, and has been tampered with, it could be immensely improved by the replacement of its glazing bars. Benedict Arthur died at Bath in 1752 and was succeeded by his natural son, John Arthur (whose mother he had married shortly before his death). Arthur's descendants continued to live at Seafield into the nineteenth century, in the second half of which it was purchased by John Hely-Hutchinson; it is now in the appreciative ownership of Mr Howard Dawes, and well cared for.

Gloster, Co. Offaly, is another instance of a notable early eighteenth-century façade and elegant interior being added to a much older house. The alterations, done about 1730 for Trevor Lloyd, are attributed to Pearce,[25] who was his first cousin, their mothers being sisters, daughters of Christopher Lovett, Lord Mayor of Dublin. The Lloyd crest is on the pediment of the old front, and something of the character of the seventeenth-century house can still be discerned. The superimposed garden front achieves an attractive balance with two tiers of fluted pilasters, the upper range with Doric capitals dividing the bays. There are amusing masks on the upper architraves of all the windows, a most unusual feature, although human, animal and grotesque masks were a favoured decoration on Irish furniture. Extending wings were added at each side of the house, and these have pedimented windows on the ground floor and niches above. The door on the garden front leads into a well-lit and richly stuccoed saloon with busts on tall pedestals in its niches, and which, as at Seafield, occupies two storeys in the centre of the house. A deep arcaded gallery, off which corridors lead to the upper rooms, overlooks the saloon: it has protective railings in the arches. From the saloon a handsome door leads into

Right: the saloon, Seafield, parish
of Swords, Co. Dublin

Above: windows on the garden
front, Gloster, parish of Ettagh, Co.
Offaly, and right: upper part of the
saloon from the gallery

the old flagged hall of the seventeenth-century house, whence rises the main staircase, a rather simple structure. The Lloyds remained at Gloster until recent years and it is now a Salesian convent and guest-house.

The old house of Clonmannan, Co. Wicklow, is an anomaly. Built entirely of red brick, its frontispiece seems to be straight from Inigo Jones, which has led to it being regarded as a seventeenth-century house. The house is of remarkably small proportions: were it bigger it might reasonably be considered a product of the red-brick Classical building phase of the 1650s and 1660s, but in view of its size and the unlikelihood of so small and indefensible a house being built in this part of the country in the mid-seventeenth century, it seems more probable that it was built for Holt Truell (born 1700) about the time of his marriage to the daughter of Abraham Yarner. By the end of the eighteenth century the house was too small for the Truells, who built themselves a larger residence in the demesne.

By the 1730s the use of brick had become quite widespread. Saunders Grove (1718), Clermont (1730), both in Co. Wicklow, Barbavilla, Co. Westmeath (1730) and Ballyhaise, Co. Cavan (1730) were all red-brick houses. Ballyhaise has nine bays in its centre block, to which a later owner, William Humphreys, added two broad single-bay wings, breaking slightly forward. The general effect is ponderous, largely due to the additions. The centre bay at the back is curved, and on the main floor accommodates a pretty oval room with good plaster-work, curved doors and fireplace. As in the King house at Boyle all the storeys are vaulted over. When Ballyhaise was built, its owner was Brockhill Newburgh, whose family had been there since the seventeenth century, and who made his will there in 1739. He was succeeded by his son, Colonel Thomas (1673–1776), who in turn was succeeded by his nephew, William Perrott Newburgh. The next heir was a cousin, another Brockhill Newburgh who made his will there in 1797 and was succeeded by his son Arthur.[26] Subsequently the property was acquired by William Humphreys, whose descendants remained there into this century, when it became an agricultural college.

Frontispiece, the old house, Clonmannan, parish of Rathnew, Co. Wicklow

Above right: centre bays of the façade, Ballyhaise, parish of Castleterra, Co. Cavan

Ballyhaise was designed by Richard Cassels, a German architect, born about 1691, who settled in Ireland in the 1720s and anglicized his name to Castle, by which version he is usually known. He married an Irish-born wife of Huguenot origin, and became the leading architect in Ireland after Pearce's death, carrying out a prodigious amount of work, both in Dublin and the provinces, before his death at the age of about sixty in 1750. Castle's main works in Dublin were Tyrone House (1740–45), still standing though considerably altered externally, and the great Leinster House (built in 1745 as Kildare House for the Earl of Kildare, who became 1st Duke of Leinster), now the seat of the Irish Parliament (*Dail Eireann*, p. 2). He designed several important seats in the neighbourhood of Dublin, including Russborough, Co. Wicklow, considered Ireland's greatest example of the Neo-Palladian style, which was built in 1741 for Joseph Leeson, heir to a great Dublin brewing fortune and later 1st Earl of Milltown. Other great houses built by him in the same vein are Carton, Co. Kildare, which he remodelled for his patron, the Earl of Kildare, and Powerscourt, Co. Wicklow, begun in 1731 for Richard Wingfield, later Viscount Powerscourt. These three houses are all described and illustrated in *Irish Houses and Castles*.[27]

In Connaught, Castle built Westport House, Co. Mayo, for John Browne about 1730, and Hazlewood, Co. Sligo, for Owen Wynne. This latter house is one of his earliest essays in the centre-block-and-pavilion type. The exterior is not at all as pristine as his later work, and has some fussy elements. Though the façade is not improved by having lost most of its glazing bars, it still retains some of the fine original stonework, and there is excellent decoration in the hall, which in 1808 Mrs Beaufort found used as a summer sitting-room, furnished with a sofa and family pictures. Her husband's comments on the house in 1787 are interesting. He called it 'a noble place, delightfully situated in a peninsula . . . and laid out in great taste. The house is not large and rather heavy having too few windows but altogether a handsome building and laid out by Cassels who also built the handsome large church at Sligo.' After being inhabited by the Wynnes for generations, the house is now the Irish headquarters of the Italian industrial concern, SNIA.

Entrance-hall, Hazlewood, parish of Calry, Co. Sligo

At Strokestown, Co. Roscommon, there is another Neo-Palladian house, parts of which have been attributed to Castle.[28] The present owner, Mrs Pakenham-Mahon, whose family has been continuously resident there for centuries, recounts the tradition that her ancestor, Nicholas Mahon, returning from exile at the Restoration, brought with him a Dutch architect to build a house on his newly granted lands at Strokestown. This work is supposed to have taken three decades. Nicholas died in 1680, and was succeeded by his son John, who married in 1697 and died before 1708, when an inventory was compiled of the goods of John Mahon of Strokestown deceased.[29] This is not divided into rooms, so is not enlightening as to the disposition of the house at that date, though it does indicate that it was only a moderate establishment, since it lists only six feather-beds and four beds for servants, and although there were 277 ounces of plate (valued at £80) and 126 pounds of pewter (valued at £4 14s 0d) there was no important furniture.

The house has a date-stone inscribed 1696, and the family tradition is that the entire complex of house, flanking walls and pavilions was completed at that time, according to the design of the 'Dutch architect'; the present facing of the main block being, of course, a later addition. In support of this tradition the present owner points out that it would have been unlikely that the house alone, without walls and pavilions, would have been placed on such a sharp declivity. When this was done elsewhere it was usually to secure a view, or because the building followed the lines of an ancient tower; neither explanation fits Strokestown. It seems impossible, however, that the Neo-Palladian lay-out could precede Galilei's introduction of the style to Ireland at Castletown. In the eighteenth century the term 'Dutch' was used loosely to cover also Germans (for example Pennsylvania Dutch – who were, in fact, German) and it seems that the 'Dutch' architect associated with Strokestown was really the German (*Deutsch*) architect, Castle. The arrangement at Strokestown of the galleried kitchen in one pavilion and the columned and vaulted stable in the other closely matches that at Ardbraccan, Co. Meath, known to be by Castle. Undoubtedly, John Mahon (son of the first Nicholas) must have built or completed a house in 1696 which forms the core of the present one. His son Thomas (1701–82), Member of Parliament for Roscommon, married in January 1735 the eldest daughter of Lord Brandon, and it is likely that he then brought Castle from Dublin to smarten and extend his house, refacing the front and adding the pavilions and linking walls. Later in the eighteenth century a drawing-room was added, and other changes made at the back. At this time some superb furniture was installed, including a particularly fine Chippendale bookcase and an inlaid marble table made for the house by Bossi. There is also a claret-table, a rare item evocative of the high living of the eighteenth-century gentry: they sat round these semicircular tables, in front of the hearth, drinking copious quantities of claret (indeed, the vast consumption of French wine in Ireland was considered a national calamity) and throwing the empty bottles into the netted section.

Until the turn of this century the windows in the main block retained their glazing bars: their replacement by plate-glass has now rather spoiled the graceful façade, though the pavilion windows are intact. The old kitchen in the left-hand pavilion is interesting; it is crossed lengthwise by a gallery with a Carolean-style balustrade of robust turned balusters. Their style is perplexing, and it is possible they were copied from a seventeenth-century stone balustrade. Access to the gallery and its communicating storeroom is only through a lockable door, and from the gallery the mistress of Strokestown or her housekeeper could survey proceedings

in the kitchen below and lower baskets of stores to the cook. In the centre of the ceiling is a round contraption, regulated by a weathercock on the roof, which serves to ventilate the kitchen. Off the kitchen is a dairy – still in use – and pantries. The kitchen pavilion is linked to the main house and to its basement (where the present kitchen is now installed) by two corridors masked by the curved curtain wall. On the other side only the curtain wall (without a corridor) joins the house to the stable pavilion, although in the interests of symmetry the wall has been supplied with a door, niches and fake windows. The stables have beautiful cross-vaulting and the stalls, whose timber partitions have vanished, are separated by a single row of Doric columns. The walls of the court at the back of the stable appear to be the remains of the bawn of the seventeenth-century house. A brick tunnel underneath the house links the stable-yard to the kitchen-yard.

The first Nicholas Mahon of Strokestown married Magdalene French of Movilla Castle, Co. Galway, and the Mahon family tradition is that their 'Dutch architect' also built the now-derelict Frenchpark, Co. Roscommon, for a branch of the French family. Frenchpark's old name was Dungar, and so Dominick French called it when he made his will there in May 1670.[30] In 1913 it was reported that the date 1667 was painted on a wooden shutter to the circular aperture in the centre of the gable but that this inscription was quite recent, though it was then alleged to have replaced an earlier one. It appears that Dominick French had a house at Dungar about the same time as Nicholas Mahon had one at Strokestown. Evidently Dominick's son John named the estate Frenchpark, and both he and his widow made their wills there in 1734.[31] John French left his son Arthur a substantial fortune: his funeral and wake were an extravaganza – his body lay in state in the park for three days and nights while the county was feasted around it. Obviously there were several spates of building at Frenchpark, and inasmuch as the linked pavilions and some of the other building definitely appear to be the work of Richard Castle, it is reasonable to conclude that Arthur French, with his new inheritance, employed Castle to renovate

x Left above: East front, Drishane, parish of Castlehaven, Co. Cork (p. 172)

xi Left below: doorway of the Dobbin House, Armagh (p. 208)

Left: the stables, and right: the old kitchen, with stoves and moving spit added in the nineteenth century. Strokestown, parish of Bumlin, Co. Roscommon

and add to the old house about 1735, which would fit with the period when it is assumed Castle was at Strokestown. An illustration in Volume V of the *Georgian Society Records* depicts a wrought-iron gate at Frenchpark with the initials AF and the date 1704 – apparently 1764 with the 6 broken. This must refer to Arthur French, who married in 1722, succeeded to Frenchpark at his father's death in 1734 and died in 1769.

Castle's plans for Ardbraccan, Co. Meath, have recently come to light and are now in the National Library of Ireland. By the time he designed this large stone house with its linked pavilions as a palace for the bishops of Meath, he had gained considerable experience and the result is highly accomplished (p. 86). He achieved a satisfying and tranquil symmetry, much suited to the rich flat lands of Meath. The doors to the pavilions exactly match the main door; the curved curtain walls, which mask two storeys on the kitchen side, are carefully twinned, having two tiers of matching niches. The vaulted and columned stable is very like that at Strokestown, save that it has an upper floor containing groom's quarters and a hayloft under the roof. Whereas elsewhere at Ardbraccan the design is more refined than at Strokestown, the kitchen is not so large or so grand, although it rises two storeys high. Like Strokestown, it has a gallery, but one carried on corbels and without a balustrade. There are three small extractors in the kitchen ceiling of the same type as the big one at Strokestown. Most of the interior decoration dates from later in the century, and was designed by James Wyatt (pp. 159–60).

Following the same idiom as Ardbraccan, and in the same county, is Bellinter, built for John Preston, MP. It is thought to be one of Castle's last houses. Here the

Bacchantic mask on the chimney-piece, and right: stucco-work in the entrance-hall, Bellinter, parish of Assey, Co. Meath

Pigeon-house, Waterston House, parish of Kilkenny West, Co. Westmeath

Left: Ledwithstown House, parish of Kilcommick, Co. Longford

pavilions are connected to the main house by straight arcades in the same manner as at Powerscourt. The Prestons remained at Bellinter until the second half of the nineteenth century. It is now a Convent of Our Lady of Sion, and although the pavilions have been considerably altered internally the whole complex is excellently maintained (p. 86). The entrance-hall is finely decorated with panels of stucco-work trophies and a massive stone chimney-piece embellished with a Bacchantic mask, reminiscent of one on a marble chimney-piece of about 1740 at Rushbrooke Hall in England.[32] It was about this time that the idea of landscaped grounds with long winding avenues was introduced to Ireland; by the 1750s this seems to have gained almost universal acceptance. No longer was the approach short and straight, aligned on the front door like Beaulieu (1666), or Bonnetstown (1737): instead the length of the avenue became a yardstick of grandeur. Gardens, which previously had been adjacent to the house, were banished to walled enclosures, sometimes at a great distance from the house – half a mile was not unknown – and the park in which the house was situated was planted with trees, often with most beautiful effect.

Castle also designed smaller and simpler houses for less opulent clients, but usually adhered to the principles of the Neo-Palladian school. His hand can be discerned at Ledwithstown, Co. Longford, a small square house with a cut-stone façade built about 1740, and now in great disrepair.[33] The house at Waterston, Co. Westmeath, built for Robert Handcock, has likewise been attributed to Castle.[34] The house is now demolished; all that remains is the pigeon-house in the gardens, which is a highly original construction, though, of course, pigeon-houses were a regular feature of all great establishments.

The 1740s saw a good deal of building. It was then that Sir Marcus Beresford, who had married Catherine Le Poer, heiress of Curraghmore, made extensive improvements to her house in Co. Waterford, already an amalgamation of several buildings.

Doorway in the curtain wall between house and stables, Curraghmore, parish of Clonagam, Co. Waterford

Right: the garden front, Bonnetstown, parish of St Canice, Co. Kilkenny

In the late seventeenth century a house had been added on to and behind the ancient keep, and Sir Marcus now gave the ground floor of this old tower, which had become the entrance-hall, a coved plaster ceiling richly decorated in stucco-work with busts in medallions above the cornice. The stucco-work is attributed to the Francinis[35] – Italian brothers then the most fashionable stuccodores in Ireland. He employed John Roberts, a Waterford man, to lay out the impressive forecourt (550 feet long and 192 feet wide), perhaps inspired by Vanbrugh's Blenheim. Along two of its sides Roberts built two-storey pedimented stables. These have rusticated Doric columns and arched doorways with moulded architraves topped by large lunettes, whose surrounds rest on their keystones. To form the whole complex into one unit he added two wings *en échelon* to the house (p. 122), and by curved curtain walls with niches linked wings and stables. The entire effect of space, symmetry and grandeur is dramatic and almost Baroque.

Many country gentlemen, though moderately wealthy and fired with building zeal, could not afford the services of so eminent an architect as Castle or even Roberts. At best they employed one of their assistants, or at worst, tried to impart the relevant ideas to a local builder. This, however, did not prevent the construction of some quite beautiful smaller houses, such as Bonnetstown, Co. Kilkenny, built for Samuel Mathews (p. 85). His name 'Sam^{ll} Mathews Esqr' and the date 'May 14th 1737' are cut on front cornerstones. The house, which stands at the end of a long straight avenue aligned on the front door, has remained unchanged externally, even to the glass in an upper window-pane where an eighteenth-century Mathews lady scratched her name with her diamond ring. On the garden front the fenestration is most unusual. The interior has lost some of its original chimney-pieces and panelling, although good simple panelling remains in the little room to the left of the hall which was probably a gun-room, and all the windows are fitted with panelled window-seats. The staircase is similar to that in the Bishop's Palace in near-by Kilkenny. This delightful house now belongs to Miss Daphne Knox, who was born there.

Floor-plan of the Bishop's
Palace, Kilkenny, and
above: the staircase

The same artisans who worked for Samuel Mathews were probably also employed
at the Palace in Kilkenny. In the fourteenth century Bishop Ledred had demolished
three churches outside the city walls and used their stone to build an Episcopal
Palace beside St Canice's Cathedral. The floor-plan shows the thick walls of the old
square tower and its adjoining house. This had become derelict by 1661, but was
restored by Bishop Charles Este who was appointed to the See in 1735/36.[36] When
Este had completed his renovations the façade looked much as it does today, except
that the roof has been raised and his dormers replaced by full windows on the top
storey; the windows also had rusticated surrounds to match that of the door. The
entrance-hall is part of the ancient structure and its groined vaulting is similar to
that in the Cathedral. Este made an addition to the back of the house in order to
accommodate his new staircase, which has very finely turned balusters and newels
that are fluted columns of the Composite order. There is much elaborate carving
in wood, including a little seated dog at the end of the handrail on the first floor,
and the frieze round the staircase gallery and the arched architraves of some of the
doors have small grotesque masks. Crowning the masks on two of the doors are
carved episcopal mitres: these doors lead to the Bishop's study and his bedchamber.
Twenty-five years later Bishop Pococke built the graceful Robing-room in the
garden; it was once joined to the house by a colonnade. The big dining-room and
the drawing-room above it were added still later, probably after 1779 when Mrs
Beaufort commented that the Palace was small and gloomy.

In 1740 Bishop Este was translated from Ossory to Waterford, which provided him with scope for further building activity. His predecessor had already had designs drawn for a new Palace at Waterford by the English architect William Halfpenny, and when, in 1741, Este commissioned Castle to erect a superb new Palace, it seems that Castle adapted some of these.[37] Este was undoubtedly already familiar with Halfpenny's work, as the doorway to the Kilkenny Palace is taken from one of the architectural manuals that Halfpenny published for country gentlemen and builders. The Waterford project was grandiose, to say the least. Unfortunately Este did not live to see it finished and his successor regarded it as rather a white elephant.

There is a good example of another such doorway on an early eighteenth-century house on the edge of the town of Athy, Co. Kildare, called Mount Ophaley or, erroneously, Mount Ophelia. In 1750 this was the residence of Richard Fitz-Gerald who married a daughter of the 4th Lord Kingston.

John Sabatier, a member of one of the Huguenot families settled in the vicinity

of Portarlington, Co. Leix (where there was a French Church) lived in the town of Mountmellick until he purchased the lands of Garroon in December 1736.[38] There, apparently between 1737 and 1748,[39] the Sabatiers built a stylish house of small grey ashlars with two matching bays on each side of a wider centre bay, which they named Summer Grove. The doorway, with its fine Gibbs surround, leads into a pretty entrance-hall, across the back of which the architect devised a tripartite screen to mask both the descent to the kitchen and the simple staircase. The right-hand door leads to the staircase and the backquarters, the centre door is a dummy and the left-hand door opens into a cupboard beneath the stair. At the back of the house are two Venetian windows, and the entrance to the kitchen (which is beneath the main floor as it appears at the front) is at ground-level. The drawing-room has Rococo plaster-work which includes birds, a favourite motif of the great stucco-artist Robert West, though the Summer Grove work seems to be of a less-expert craftsman. The house has changed hands many times and is now happily in the possession of Mr and Mrs Barrie Whelan.

Opposite below: front doorway, Mount Ophaley, parish of Athy, Co. Kildare

Opposite above: frontispiece, the Bishop's Palace, Waterford

Centre: entrance-hall, Summer Grove, parish of Rosenallis, Co. Leix.

Above: the frontispiece.

111

Porthall, Co. Donegal, was built about 1746 for John Vaughan, merchant, by an Ulster architect, Michael Priestley. In order to meet his client's need for a dwelling-house, warehouse and offices, Priestley placed two long, low, gabled office buildings behind the five-bay house. The façade has a Diocletian window set in the pediment and over the breakfront like the one at Summer Grove, and the windows and doors have rusticated surrounds, though in general the treatment here is less refined.

A plain lunette appears instead of a Diocletian window in the pediment at Allenton, Co. Dublin, a pretty but altogether simpler house, undoubtedly the work of a master mason without the help of an architect. The windows have no architraves and the treatment is generally unpretentious. The single-pile five-bay house, which was once weather-slated, has external chimneys and a very narrow return at the centre back. It must date from the second quarter of the eighteenth century, and was once the residence of Sir Timothy Allen, who married in 1757.[40] It was he who gave it its present name, but it was almost certainly a house in being when he acquired the property. Allenton has no claim to great merit or importance, but it has an unostentatious charm; and it is sad that, as most of the demesne has been sold for development, it may soon be demolished.

When Jemmett Browne, Bishop of Cork, decided to renovate his father's house at Riverstown, Co. Cork – a plain, late seventeenth-century single-pile – he expended his energies and money (he had plenty of both) on beautifying the inside. Although he did enlarge the house, it is clear that he was not at all preoccupied with its external aspect which was left stark and unadorned. This, however, was not because he failed to keep abreast of fashionable developments, for he employed the famous Francini stuccodores who had worked at Castletown and Curraghmore. Their decoration of the little Riverstown dining-room was already completed by 1750.[41] By then the aesthetic trend was to replace wainscot by stucco, so that the dining-room walls were decorated with a series of elaborately framed panels of classical figures, and an allegorical scene in stucco was placed on the ceiling. Most of the panel-frames are surmounted by festoons and floral motifs, a design they also used at Castletown. The panels between the windows contained mirrors instead of figures (p. 68).

Garden front, Porthall, parish of Clonleigh, Co. Donegal

Although Jemmett Browne retained the old hall and staircase, he radically changed the hall's shape and appearance by means of a thin, semicircular partition screening the staircase, whose entrance was masked by one of the new doorways. The addition of classical columns and an ornate stucco frieze completed the transformation, which is in total contrast to the unprepossessing exterior. In 1788 Beaufort commented that it was 'by no means a fine place or handsome house . . . rooms low and yet adorned with large figures in basse relieves by Franchinis – no prospect at all.'[42] The final comment is certainly true. The Brownes remained at Riverstown into this century. After the Second World War, when the house was acquired by Mr and Mrs William Allen, Mrs Allen removed the original marble chimney-pieces to her house at Whitechurch, Co. Waterford (where they now are) and also took a hopper dated 1753 for its courtyard. It is to be hoped that others in the past did not indulge in this transferring of dated hoppers or date-stones around the countryside, as the confusion produced thereby is obviously enormous. Riverstown is now the property of Mr and Mrs J. J. Dooley, who with great enthusiasm and with help and guidance from the Irish Georgian Society, have brought it a new lease of life by restoring the Francini work and opening it to the public.

Allenton, parish of
Tallaght, Co. Dublin

Unlike Jemmett Browne, the owners of Lodge, Co. Tipperary, directed their attentions wholly to the outside of their house, another late seventeenth- or early eighteenth-century building to which additions were made in the 1740s with the aim of giving it a smarter appearance. There is an unverified tradition that it was built by a chaplain in William III's army and a brochure rather wildly describes it as being in the 'Dutch colonial style'. Admittedly it is stylish, but the style is its own. The five-bay body of the house may well be a farmhouse of the Williamite period, of the type of Morgans, Co. Limerick, and Berwick Hall, Co. Down. The third bay to the left of the door is on a lower level than the rest of the centre block, though on the same level as the wing. The lunette (or possibly Diocletian window) once under the pediment on the right wing has been blocked up; that on the left wing is still clearly visible. The gable on the right wing is a functional one, carrying the roof and meeting the ridge-tile at its apex, but the gable on the left is merely ornamental. It is pompously crowned by a double-headed eagle displayed and two urn finials. The right-hand gable has lost these objects, but the gables did once match, for the missing finials now lie on either side of the front door. These decorations and the Venetian windows with their surrounds give the exterior a spurious air of importance, while the interior remains very plain. The whole complex is an intriguing puzzle with undeniable charm, and it is disappointing that nothing more could be found regarding its eighteenth-century owners.

Sometimes local builders contrived houses curiously; not infrequently a stair-case was carried across a ground-floor front window, as though it were an after-thought. There are good examples of this at Knockgraffon Rectory and at Bally-steen, Co. Limerick. Ballysteen is a well-built house with good, handsomely proportioned rooms, and the symmetry of its façade is pleasing. The entrance-hall occupies the entire five bays across the front of the house, and the stair rises from it in such a way that, on approaching the house, one can clearly see the string and nosing of the treads and risers and some balusters as they traverse the upper half of the window of the first bay.

The Catholic clergy, of course, had no official residences at this time, and the glebe houses of the Protestant rural clerics were often primitive and a far cry from the palatial homes of their bishops. In December 1753, when the Reverend George Bracegirdle, the new Rector of Donagheady, Co. Tyrone, arrived from England, he lodged with the curate and wrote to his patron, the Earl of Abercorn, that:

> the glebe-house (where I am, for a few days, very comfortably with Mr Law) is by no means so bad as represented. There is a parlour twenty feet square, out of which two tolerable rooms with beds; in one of them a chimney and closet, a large kitchen, open to the roof, two other little rooms where the servants lay – all these of a floor – your Lordship knows in this country they have not the art of building a staircase. I must not forget a very good cellar and also six magnificent sash windows in front. The house is convenient enough for a single man, though not fit for a family.[43]

This reflection on the ability of the artisans to construct a stair seems unwarranted, unless it was limited to the villagers of Donagheady who may have lagged behind the norm. Certainly in the city of Derry, within easy reach of Donagheady to the north, and in the town of Dungannon to the south-east, quite accomplished work was being carried out at the time. Two months before Mr Bracegirdle's arrival the Earl's agent had reported that the glebe house 'exceeds a good deal the common farmhouses but is somewhat out of repair . . .'.[44]

The line of demarcation between the status and residence of strong farmers and of the minor gentry was indeed slim. Due to inheritance by primogeniture, younger sons of even prosperous families, unless they sought a career in the Army, the Navy, the Law or the Church, were often left impoverished and nearly landless. In the next generation, the younger sons of these younger sons, unless they had been able to secure an heiress-bride, found themselves poor indeed, and only their pretension to the status of gentlemen by descent and the patronage of their grander relations separated them from their farmer and shopkeeper neighbours. William Lysaght (born 1721) was such a gentleman, descended of an ancient Munster family who had lost some of their property when they were transplanted to Co. Clare by Cromwell, but who had later conformed to the Established Church. His kinsman and patron, John Lysaght, was created Baron Lisle in 1758, and it is he who is referred to as 'Mr Lysaght' in the following extracts from William Lysaght's journal:

> In May 1744 I took East Johnnea, 202 acres, at 10/– per acre for three lives from Mr Lysaght, which improved by ditching; and in 1748 I took Kilcranathan from the exors. of Minor Purdon. In 1749 I took Clogheen from Lady Middleton, 348 acres, at 10/– per acre, a lease of three lives renewable for ever. . . . In 1749 I took West Johnnea, 110 acres, from Mr Lysaght at 10/– per acre during his life and 12/– afterwards, and I gave him in exchange Kilcranathan, for his convenience and he paid half a year's rent by way of fine to me. In 1749 I built a pretty little thatched house at Clogheen, a parlour, kitchen, cellar, dairy and little hall, three lodging rooms over and garrets. I was ever fond of industry and improvements, which I showed now to some purpose. The times were low, lands very dear for the prices, but I both paid the rents and improved the land. For five years before this period I contracted a great liking for the eldest daughter of Mr James Knight, of Newtown, a near relation to Mr Lysaght, and

Lodge, parish of Killodiernan, Co. Tipperary

115

Thatched house at Tara, Co. Meath, now the Post Office

by her permission I spoke to her father . . . but it came to nothing; then I continued my industry for myself and business for Mr Lysaght with whom I lived. In some time Mr Knight finding that his daughter had also fixed her liking for me, and would not hear of any other, and that I did not come to his house, came to me at Clogheen and invited me to his house to renew the family intercourse . . . said he would send for his daughter who was then from home, and that he would contribute all in his power to make us happy. Tho' I was sensible by this time that I was not in a proper situation both in years and fortune to marry, yet for what engagement subsisted between Miss Knight and me I received the proposal cheerfully. . . . Affairs were settled. I was promised £350, viz. her grandmother Gubbins gave her £200, an uncle Blakeney Gubbins she had had left her £50 and her father £100. The 24th Febry we were married at her father's house . . . privately. I am sure no one felt the satisfaction we both did. I had now a great deal of business, my own and Mr Lysaght's, who lived then in Dublin with his family. . . . In some little time her father's house became not pleasing to my wife, some unhappy bickering &c, and my house at Clogheen not finished or furnished, low in cash, getting none on my marriage, keeping it on mortgage on part of his land as provision for his daughter, until there was an opportunity to lay it out in some lasting interest; my lands then not appearing to be of sufficient interest and my personal fortune computed by Mr Knight to be but £600 as per marriage articles. She lived with me at Clogheen until December following, when she went by kind invitation to her uncle Henry Knight at Ballynlina, both to lie in and to Xmas. The 21st Decr she was safely delivered of a Daughter; when I heard of the event was at Mallow Fair. She sent the child to nurse. In Feby. she came to Clogheen and brought her grandmother home with her; differences increased in her father's house and we kept much asunder.[45]

William Lysaght's thatched house was at Clogheen in Co. Cork. His father-in-law, James Knight, lived at Newtown alias Ballynoe near Charleville. Grandmother Gubbins was the widow of Joseph Gubbins, Justice of the Peace, of Knocklong, Co. Limerick, and a sister of Major-General William Blakeney, then Governor of Minorca, created Baron Blakeney in 1756. These close connections between the lords and the struggling family in their 'pretty little thatched house' with its parlour, kitchen and three lodging-rooms above, were quite usual in Ireland at that time.

The thatched house at Tara, Co. Meath, now the Post Office, is of about the same date as William Lysaght's, and undoubtedly similar in appearance. Also in Co. Meath, but one degree down the scale of prosperity, is the two-storey thatched house at Crossguns which has eight rooms but no hall, the stair leading directly out of the kitchen, where there is a great hearth and a spyhole-window to the front door. Edmund Burke, the famous politician and orator, born in Dublin in 1729, the son of an attorney, spent his early childhood in his maternal grandfather Nagle's long, low, thatched cottage at Ballyduff, Co. Cork. In 1832 another storey was added to this old cottage, and later its roof was slated so it lost its original character. The cottage on the townland of Wardhouse, Co. Leitrim, is of the same period as that in which Burke spent his childhood, but has not undergone alteration: it has two rooms each with a chimney, and there is a barn within the house, the barn window being identical to those of the dwelling.

Cottage at Wardhouse, parish of Rossinver, Co. Leitrim

Other examples of these long, low, thatched buildings survive in various parts of Ireland. On the townland of Esker, Co. Leix, there is a small version: Mrs Ryan's robust two-roomed cottage which in its dignified simplicity has an almost fairy-tale quality. It is still warm and cosy, and virtually the only changes in over two hundred years have been the installation of new window-panes and of electric light. The illustration shows the back as seen from the kitchen garden.

Wood Village, Lisheenanoran, Co. Galway, is a cluster of about a score of early eighteenth-century thatched cabins of the simpler kind that have now all but disappeared from Ireland. These were the homes of smallholders. Below these was the wretched category, graphically described by Madden in 1738:

they the tenants – I speak of the poorest and greatest part of them – have rather huts than houses and those of our cotters are built like Birds Nests of dirt, wrought to-gether and a few sticks and some straw . . . numbers of them have no chimney either from want of wood or skill to build one but vent the Smoak like those of the Hottentots.[46]

Mud houses were still in use in the towns as well as in the country, for in 1740 Michael Echlin wrote of Bangor, Co. Down, 'the houses are built with stone and are ruff casted not built with Mudd like the rest of Bangor houses'. These mud houses were not as perishable as they sound, for the clay was coated with roughcast on the outside and lime-washed inside. Some of them even survived into this century.[47] Elsewhere in the small towns brick was beginning to be used for the better small houses, indeed so early as 1714 Colonel Flower granted a brick house in Durrow on a repairing lease to a butcher who was to build his own slaughter-house.

Consciousness of the styles imported by Pearce and Castle for the wealthy slowly permeated down the social scale through the illustrated manuals of such architects as Halfpenny, but the Neo-Palladian style as it developed in Ireland remained mainly the perquisite of the rich, never proving really popular with the ordinary country gentry. As a result most of the building in the third quarter of the eighteenth century was to be done by those in the upper income bracket.

Cottage at Esker, parish of Clonenagh and Clonagheen, Co. Leix

Wood Village,
Lisheenanoran, parish of
Annaghdown, Co.
Galway

XII Right: one of the
pavilions, Belline, parish
of Fiddown, Co.
Kilkenny (p. 177)

CHAPTER 5

The lack of a master hand

1750–1780

IN THE MID-EIGHTEENTH CENTURY the appearance of Ireland varied enormously from village to village, from town to town and indeed from street to street within the towns, perhaps more so than at any other period. The aspect of individual villages depended not only on the degree of local prosperity, but also on the interest and attitude of their landlord. Some landlords, particularly those whose house was near their village, were extremely conscious not only of the need to build neat and adequate accommodation for their tenants, but also of the desirability of laying out streets in a pleasing manner. An instance of this was at Cookstown, Co. Tyrone, a village founded in 1609 by Allan Cook. Here, about 1750, William Stewart of Killymoon, the then landlord, laid out the present town on a rectilinear plan, the tree-lined main street (130 feet wide) being crossed by small straight streets that connected with the old country lanes. The Earl of Grandison was another improving landlord. He imported experienced weavers from Ulster to his estate at Dromana, Co. Waterford, and built two villages for them, Villierstown and Mount Stuart. In 1752 Bishop Pococke wrote:

> I went with Lord Grandison . . . to see a new town he has built called Villiers Town, the design is two streets crossing each other with a square in the middle for a market and chapel. There are twenty-four houses built with a garden to each of them, his Lordship is bringing in about eighty acres of land at great expense for pasturage for the town, for as they are all linen weavers they are not to be diverted by farming.[1]

The town of Dundalk, Co. Louth, owed its prosperous and consequential appearance to its principal landlord, the Earl of Clanbrassil, who patronized building activities there. Two of the chief builders were the Elgee brothers from Raby, Co. Durham. William Elgee built the Dundalk court house and also did work at Carrickmacross in Co. Monaghan; Charles, variously described as bricklayer, builder and carpenter, was responsible for several houses in Dundalk. He was the great-grandfather of Sir Robert McClure, explorer of the North-West Passage, and of the poetess Speranza, mother of Oscar Wilde. In contrast to Dundalk, Carlingford in the same county had sunk from its medieval importance to a poor, shabby place, consisting of mean cabins clustered round the ruined castles, just as other previously important towns such as Athenry and Athlone had fallen into poverty and neglect.

Downpatrick, Co. Down, provided an exception to the generally unprepossessing appearance of the towns. It had neat, well-constructed buildings in English Street, including some three-storey five-bay houses as well as the two-storey

XIII Left above: Emo Park, parish of Coolbanagher, Co. Leix (pp. 169, 187)

XIV Left below: Curraghmore, parish of Clonagam, Co. Waterford (p. 108)

House in the main street, Innishannon, Co. Cork

Centre: some of the almshouses in the square, Kingston College, Mitchelstown, Co. Cork

twelve-bay block which contained the clergy-widows apartments, and there were also attractive small two-storey houses in Irish Street. Limavady, Co. Derry, like-wise had a pleasing appearance, and in 1765 Beaufort described it as 'neat with pretty cabins'; but Maghera, in the same county, was a small, miserable place. Belfast was still a nondescript little town, and Monaghan remained poor and dirty, not to be improved until the late 1760s. Swanlingbar in Co. Cavan had not a single house, but cabins only, and Westport, Co. Mayo, was only a cluster of cabins round the Big House. The old town of Abbeyleix was an unwholesome, damp place, sited on a bog, and the new town improvement of the landlord, Thomas Vesey, was not yet under way. Ennis, Co. Clare, was a maze of crowded, narrow and populous lanes: even the better stone houses stood in these dirty alleys with stinking cloacinas at the ends of their yards. This labyrinth of streets can still be seen today, and new shop-fronts conceal many old houses. Tralee, Co. Kerry, was a rambling, dirty place, its Mall as yet unbuilt. Dingle had retained a rather exotic appearance but was in decay: the stone houses had balconies and oriel windows like the old houses of Galway, and travellers remarked on its 'Spanish' character. These houses were all gone by 1788. Kinsale was clean and tidy but, like most of the old towns, had narrow winding streets. Many of its houses had canted oriel windows without corbels, projecting from the first floor over the street, where the good wives could sit and observe every coming and going in the thoroughfare below. Some bow-shaped examples of these windows survive; by no means uncommon in England, they were decidedly rare in Ireland. Beaufort noted one on the parlour of Mr Weir's inn in the 'respectable town' of Carrickfergus, Co. Antrim, and likened it to some he had seen in English inns. He also found several of these oriels in Mallow, Co. Cork (where they were painted green), and most of the old houses in Bandon had them.

Innishannon presented a tidy appearance, undoubtedly due both to its relative

124

Above: doorway of a
house in the main street,
Banagher, Co. Offaly

prosperity, based on cotton-weaving and boat-building, and to the vigilance of
its proprietor, Thomas Adderley, M P, who promoted both industries, and was
one of the first Commissioners appointed to regulate town-planning in Dublin
in 1757. Its single street had some quite superior houses, like that illustrated, which
would have been occupied by a master shipwright or other leading townsman.
The town of Mitchelstown in the same county belonged to the King family, and
when the fourth Baron Kingston (1693–1761) began the erection of a range of
almshouses, which he named Kingston College, he endowed them with £25,000,
stipulating they should be for the use of decayed Protestant gentlefolk, a purpose
they still serve. They were built by John Morrison of Midleton, and formed half
a square, which was later completed with private houses belonging to professional
people of the town. Morrison's original arrangement was a central chapel with a
five-bay house on either side, one for the chaplain and one for the doctor. Beyond
these, on each side, were seven three-bay houses, all two storeys over basement,
in perfect symmetry. The entire complex is still very attractive though changes
have been made: doors transformed into windows and vice versa, and inside
walls removed to increase the capacity to thirty-one individual dwellings.

There had long been a French Huguenot settlement at Portarlington, Co. Leix,
and in the 1750s the town acquired a unique character with a number of good
houses in its main streets, many having handsome façades, and some facing the
river with their backs to the street. Several of these houses survive, but their appearance has suffered sadly from the recent misdirected zeal which has prompted the
inhabitants to coat them with pebble-dash or cement rendering.

Banagher, Co. Offaly, had a few substantial residences, and the three-bay house,
whose centre bay with rusticated pedimented doorway beneath a country builder's
naïve attempt at a Venetian window must have been the home of some local
worthy such as an attorney.

125

Two house-shops, Askeaton, Co. Limerick

Right: house-shop, Cappoquin, Co. Waterford

Shops in these small towns were accommodated in private houses, and a shop window like that in the house-shop at Cappoquin, Co. Waterford, was a definite refinement. This was one of a row of four, but the others have now been altered. Neat little former house-shops of this period still survive at Askeaton, Co. Limerick. Outside the big cities such a thing as a display window was unknown.

The city of Waterford, apart from its long broad quay, consisted of narrow, crooked and dirty streets, reportedly very evil-smelling, and even the better houses were dark because of their cramped situation. Kilkenny, too, had narrow, dank streets – the legacy of the medieval town – with its old houses in poor condition and its new ones irregular and badly built. Sligo, which had grown up mainly since the beginning of the century, had mushroomed haphazardly so that even the old Abbey had become choked up with cabins. Limerick consisted of a muddle of dilapidated cage-work houses, half-timber and half-stone houses, the old black basalt houses and tall red-brick Dutch-style houses all interspersed with ramshackle small houses and single- and double-roomed cabins, as well as a few exceptional new houses such as that of Bruce the banker in Patrick Street. Excluded from the general disorder was John's Square (then called New Square), begun in 1751 and built up on three of its sides with terraces of three-bay houses, the corner sites being filled by larger five-bay houses with façades in the Palladian tradition of Castle, and possibly designed by Francis Bindon. Trade was thriving and these houses were built for prospering merchants and businessmen, and also as town residences for some of the country gentry.

Though most of Drogheda's old cage-work houses had fallen into decay, rows of little two-storey artisan dwellings like those in Francis Street were being built. These had a kitchen downstairs and two rooms upstairs, and the inevitable large families were crammed into them.

126

The few remaining cage-work buildings in Dublin were in such an advanced state of decay that they were generally called pest-houses. Five ruinous specimens at the corner of Thomas Street and Mass Lane, which had been in a tottering condition for some time, were pulled down in 1782; three were of three storeys and the other pair of two storeys. In 1750 there were still cage-work houses in Cornmarket, Back Lane, Patrick's Street, Coal Quay and Rosemary Lane, as well as one at the corner of Trinity Street and the Old Crane. The last survivor was a four-storey house on the corner of Werburgh Street and Castle Street, which was taken down in 1813.[2]

By 1750 a building boom was in progress in the capital. The wave of public building, as well as the construction of the great town-houses designed by Pearce and Castle, had provided work for many and played its part in contributing to the general increase in prosperity. St Patrick's Hospital, endowed by Dean Swift, was begun in 1749 for the accommodation of the rising number of lunatics in the metropolis, and was opened eight years later. In 1745 the first maternity hospital had been inaugurated by Dr Mosse in a converted house in George's Lane. The doctor was a friend of Castle's, and in 1748 when he leased a plot in Sackville Street for the erection of a purpose-built hospital, it was Castle who prepared the designs. This hospital was begun in 1751 just after Castle's death, and is now the world-famous Rotunda. Behind it lay the popular Assembly Gardens with their bowers and temples of refreshment. The Music Hall, in Fishamble Street, was also built to a design of Castle's, and was the setting not only for theatrical productions but of gatherings as diverse as masquerades, debates, lotteries and meetings of Lord Mornington's Music Academy.

With so much of interest going on in the city, such of the richest nobility as had not already built an impressive mansion there now hastened to do so, and the new

Francis Street, Drogheda, Co. Louth

Stucco-work on the
staircase-gallery, No. 20
Dominick Street, Dublin

peers, who were constantly being created, deemed it necessary, if at all financially
feasible, to maintain a mansion in Dublin. Any country gentleman who could
afford it – and some who could not – likewise wanted a town-house, not as hitherto
in their county town, but in Dublin, and this despite the fact that on their estates
many of them were living in uncomfortable converted tower-houses. Some of
the lesser country gentlemen, prudent enough to perceive the limitations of their
means, settled for elegant lodgings during their sojourns in the city, as did the many
bucks, rakes and expensive whores with whom Dublin abounded. Merchants
and shopkeepers were becoming affluent, artisans had employment and the time
was ripe to replace the old cage-work houses and cabins by new dwellings. Indeed
it was a heyday for speculators, of whom there were many, with Luke Gardiner
to the fore. About 1750 Gardiner drove a great road, 72 feet wide, through part of
north Dublin near the Rotunda and thus launched an orgy of street-building in the
area. Development was so rampant that in 1757 the Government passed an Act
setting up a Commission for Making Wide and Convenient Streets. The 'Wide
Streets Commissioners', as they came to be called, were twenty-one citizens,
including the Lord Mayor, who had compulsory powers to purchase houses and
land, and it is thanks to their vigilance that Dublin acquired its gracious aspect in
the late eighteenth century. The wide streets it boasts today are the fruits of their
determined planning. By the late 1750s the area south of the Liffey was also becoming fashionable, as the Earl of Kildare had predicted it would when he built Kildare
(now Leinster) House there. The Leeson and Fitzwilliam properties there were
being developed, and by 1762 Merrion Square had been planned and houses were
going up on its north side.

The lands on which Dominick Street (not far from the Rotunda) were laid out belonged to Ussher St George of Headford, Co. Galway, and his wife, Elizabeth Dominick. Robert West, a Dublin master builder and one of the best stuccodores of his day, leased several plots there from the St Georges between 1757 and 1765. By the autumn of 1758[3] he had completed a large, commodious dwelling-house which, along its front, extended the length of *two* lots (i.e. 56 feet), and it seems this must be No. 20, which is indeed double the frontage of the other houses in the street. In October 1758 he sold this house to the Hon. Robert Marshall, one of the Justices of the Court of Common Pleas, for £3,200. It is a four-bay house with two windows on one side of the front door and one window on the other. The staircase rises from the entrance-hall to the first floor, and West decorated its walls and ceiling with fantastic stucco-work. His art is plastic, blending a medley of subjects in both high and low relief with consummate skill. He worked with unrestrained verve, and although the swirling garlands of flowers and fruit, the draped busts of girls and the sweeping birds with their outstretched wings and craning necks are not arranged with any symmetry, the effect of the whole exuberant decoration is one of balance, grace and movement. On the wall of the staircase-gallery some of the birds are free-standing models. The drawing-room, which leads off this gallery, also has excellent stucco-work; here the centre group in the ceiling is of children at play with a bird perched on one of their hoops, and scattered about the walls are more children, musical instruments and birds.

Indeed, Robert West's partiality for birds has led to them being considered almost his trade mark, so that whenever they occur in stucco in Ireland – some possibly by his brother John, also a stuccodore, or by one of his assistants or even by crude imitators – the work is instantly labelled 'West'. There is no doubt that West excelled at birds. In No. 86 Stephen's Green, which he decorated for Richard Chapell Whaley (1700–69), as many as sixty-three birds are to be found throughout the house.

The Rococo plaster-work in Ireland at this period surpassed most in England, and many examples of it survive, both in houses near Dublin, such as Newbridge (which has a splendid drawing-room ceiling done by West) and Rathfarnham Castle, and in other parts of the country, though it is not always of the superb quality of West's work. Much, too, has perished, such as the state rooms at Kenure Park, Co. Dublin, which West decorated for Francis Palmer, and which is now in ruins. Presumably a good deal was also lost when Rococo ceased to be fashionable and rooms were refurbished in Wyattesque or later taste.

When Pearce died young, Castle had stepped ably into the breach; but when Castle died in 1751 there was no one of his stature to take his place. Several individuals tried – notably Clements, Bindon and Ivory – but none of them really succeeded.

Nathaniel Clements (1705–77), an able and talented man, became a Member of Parliament when he was twenty-two and rose to the powerful position of Paymaster-General for Ireland. He knew Pearce, was a friend of Castle and a business associate of the ever-enterprising Luke Gardiner, who regularly consulted him both on technical questions and matters of architectural taste. He acted as a contractor supplying materials for Gardiner's development schemes, and also leased land from him in Dublin on which he had houses built as speculation. In 1751 he obtained the appointment of Ranger of Phoenix Park for himself, with reversion to his sons, and proceeded to design and build a lodge there. An engraving of

Newberry Hall, parish of Carbury, Co. Kildare. Right: the garden front

1783 shows the building to have been a five-bay three-storey block with linked single-storey pavilions, very much in the tradition of Castle. The two end bays on either side had mezzanine windows on the first floor and the centre bay had a Diocletian window over the front door, lighting the hall. Like Pearce's Bellamont Forest, it owes its inspiration to some of the features of Palladio's Villa Pisani, and unless Clements was a very skilful dilettante, its design must surely have been based on one prepared by Castle. Clements is believed to have designed a number of houses,[4] one of which is Beauparc, Co. Meath, a three-storey house of the centre-block-and-pavilion type, whose façade is identical with that of the town-house in Ann Street, Dungannon, mentioned in the last chapter. Another house attributed to him (Williamstown, Co. Kildare) has only two storeys, but retains the same door-surround with a Venetian window above as at Beauparc, while two other of the houses attributed to him (Colganstown, Co. Dublin, and New-berry Hall, Co. Kildare) have a two-storey variation of the Beauparc façade.

Arthur Pomeroy, later Lord Harberton, obtained the lands of Newberry by his marriage to Mary Colley in 1747, at which time the Colleys were still living in the old castle at Castle Carbery, although a mere twenty years later it had become a roofless ruin. Pomeroy owned a house in Dublin, but soon after his marriage built a country seat of the centre-block-and-linked-pavilion type at Newberry. It is well constructed in red brick with stone dressings and some unusual features. The third storey has no windows to the front, and its half-windows on the garden front are fitted into the cornice. On the garden front none of the windows has a stone sur-round, although urns and parapet continue round the house. The L-shaped two-storey pavilions have three-sided projecting bays at the front. The curtain wall

which links house and kitchen pavilion has a corridor behind it and a central door giving access to the forecourt, whereas the wall between house and stable pavilion has no corridor and the matching door is a dummy. The ground floor of the main house is compactly arranged. The dining-room has a good Rococo stucco frieze with birds and flowers in high relief in the style of West. The Pomeroys left Newberry Hall about 1840 and it passed first to Edward Woolstenholme and then to William Pilkington, a Dublin publisher. In 1911 it was bought by the family of Mr Richard Robinson, the present owner.

Lodge Park, in the same county, was built about 1773–75 as a country seat for Hugh Henry, a wealthy Dublin banker who in 1770 married his first cousin, Lady Anne Leeson from Russborough. It is the last house attributed to Clements, who died in 1777. Here the Palladian lay-out is extended into a five part composition, there being a pair of detached two-storey pavilions on either side of the five-bay, two-storey house over basement. There may be some truth in the tale that the Henrys asked that the front of their new residence should be stretched out to make it as long as the magnificent Russborough. Two unusually emaciated and expressive stone lions sit on each side of the doorway; between them, in the illustration, is the lion-dog of Mr Richard Guinness, the present owner.

The Palladian lay-out was not necessarily confined to new houses, and some older buildings were given a Palladian dress, chiefly by the addition of pavilions linked to the house by curtain walls. This was done at Florence Court, Co. Fermanagh – one of the most beautiful houses in Ulster and now in the care of the National Trust – when, about 1770, pedimented pavilions were attached to the house by graceful arcades topped by balustrades. Likewise at Rathbeale Hall, Co.

131

Dublin, curved curtain walls pierced by central doors and with niches containing and surmounted by statues were introduced, joining the house to two-storey pavilions.

A similar arrangement occurs at Moone, Co. Kildare, where straight curtain walls with windows, niches, statues and central doors link the house to rather unusual pavilions with shaped gables and round-headed windows. Here, too, the centre block may be a conversion of an older house, even though it has the favoured Diocletian window in its pediment; it was further altered in the nineteenth century by the addition of a third storey, but the print of 1792 shows it before this change took effect. The Palladian work was done for the Yeates family. In 1748 Samuel Yeates of Colganstown (another house attributed to the architect, Clements) obtained the lands of Moone from the heirs of Thomas Ashe[5] and in 1757 transferred these to his eldest son, also named Samuel Yeates.[6] In 1752 this younger Samuel had married a daughter of Benedict Arthur of Seafield and it is almost certainly he who was responsible for the Palladian conversion at Moone, where he appears to have been resident as from 1759. Moone was still in the possession of Benedict Arthur Yeates in 1837.

On the reverse side of the coin, some houses have now lost their Palladian dress. One such is Leslie Hill, Co. Antrim, built about 1755 for James Leslie (1728–96). When Mrs Delaney was his guest there in 1758 she reported the house to be both unfinished and full of company. It had two-storey pavilions accommodating stables and kitchen, but these and their straight curtain walls are now demolished, although the façade of the main house – three storeys over basement with a half-oculus in the pediment above the three-bay breakfront – is still intact save for the loss of the glazing bars in a couple of windows. It is occupied by Mr James F. Leslie, a descendant of its builder's brother.

Moone Abbey, parish of Moone, Co. Kildare. An engraving of 1792

One of the relatively few houses of this period built for a gentry family of moderate means is Crosshaven House, Co. Cork. The lands had been purchased by the Hayes family a century before William Hayes built the present house in 1759.[7] Here the two-storey pavilions with oculi in their pediments are not joined to the main house, and their height is not in proportion to it. One of them can just be seen in the illustration, on the right.

Another architect who strove to continue the Pearce/Castle tradition was Francis Bindon (*c.* 1690–1765), who came of country gentry stock in Co. Clare and whose brother married Pearce's first cousin, Anne Coote of Bellamont. As a young man he travelled in Italy, and on his return practised in Dublin as a portrait-painter and architect. An obituary in Faulkner's *Dublin Journal* credits him with Bessborough, Castle Morres and Woodstock, all in Co. Kilkenny, and also Russborough, Co. Wicklow, which is known to be by Castle. Bindon probably collaborated with Castle and completed such work as remained unfinished at Castle's death. A number of other houses have been attributed to him on stylistic grounds,[8] including Raford, Co. Galway, Newhall and Carnelly, both in Co. Clare, and Castle Park, on the outskirts of Limerick. The last three houses are of interest as being among the few examples of country seats built or remodelled for gentlemen of moderate means at this period. Carnelly belonged to Bindon's brother-in-law, George Stamer, and both it and Newhall are of mellow pink brick. Newhall is the most accomplished of the houses attributed to Bindon, as distinct from those known to be by him. It was built for Charles McDonnell, Member of Parliament

133

Newhall, parish of
Killone, Co. Clare.
Below: organ-case in the
octagonal entrance-hall

for Co. Clare from 1761 to 1768, and for Ennis from 1769 to 1776. The brick house is placed across the gable-end of a seventeenth-century stone house, which has dormer-windows and tall chimneys rising from the gables. This stone house was retained to provide kitchens, nurseries, etc. A five-sided bay, accommodating, on the ground floor, the octagonal hall behind it, breaks the front of the brick house, and rises to the roof, crowned by a stone balustrade with finials at the angles. The octagonal hall has a rich frieze whose metopes are decorated with bucrania, masks of smiling beasts and the McDonnell crest. The painted and gilded organ-case across the back of the hall facing the front door is a quaint conceit, for there is no musical instrument behind it; it is merely a cupboard. Newhall now belongs to Mr Patrick Joyce, whose father bought it about sixty years ago.

Castle Park is another instance of a new house being built in front of an older one, with the further complication of being beside the stump of an ancient tower-house. The new house was joined to the tower stump by a curtain wall with a passage behind as though the stump were a Palladian pavilion. Both the stump and the frieze of the high cornice which masks the front of the house itself have been given stylized battlements, early in the nineteenth century. The house attributed to Bindon is basically a plain, five-bay construction whose breakfront is embellished by a Venetian window on the first floor and a lunette in the pediment. The disposition of these elements is handled clumsily – a Bindon characteristic – since the surround of the lunette actually rests on the keystone of the architrave of the Venetian window. Castle Park was a sub-denomination of Ballygrenan in the north liberties of Limerick, and was leased by Edward Ormsby to Nicholas Smith of Limerick, barrister, for a long term.[9] It is not clear whether the house was built

Diocletian window above
front door, Raford, parish
of Kiltullagh, Co.
Galway. Right: the
staircase-gallery

for Ormsby or for Smith, but probably the latter. An advertisement in the *Limerick Chronicle* of 3 October 1771 states that 'Mr Nicholas Smith being now settled at Castle Park will let his late dwelling house in Limerick. . . .' Smith's town-house was in the same parish as Castle Park and the registers show the baptisms and burials of his children between 1754 and 1764. He died in Wales on his way home to Limerick in 1789 and was succeeded at Castle Park by his son Charles, also a barrister, whose sister Rebecca married Richard Maunsell. After Charles's death in 1792, Castle Park was acquired by William Maunsell, husband of Richard Maunsell's niece, Dorothea Gabbett. In the second quarter of the nineteenth century it was bought by Christopher Delmege (1785–1863), a successful Palatine from Rathkeale.

From the seventeenth century the Dalys owned the lands of Raford, Co. Galway, and had a house there. The exact date of the present house is not known: it could have been built during the lifetime of Denis Daly the elder, who died at Raford in 1759; but it is more likely to have been built for his son, Denis the younger, who in 1735 had married Lady Anne Bourke from Portumna Castle. In 1741, when the elder Denis was still alive, the young couple were living at Rathmore,[10] and unless they joined forces with old Denis before his death, the probability is that they built themselves a new house on inheriting the property in 1759. Here again the disposition of the various elements in the façade is awkward. Above the tripartite pedimented door is a Diocletian window with a fussy surround resting unconvincingly on four consoles, above which again, on the top storey, is an oculus flanked by two small windows, an identical arrangement to some of the houses in John's Square in Limerick. Raford's rooms are spacious and well proportioned. The Diocletian window lights the staircase-gallery, whose ceiling has rather sober Rococo plaster-work, symmetrically arranged, showing groups of musical instruments – horns and recorders – set off by foliage in low relief.

136

Ballydonellan, parish of Kilcoona, Co. Galway. Based on a sketch made by the Rev. Daniel Beaufort, 1787

Denis Daly had family ties with a number of interesting houses in Co. Galway. One of his sisters, Mrs Kirwan, lived at Castle Hacket, another, Mrs Blake, at Oranmore: his wife's brother owned Portumna; a second cousin, James Daly of Carrownakilly, built the fine five-bay three-storey house at Dunsandle, with linked three-sided two-storey wings round courtyards, which is now a total ruin. Denis Daly's daughter married Sir George Browne of The Neale, and his son, a third Denis, married Anne Donellan of Ballydonellan near Loughrea. This last house was a most unusual place, which fascinated Beaufort when he visited it in 1787. The long eight-bay two-storey single-pile was flanked by turrets, crowned with cupolas topped by finials. The turret to the right had been an old castle on to which the house was built, and this accommodated a back stair; the turret to the left contained, on the ground floor, a 'great room' with a tripartite window to the front and three windows in the bow on the garden front. It had five chambers on the floor above, and in the attic a single barrack-room lit by the cupola.[11] The lay-out of the main part of the house was also singular, being divided into three sections: the centre formed the drawing-room with windows to the front and garden; on the left was the entrance-hall with the main staircase; to the right at the front a passage to the secondary stair in the turret, and behind it a breakfast-room. To achieve a symmetrical appearance the façade had twin front doors approached by steps, that on the left being the entrance to the hall and that on the right a dummy. It is not clear which of the Donellans built this remarkable house; almost certainly not the Malachy Donellan whose will was proved in 1729, but perhaps the Malachy Donellan of Ballydonellan who died at Galway in 1758, or his son John who died at Ballydonellan in 1772.[12]

As the century advanced, many Irishmen joined the East India Company and made their fortunes in the Far East. One such was Robert Gregory of Galway, who rose to be Chairman of the Company, and who in 1768 bought the estate of Coole in his home county. There he built himself a house, choosing a style popularized by Gibbs's manuals and favoured by those who could afford it – three storeys and six bays, the centre bay having the customary Venetian window on the first floor and the Diocletian window above. For half a century Coole was the home of Augusta, Lady Gregory, author, playwright and patron of the arts, who died in 1932. There she kept open house for J. M. Synge and Sean O'Casey and for W. B. Yeats, who immortalized the place in his poetry.

Most of the building at this period was being done by the very wealthy, which in general meant the nobility. The 1st Earl of Carrick who, having been 8th Viscount

Ikerrin, was advanced to an earldom in 1748 (three years after his marriage to Lady
Juliana Boyle) built himself a new seat at Mount Juliet in Co. Kilkenny. Traditionally it was built in the 1750s and named after the Countess, who was known as
Juliet. Though this date may be correct, it is noteworthy that Kimber's *Peerage* of
1768 gives the Earl's seat as Ballylinch House (just across the river from Mount
Juliet), whereas a newspaper announcement of October 1771[13] states that his
daughter was married at Mount Juliet. It thus seems probable that the house was
finished between 1768 and 1771, which would fit the appearance of the front, now
the garden front, which has had its door replaced by a modern window with
Adamesque astragals. The interior of the house was remodelled by the 2nd Earl,
and will be discussed in the next chapter.

On the evidence of Beaufort, the present Bantry House, Co. Cork, was built in
1771, for on his visit in 1788 he described it as 'a large old fashioned house but
seventeen years built and nobly situated over the bay'.[14] Its situation is incomparable,

standing on the south side of Bantry Bay with a superb view across the water to the Caha Mountains on the Bere Peninsula (p. 103). The first house at Bantry was built by Hugh Hutchinson, who married in 1698; he was certainly living there by 1728 when his elder daughter married William Cox of Ballynoe, Co. Limerick, and Hugh himself made his will there. Ten years later his sons Samuel and Emanuel are described as 'of Blackrock', which was still its name when Beaufort went there in 1788. The property was subsequently acquired by Richard White, who took up residence there in 1766, presumably in the old Hutchinson house. Possibly the house of 1771 was only a rebuild of this: in any event the first building forms the core of the house as seen today, but has been subject to various additions. The house – the first in Ireland to be opened to the public in modern times – is in the possession of his descendant, Clodagh Shelswell-White, and contains a remarkable collection of furnishings, thanks to the zeal of his grandson, the 2nd Earl of Bantry, a connoisseur who travelled all over Europe seeking objects of fine art to bring back to Bantry: Gobelin tapestries, Aubusson carpets, paintings, prints, Russian icons, Chinese lacquer, Buhl and other French furniture. There is also some beautiful Irish Chippendale furniture. Much of the interior decoration is ornate. Both dining-room and library have free-standing Corinthian columns of coloured marble with gilded capitals, and there are a number of handsome mantelpieces.

In the absence of any great master to succeed Castle, it was presently apparent that in Ireland nobody could build in the height of fashion – because there was none. Under these circumstances a number of rich Irishmen sought to give their houses a *cachet* by demanding 'something different', as had evidently been done at Bally-donellan. All too often, however, this desire produced an irrational use of a variety of elements abstracted from a synthesis of the Palladian conceptions of Inigo Jones, Vanbrugh, Burlington, Campbell, Pearce, Castle, Gibbs and others, without the infusion of any new spirit. Had Galilei settled in Ireland, or had there been direct contacts with Austria and Italy in the early part of the century so that the later continental Baroque style was introduced, this might have suited the Irish aristocracy and found considerable favour; but – with rare exceptions – architectural ideas only filtered into Ireland by way of England.

There is an example of a house built to a Baroque plan at Castlecore, Co. Longford. The Reverend Cutts Harman (1706–84) married in 1751 and held several livings before being made Dean of Waterford in 1759. When his brother died in 1765 he succeeded to the family estate at Newcastle, Co. Longford, and took up residence there; at his own death in 1784 he was described as having two seats, Newcastle and Castlecore, only three miles apart. He may have built Castlecore before inheriting the family estates, but it seems much more likely that he built it as a hunting-lodge after 1765, particularly as in 1815 Mr Atkinson, who had stayed there for two days, wrote of the late Dean as 'the founder of this hunting lodge'.[15] Harman's lodge stands on an eminence, in the best tradition of hunting-lodges, and consists of an octagon with single-room wings projecting from four of its sides, and communicating with the octagon, whose entrance was on the first floor, by way of a stair and vestibule. The ground floor contained the kitchens. This plan for a hunting-lodge – kitchens on the ground floor and the main entry on the first floor by a stair and vestibule – had been employed for Speaker Conolly's summer-house/hunting-lodge, built on top of Mount Pelier, Co. Dublin, about 1725. At Castlecore the first-floor octagon room has a centre pillar rising from a plinth and containing a chimney. On the sides of the plinth, separated by marbleized columns with ornate gilded

XVI Left above: the garden front, Kilruddery, Co. Wicklow (pp. 197–8)

XVII Left below: eighteenth-century Gothic gateway, Portumna Castle, Co. Galway (p. 191). Through the gates the Jacobean mansion can be seen (p. 53)

141

Composite capitals, are four fireplaces. These once had mirrored overmantels to reflect views of the surrounding country – the River Inny can be seen on one side and the land down to the Royal Canal on the other. The frieze above the overmantel has entablatures adorned with carved gilt sunbursts and ornate swags of gilt roses, the whole resting on consoles, all very Italianate. The illustration shows it in its present dilapidated condition, with inset Art Nouveau tiled grates, etc. The octagon room has a marble floor, a fact over which several nineteenth-century observers marvelled, noting that though cool in summer it was unpleasantly cold in winter. Fortunately the four communicating chambers have timber floors.

After the Dean's death in 1784 his estates passed to his nephew, Laurence Parsons, later 1st Earl of Rosse, and in 1814 Mr Peyton Johnston was living at Castlecore as a tenant of Lord Rosse. It may have been during his tenure, though more likely in that of his successor, Thomas Hussey Esq. (whose seat it had become by 1826), that the two-storey three-bay boxy house was added to the front of the hunting-lodge to make the place domestically feasible. This new house communicated with the octagon by means of the old vestibule and part of the stair, which now form a sort of corridor between the two premises. Castlecore is now the Ladies of Mary Rosary Convent.

Writers in 1819, 1826 and 1844[16] opined that Dean Harman had taken Windsor Castle as a model for his unusual house. The first of these writers, the Reverend John Graham, a native of the parish, even likened Castlecore to the round tower there. In modern times attention has been drawn to the resemblance between the plan of Castlecore and that of the hunting-lodge of the kings of Sardinia at Stupinigi in Piedmont.[17] Perhaps Graham, when a boy at Shrule, had heard that the Dean's strange house was based on a royal residence and decided this must be Windsor Castle. However, in view of its Baroque plan, its marble floor better suited to the Mediterranean than to Ireland, and its kinship to the King of Sardinia's Stupinigi, may not this be one of the first essays in Ireland of Daviso de Arcourt (later known as Davis Ducart)? This Sardinian architect, who must have seen Stupinigi, came to Ireland in the early 1760s and worked as a canal engineer in Co. Tyrone before becoming preoccupied with designing houses.

In his known work Ducart mingled some Italian Baroque details with the traditional Neo-Palladianism then current in Ireland, and with ideas culled from earlier published works such as Campbell's *Vitruvius Britannicus*, already long outmoded in England. Ducart was skilful and suited the Irish, who were in search of 'something different'. Indeed, two of Ireland's loveliest surviving country-houses were built to his designs – Castletown Cox, Co. Kilkenny (begun in 1767, and based on Buckingham House in London, built in 1703) and Kilshannig, Co. Cork, both of which are illustrated in *Irish Houses and Castles*.[18] Kilshannig, now the residence of Commander and Mrs Douglas Merry, is particularly interesting, with an ingenious lay-out and very superior stucco-work on the ceilings of the saloon, ballroom and library. This was perhaps done by Patrick Osborne, who also worked for Ducart at Castletown Cox and in the Cork Mayoralty House. Its most impressive feature, however, is the circular staircase beneath a dome. The arcaded curtain walls which join the house to the pavilions are similar to those added to Florence Court, but have no balustrades. Kilshannig was built for Abraham Devonsher (1725–83), born a Quaker of Cork merchant stock, who became a banker and Member of Parliament for Rathcormac. He died childless, and Kilshannig descended to his sister's grandson, John Newenham, who took the name of Devonsher and in 1792 married an American, Cornelia Schuyler. Their son Abraham John Newenham Devonsher (1796–1880) succeeded to Kilshannig, but between 1820 and 1837[19] sold it to Edmond-Edward Roche of Trabolgan (1771–1885). Trabolgan is sited so as to face the sea and fully exposed to the east wind, making it intolerable in cold weather, so that the Roches (Lords Fermoy) used Kilshannig as a winter residence into the present century.

The Rogers were another Cork family of Quaker origin who employed Ducart. On the death of Robert Rogers in 1718 the estate of Lota, near Glanmire, passed to his third son, George, who died in 1721/22, bequeathing it to his brother Christopher, who died in 1740/41, leaving it to his son Robert, who died unmarried in 1787. It was this Robert who commissioned Ducart to redesign the house. The exterior has now been considerably altered, but Ducart's portico, with its distinctly Baroque rusticated columns and pilasters with a balcony above (formerly balustraded) can still be seen. In connecting Ducart with Lota it has been wrongly stated 'that the house was built for Noblet Rogers, Mayor of Cork in 1768 while the Mayoralty House was under construction.'[20] Robert of Lota's uncle, Noblet Rogers, was indeed Mayor of Cork, but in 1709, and was long dead at the time of Ducart's activities. The 1768 Mayor was Noblet *Philips*.

By English standards Ducart's work was hopelessly out of date. The 1760s in England had witnessed the inception of Neo-Classicism, which had as yet hardly penetrated Ireland. England's architecture was dominated by the rivals Sir William Chambers (1723–96) and Robert Adam (1708–92). Adam built several important country houses there in the 1760s, and Chambers, the King's architect, was associated with the foundation of the Royal Academy in London. Neither of them had any immediate impact on Irish designers, although Chambers as early as 1765 had submitted to the Earl of Abercorn a plan for a Market House in Strabane, Co. Tyrone.[21] He also designed the strictly classical Casino at Marino, Co. Dublin, for the Earl of Charlemont, which was completed in 1769. Possibly the many who admired this latter work may have been discouraged from emulating it when they learned of the expense involved – the small, perfect Casino having cost some £60,000.

Interior of the porch,
Browne's Hill, parish of
Carlow, Co. Carlow

One of the few bold enough to make an early venture into Neo-Classicism was Robert Browne (1729–1816) who in 1763 – a year after his marriage – built a seat at Browne's Hill, about two miles from the town of Carlow. This six-bay grey stone house is reputed to have been designed by an architect named Peters.[22] Its details are expertly executed, such as the gutters with carved animal heads on the cornice above the taenia on each side of the porch. Inside the porch the metopes of the handsome frieze are decorated with scenes in high relief of satyrs battling with beasts. Both the curved hall and the staircase-hall have good plaster-work, and the drawing-room has stucco birds in high relief after the manner of West. In 1961 this excellent house, with three reception-rooms, ten bedrooms, two bathrooms, oil-fired central heating, fifteen stables, loose-boxes, garages, dairy and a groom's house, all in good repair and standing on five acres, was for some considerable time on the market at the seemingly absurd price of £2,500 without finding a purchaser, even though a further sixty-eight acres was optionally available at £7,000. It is now the property of Mrs Tully. The unusually handsome, pedimented entrance gate, with its rusticated doorways and recumbent lions, has been removed to Lyons House, Co. Kildare.

Concurrent with Neo-Classicism in England at this period was the movement known as Gothic Revival. As with Neo-Classicism, Irish excursions into Gothic Revival were relatively rare in the middle of the eighteenth century, though it was to become highly popular several decades later. In the 1760s, like the first strictly Neo-Classical essays, it was mostly reserved for the rich, and more especially for those who travelled to England and admired it there.

In 1759 Bernard Ward, Member of Parliament for Co. Down, inherited his father's house at Castleward near Strangford. The following year Mrs Delaney

described it as one of the finest places she had ever seen, but it was not fine enough for Bernard and his wife, Lady Anne, and by 1763 they were building a new house. They had, however, been unable to agree on the style. He wanted a beautiful but sober classical house, but she had other ideas. Her desire was for something in the manner of Horace Walpole's Strawberry Hill in England, which was all the rage there and had set the fashion for Gothic Revival. Lady Anne was not only whimsical: she was also rich, being the daughter of the Earl of Darnley and – when she married Bernard Ward – the widow of Robert Hawkins-Magill of Gill Hall and the mother of its child-heiress. As a result Castleward was built half in the way he wanted it, and half in the way she wanted it, recording for posterity their divergence in taste and personality. The façade is classical: the garden front castellated with Gothic windows and glazing bars. The reception-rooms of Mr Ward (or Lord Bangor, as he became) are classical and chaste. Her ladyship's drawing-room is in the Gothic style initiated in England by William Kent, as are her sitting-room and library, both of which have elaborate Neo-Gothic ceilings, the sitting-room vaulted and the library ribbed with icing-sugar pendants.

A somewhat similar result was effected at Lisanoure, Co. Antrim, where Lord Macartney rebuilt the old castle. In 1768 he married a daughter of the Earl of Bute, and it would seem that building began soon after the marriage, for in the 1770s he left Ireland to take up appointments abroad, becoming Governor first of Bengal, then of Madras, and finally Ambassador to Russia. An undated sketch pasted into a volume of estate maps of 1772 shows the new house as having one rather dull classical front and another front castellated with some pointed and some quatrefoil windows. Perhaps the Macartneys had the same dispute as the Wards; or – even more likely – decided to copy them.[23]

145

Another early venture into Gothic Revival was that of the 6th Earl of Drogheda
(1730–1821), who built the enormous fifteen-bay Moore Abbey in Co. Kildare.
The castellated house is three storeys over basement, and all its many windows on
all floors (including the basement) match exactly, with pointed arches and elegant
Gothic glazing bars, producing a stupendous monotony. Scarcely any change has
been made to the façade save for the enlargement of the porch and front steps and
the addition of the low, pierced wall round the basement area. The house is now a
hospital of the Sisters of Charity.

An alternative use for Gothic Revival was to provide a face-lift for an old castle,
as at Leap, Co. Offaly, an O'Carroll stronghold which passed to the Darby family
in the seventeenth century. Jonathan Darby of Leap (1713–76) married Susanna
Lovett, whose father and mother were both first cousins of Sir Edward Lovett
Pearce. As a girl she may have known the architect, and must certainly have heard
his work discussed, although he was dead before her marriage. Several of her
relations were well housed: the Cootes at Bellamont Forest, the Lloyds at Gloster
and her Lovett kinsfolk at Liscombe in Buckinghamshire. There is no certain
evidence that Jonathan Darby and his wife actually visited England, but it is
probable, since one of their younger sons became an Admiral (commanding the
Bellerophon in the Battle of the Nile); another was a General; another, who
eventually inherited Leap, lived in Sussex, and a daughter married her cousin, Sir
Jonathan Lovett of Liscombe. When Jonathan Darby renovated his ancestral castle
he gave it a Gothic Revival dress, with, among other things, a doorway taken from
one of the designs of Batty Langley, published in 1741 in his *Gothic Architecture
Restored and Improved*. The castle is now uninhabited and in disrepair. The Gothic
staircase-gallery which ran round the high hall has collapsed, and the place has an
eerie quality. Indeed, it is famous for possessing one of the most persistent elementals
in Ireland – a headless sheep which frequents the old tower stair.

Leixlip, Co. Kildare, is another example of an old castle being given a Gothic
dress in the mid-eighteenth century, probably while occupied by the rich Conollys
who journeyed frequently between England and Ireland. Pointed windows were
pierced through the thick walls and glazed in the Gothic Revival manner, with very
attractive results.

As has been seen, during the third quarter of the eighteenth century most of the
building outside the cities was done for the richest strata of society, which in effect

meant the nobility. Most of the middle-income landed gentry were still living in their converted tower-houses, or in houses built fifty to seventy years before. They seem to have been tolerably satisfied with them, and at most gave them a face-lift and a refurbishing; new medium-size residences like Carnelly or even Lota were the exception. Palladianism had little real appeal for this class, notwithstanding that there were some competent and inexpensive builders in the provinces. One such refurbishing was done at Ballynoe, Co. Limerick, which belonged to the Coxes, a comfortably off country gentry family. The first house at Ballynoe was built between 1654 (when there was none) and 1659 when William Cox, who had previously lived in the little town of Bruff, was resident there. His son Sampson (1665–1734) married a daughter of the 20th Lord Kerry, the widow of John Odell junior of The Turret, and had a large family born at Ballynoe.[24] It is likely they rebuilt the Cromwellian house, particularly since the tall windows on the ground floor appear to be survivors from an early eighteenth-century house. Their son William married Margaret Hutchinson of Blackrock, Bantry, in 1728 and also had a large family born at Ballynoe, where he certainly lived until 1750;[25] he died in

The Gothic doorway on the old castle, Leap, parish of Aghancon, Co. Offaly

147

1762, and in his will describes himself as 'of Ballynoe but now of Cork'. There is
evidence that he was living in Cork from at least 1758, and the old house at Ballynoe
had apparently become uninhabitable, for after William's death his eldest son Hugh
lived near Charleville, Co. Cork, where all his elder children were born up to 1769.
It was Hugh who renovated the old single-pile house, adding a second pile at the
back, possibly an additional floor and a second staircase, the original staircase
becoming the service stair. He and his family moved in in 1770, and this is the house
as seen today, save for the addition of the portico. Ballynoe has mellowed stable-
yards which are hard to date, but the cut-stone arched entrance with its bellcote
was certainly there in the mid-eighteenth century.

In general, however, the lesser gentry were occupied in supervising their lands,
hunting, eating, drinking, wenching and raising dowries for their many daughters,
without much time to spare for sensitivity to architectural fashion, although they
did demand elegant lodgings for their occasional sojourns in the cities. It is also true
that for many of them a house on the lines of those designed by Castle or his
imitators was out of reach, and that if faced with a choice between a lease of some
extra acres, a new hunter, some hogsheads of claret or a Diocletian window, few
would have opted for the latter. Indeed, improvements were often made to the
stables rather than to the house, and many a house described by Beaufort as old.
old fashioned or uncomfortable, had a good stable-yard. Many a stable-yard
lying behind a Neo-Classical box-house is considerably older than the house. Nor

does there seem to have been any stigma attached to living in a good thatched house, like that built by William Lysaght, so long as it had two storeys to elevate it – and its owners – above the *hoi polloi*. When Arthur Young made his tour through Ireland in 1779, he observed 'another circumstance to be remarked is the miserableness of many of their houses; there are men of £5000 a year in Ireland, who live in habitations that men of £700 a year in England would disdain.'[26]

Even as Young wrote, the situation had already begun to change, and by the end of the century it had changed radically when the Neo-Classical box-house became the rage with gentlemen of moderate income. The forerunners of the box were houses such as Prior Park and Landsdown, both in Co. Tipperary. Prior Park was built by James Otway (1751–1839) on land inherited from his mother's family, the Woodwards of Cloghprior. He started building on 30 April 1779, and first slept in his house on 27 February 1786.[27] Unmarried, he raised five orphan cousins, laid out his gardens with considerable taste and was very hospitable. He lived extravagantly and was presently forced to let his new house, first to Mr Saunders and then to Mrs Sadlier at £300 per annum, while he stayed with relations in Wales; eventually he sold Prior Park outright to George Waller,[28] whose descendant, Miss Sally Waller, is its present owner. The lay-out is convenient: the dining-room and drawing-room lead off either side of the flagged entrance-hall, while doors at its back give access on the left to the kitchen behind the dining-room and on the right to the staircase-hall.

Prior Park, parish of Cloghprior, Co. Tipperary

149

Landsdown was built by William Parker, whose initials and the date 1779 are cut on one of the decorative lozenges on its weather-slated front. Weather-slating was not rare, though dependent on the availability of slate in the district. There is still a slate-quarry near Landsdown, which has enabled it to be kept in good repair instead of being stripped and refaced. The house is beautifully situated above Lough Derg, and its façade has a naïve charm: the round-headed window over the door with detached sidelights and its twin on the side of the house seem to be illegitimate offspring of a Venetian window. The property remained with the descendants of its builder until sold by Mrs Reeves after the First World War. It now belongs to and is carefully maintained by Colonel and Mrs White-Spunner.

The Wards imported materials from England to build their house at Castleward; they probably also imported the architect and principal workmen. In 1771 Sir William Chambers had complained that Irish builders were careless in perusing the designs he sent over to them, and seldom troubled to read what was written on them. In 1779, when Lord Carlow was trying to induce the architect James Gandon to come from England and settle in Ireland, he wrote to him, 'I do not see any architect of the least merit here.'[29] Whether this was just to encourage Gandon, or whether it represented the current opinion of the grandees, it was certainly an unfair comment. While it is true there was no master architect available, there were some perfectly competent men at work, such as George and John Ensor, Thomas Ivory (a Munster man, who was Master of the Architectural School of the Dublin Society in 1759 and built the Bluecoat School in Dublin) and the Englishman Thomas Cooley who worked in Ireland and built the Dublin Royal Exchange. Down in Co. Cork were Abraham Hargrave and John Morrison, the able architect-builder of Kingston College. There was also a rising generation of able designers. Lord Carlow was not to know it, but when he wrote Francis Johnston was an eighteen-year-old apprentice of Cooley's – five years later his elder brother Richard would design the new Assembly Rooms in Dublin, now the Gate Theatre – and John Morrison's son Richard was already twelve years old. This new generation of architects understood and adapted the Neo-Classical ideas, made them generally accessible, and thereby changed the face of the country and bestowed the 'Georgian' hallmark so characteristic of the Ireland we see today.

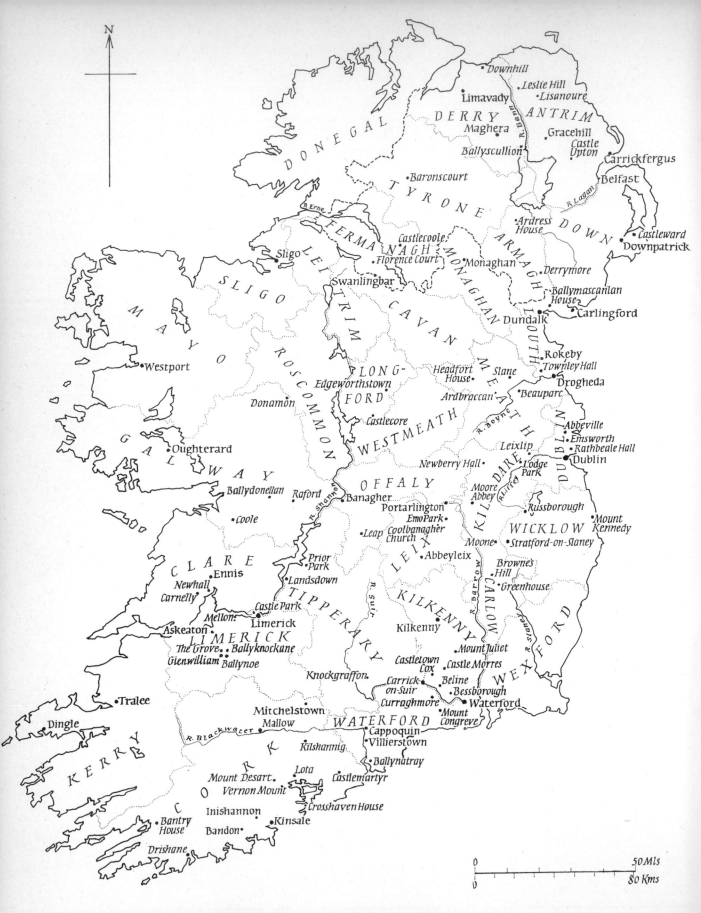

Houses and locations in Chapters 5 and 6

CHAPTER 6

Neo-Classicism comes to Ireland

1780–1800

THE ARCHITECTS WHO WORKED in the Palladian tradition had accepted without question traditional views of antiquity, but in the mid-eighteenth century a new desire to go back to prime sources awakened. This was partly aroused by interest in the excavations of Greek temples in Sicily and Paestum and by the discovery of the decorative frescoes at Herculaneum and Pompeii. Piranesi's drawings inspired a more perceptive appreciation of early Roman architecture, and Winckelmann proclaimed that the prime virtues of Greek art were noble simplicity and tranquil grandeur. These were two qualities that the Neo-Classicists tried to embody in their work, their school being born of a wish for a rational architecture based on established principles of law and reason, discarding sensational effect for the expression of an intellectual ideal. They did not strive to copy antiquity slavishly, but endeavoured to be scrupulously Classically correct. For instance, the Orders were only to be used structurally, not ornamentally; decoration was restrained and the pundits decreed that motifs not employed in Classical times should be rejected. Two of the movement's leading tenets were logical construction and truth to materials. This all led to a use of simple geometrical forms – cube, pyramid, cylinder, sphere – with each element rigidly defined, even juxtaposed. The resultant buildings with their unbroken contours were cool, well proportioned, elegant and rather impersonal. In their purest form they did not suit the Irish at all: in a slightly debased form they proved the answer to many problems.

These ideas had begun to circulate in England as early as the 1750s, when the intellectuals read and applauded Winckelmann and the Abbé Laugier. Both Robert Adam and his rival Sir William Chambers, who between them dominated English architecture for a quarter of a century, visited Italy to study the antiquities. Adam spent two years in Rome, and took draughtsmen to Spalato (now Split in Yugoslavia) to record the remains of the Emperor Diocletian's Palace. He returned to England in 1758 and published the drawings in 1764. He was erudite, meticulous and imaginative: he excelled at achieving an unostentatious opulence, lavishing infinite care on every aspect of his work down to the most minute details, so that the final product would be absolutely perfect. In addition, he introduced novelties which thrilled his clients, and his influence spread rapidly. Chambers was equally cultivated and fastidious, but more eclectic and reserved. As has been mentioned, he dispatched designs to several peers in Ireland, but Neo-Classicism was slow to take root there, and indeed the influence of Chambers and Adam was already on the wane in England before Ireland seized on its possibilities.

153

The dining-room,
Mount Juliet, parish of
Jerpoint, Co. Kilkenny

So far as is known, Adam's own designs were used in only two Irish houses. The earlier was the Earl of Bective's Headfort House, Co. Meath, for which Adam designed the lavish interior between 1771 and 1775, most of which is still in good condition. His signed and dated designs are in the collection of Mr Paul Mellon, and some have been published.[1] Headfort House still belongs to the Marquess of Headfort, descendant of its first owner, but is now used as a preparatory school for boys.

The second Irish house where Adam's work was executed is Castle Upton, Co. Antrim. This was also the commission of a peer, the 1st Baron Templetown, who had an English wife. Adam submitted his first designs in 1783: work was interrupted by Lord Templetown's death in 1785 when his heir was only fourteen. However, three years later, in 1788, Adam was re-employed to remodel the house and also to build the stables, composed of two courtyards, one behind the other, with octagonal buildings in each corner.

Though these two are the only houses in Ireland where Adam is known to have worked, such was his fame that all ceilings vaguely in his manner as well as most Neo-Classical mantelpieces are now generally declared to be 'Adam' or – worse still – 'Adams'. He is not alone in lending his name to other men's work: in the same way every Cupid painted in oils is popularly labelled 'Angelica Kauffmann', every stucco bird is automatically 'West', and even the most stylized late nineteenth-century bunch of plaster grapes is attributed to 'Francini', or 'the Italians'.

Michael Stapleton, the friend and executor of Robert West, did some very fine work in the Adam style, such as the internal decoration at Ardress House, Co. Armagh, built in the 1770s for the architect George Ensor, whose wife was its heiress. Ardress is now in the care of the National Trust and open to the public, who can admire Stapleton's elegant plaster-work in the drawing-room. This has classical plaques arranged symmetrically on the centre of each wall and festooned with delicate husk chains. There is another excellent example of similar Adamesque stucco-work, probably done by Stapleton, at Lucan House, Co. Dublin (now the Italian Embassy). This was built for Agmondisham Vesey, who had consulted Chambers concerning the project in 1781.

There were some good provincial stuccodores, too, notably Patrick Osborne who worked for Ducart and was responsible for the excellent decoration in the Morres family's town-house in Waterford, now the Chamber of Commerce. There was also a competent stuccodore at work in Kilkenny, who decorated the town-house of the Butlers in Patrick Street. He may be the craftsman responsible for the attractive Adamesque plaster-work in the dining-room at near-by Mount Juliet, which is rich but less delicate than Stapleton's usual manner. Its library, too, has a fine ceiling with a centre-piece of a rustic scene. This work was done for the 2nd Earl of Carrick, who inherited the house in 1774, the year of his marriage. He made drastic alterations, installing a new staircase with twin flights from the half-landing. The handrails of its balusters curl round the fluted Ionic columns which support an arcade crossing the hall, and there is a similar arcade on the half-landing, though free of the handrail. Mount Juliet now has a monumental collection of superb marble mantelpieces in the Adam manner, practically every room having one and one room even having a pair. These were mostly accumulated by the Hon. Lady McCalmont, grandmother of Major Victor McCalmont, the present owner. The illustrations show a centre plaque and one of a pair of medallions from these.

One of a pair of medallions on a mantelpiece, Mount Juliet. Below: the centre plaque on the library mantelpiece

Ceiling of the secondary staircase-hall, Westport House, parish of Oughaval, Co. Mayo. Right: detail of Chinese wallpaper in a bedroom

xiv Right above: cottage, Mount Temple, parish of Ahamlish, Co. Sligo (p. 202)

xix Right below: a small farmhouse near Cullenstown, parish of Bannow, Co. Wexford

The brilliant James Wyatt (1747–1813) achieved sudden fame in London as a young man of twenty-three, when he built the Pantheon in Regent Street, inspired by Hagia Sophia in Constantinople. He was in tremendous demand with clients vying for his services. The first person in Ireland to commission his designs for a house was General Robert Cuninghame in 1772.[2] Cuninghame was a Scotsman who had purchased a vast estate in Co. Wicklow and was created Baron Rossmore in 1796. Work on Mount Kennedy, however, did not begin for a decade after Wyatt was commissioned. Thomas Cooley was in charge of the execution of the work, and from the evidence of plans seems to have been assisted by Richard Johnston. The elaborate stucco-work, carried out by Michael Stapleton, has survived in first-class condition, and is illustrated in *Irish Houses and Castles*.[3]

In 1781 Wyatt drew designs for the 3rd Earl of Altamont (later 1st Marquess of Sligo) for the decoration of his dining-room at Westport, Co. Mayo, and these were duly executed, as was his design for the ceiling in the secondary staircase-hall.[4] The house had been built fifty years before by Richard Castle, and then enlarged in the 1770s, probably by Thomas Ivory who produced a set of plans for an enlargement in 1773 which were not actually employed. Wyatt's designs were not immediately implemented, and the 3rd Earl's renovations occupied several years. In 1787 Beaufort wrote:

The house is large, one or two rooms elegant but not well contrived or well furnished. Things do not appear neat. . . . There are two fine black marble chimney-pieces here from Turlough and in the drawing-room a very handsome one in an uncommon style of verd Antique and statuary. In the state dressing room the pannels of Windsor shutter on looking glass which has a good effect in reflecting the bay and the surrounding hills. The room I slept in small and uncomfortable. The Great Room or Gallery which is not finished is 60 by 18 with windows and a Venetian.

156

On his return twenty-one years later (in 1808) he dined at Westport and wrote:

> We sat in the Long Gallery which is new furnished – Great improvements and additions have been made to the house and the approach changed, and a magnificent gateway from design of Holland now erecting at the north east end of the town.

The ravishing Chinese wallpaper of about 1780, still to be seen in one of the bedrooms, remains from the 3rd Earl's interior decorating, and is said to have been specially acquired for him by Wyatt. The house has been opened to the public by the present Marquess of Sligo's heir, Lord Altamont, who, with enormous enthusiasm and a determination to preserve his family home and its remaining contents and share their beauty with others, has made an outstanding success of the enterprise. He has organized shops and a restaurant in the basement and, as an additional attraction, is now forming a zoo in the large park.

Wyatt interior decorations were also added to a number of other earlier houses, among them Curraghmore, Co. Waterford. The Earls of Tyrone were rich, and each succeeding generation spent money refurbishing the house. Wyatt's work included the staircase-hall, the library, the Yellow Drawing-room, the dining-room with grisaille panels and roundels attributed to Zucchi or Angelica Kauffmann, and the Blue Drawing-room with paintings in the lunettes attributed to Zucchi and roundels by the grisaille painter, Peter de Gree. Wyatt's designs for all these, except the staircase-hall, are now in the Metropolitan Museum in New York. Unfortunately all the windows overlooking the gardens (laid out in the 1840s by Louisa, Marchioness of Waterford) had their glazing bars removed during the nineteenth century, and the wing to the right of the garden front is an addition; but essentially the house we see today is that of Wyatt's time.

Mount Congreve near by also had a fine eighteenth-century painted room but this was obliterated in the 1960s when the Congreves had the house sumptuously renovated in a manner characteristic of the most palatial hotels.

It was during the episcopacy of Henry Maxwell in the Diocese of Meath, which lasted from 1766 to 1798, that additions and alterations were made to Ardbraccan. Though Bishop Maxwell did not meddle with Richard Castle's façade (p. 86), he introduced a touch of fashionable Gothic by inserting pointed windows in the kitchen pavilion – a rather strange divergence from his order for the Wyatt decoration of the interior of the house in the Classical manner. This was carried out during the late 1780s or early 1790s, and included new marble mantelpieces, the one in the hall having a particularly endearing centre plaque.

Good-quality stucco-work in the Wyatt manner was to be found in several houses throughout the country, indicating that the majority of those who could afford it opted for this type of decoration. It occurs in such diverse houses as Avondale, Co. Wicklow (better remembered as the home of the politician, Charles Stewart Parnell), and at Ash Hill, Co. Limerick.

Unlike Adam or Chambers, Wyatt actually visited Ireland. In 1775 he had been commissioned by the 1st Earl Conyngham to design a hall for Slane, Co. Meath, but it was for the nephew and successor, the 2nd Baron Conyngham, that he came to Ireland in 1785. The inspiration for his work at Slane was not Classical, but Neo-Gothic, a genre in which he excelled. His work at Slane was completed by Francis Johnston for the 3rd Baron, who became Marquess Conyngham in 1816, and with whom George IV stayed in 1821. The round room has a marvellous lacy fan-vaulted ceiling with a central pendant. Adam had castellated Castle Upton, and Wyatt now transformed Slane by castellation and additions. These two houses were the earliest examples in Ireland of this style, which was to have such a long and successful run in the nineteenth century.

As the century drew to its close castellation was gaining ground. Donamon, Co. Galway, a genuine fifteenth-century fortress with a broad, high arch over the entrance between the towers, as at Bunratty, belonged to the Caulfeilds, and before 1792 had been daintily castellated in the Neo-Gothic manner. There is stucco fan-vaulting on the staircase-gallery. Donamon was much altered and added to in both the nineteenth and twentieth centuries, and now belongs to the Divine Word Missionaries.

The Earl of Shannon, too, embarked on Gothic fantasy by building a large, pasteboard-thin Gothic gateway to his demesne at Castlemartyr, Co. Cork, described by Beaufort in 1788 as being 'a very bad stile in imitation of Gothick'. Regrettably it is still there, as unattractive now as it was then.

Nor were these early expressions of Gothic ideas reserved for lords or for castles. At Ballynarooga, Co. Limerick, John (FitzCharles) Odell, a very middling sort of gentleman (who was paying a kinsman £432 per annum rent for three farms totalling 691 acres) erected a Gothic gate-lodge to the plain, mediocre new house he had built shortly after 1777, now called Odellville. The avenue has since been changed, and this is now the herdsman's cottage (overleaf).

The terrace of estate cottages set back from the main road beside the entrance of Ballymascanlan House, Co. Louth, is said to have been built towards the end of the eighteenth century with stones quarried from the old castle. The windows have leaded astragals in a Gothic style and are most attractive (overleaf).

Donamon Castle. An engraving of 1792

But by and large during the two closing decades of the century Neo-Classicism was defeating Gothic in Ireland, though the latter would stage a spectacular come-back in the early nineteenth century. Wyatt himself designed a number of new houses for Ireland, among them Castlecoole, Co. Fermanagh, a great, strictly Neo-Classical mansion, built for Lord Belmore between 1790 and 1797, for which Wyatt's designs were based on drawings of Richard Johnston's. The nine-bay house with its colonnades, though splendidly appointed, is very restrained. It is still the property of the Earls of Belmore, but is in the care of the National Trust and open to the public.

Francis Johnston (1760–1829), Richard's younger brother, who had studied under Cooley, was a great admirer of Wyatt and was undoubtedly influenced by Castlecoole when he came to design Townley Hall, Co. Louth, for Blaney Townley Balfour in 1794. The exterior is stark and severe with a great Doric portico and a successfully sober front door. Inside, austerity gives way to a dramatic sense of space and restrained grandeur, as the entrance-hall leads into a central rotunda which forms the impressive staircase-hall. Stucco-work in high relief decorates the ceiling and the lunettes on the frieze. Johnston paid great attention to detail in this house, and his door-surrounds are exquisite, a marvellous foil for the perfectly proportioned panelled doors in figured mahogany.

Not all the very rich, however, were employing Wyatt or Johnston. The 8th Earl of Abercorn (1712–89), the greatest landlord in Co. Tyrone, engaged the architect George Stewart to build him a new seat at Baronscourt. The old house was to be converted into stables and farm-buildings, retaining, nevertheless, its former appearance. The work was finished by September 1781 and Stewart presented his accounts, plus drawings for lodges with temple-fronts and for the

The garden front,
formerly the front,
Baronscourt, parish of
Ardstraw, Co. Tyrone

stable conversion. Up to that time he had been paid just over £8,000, presumably for building the main house. The 8th Earl was succeeded by his nephew, who – having been created a Marquess in 1790 – decided to alter the house, built only ten years before and described by Beaufort in 1787 as 'excellent and noble'. To do this the Marquess employed John Soane (1753–1837, later Sir John, the designer of the Bank of England), the son of a mason and protégé of the Earl Bishop of Derry. Soane's scheme was to reverse the house. The old front became the garden front; the dividing walls to the right and left of the old entrance-hall were thrown down and replaced by pillars, while the pillars that had been at the back of the old entrance-hall were replaced by a hall, thus creating one great gallery running the full length of the back of the house. The butler's room, pantry, housekeeper's room, etc., which had been at the back were removed; the portico from the old front was brought to the centre of the colonnade at the new front, and the back of the old hall – the part behind the pillars – became the new staircase-hall. Still further additions were made in the nineteenth century, enlarging the front of the house, but the original pedimented seven-bay house, built by Stewart and reversed by Soane, still forms the garden front.

A very similar house externally is Ballynatray, Co. Waterford, though it is somewhat larger, having eleven bays. It has not been added to since it was built in 1795 for Grice Smyth and his heiress-bride, Mary Brodrick Mitchell. It stands in an idealized deer-park overlooking a lower reach of the Blackwater, its gardens sloping down to the river where tall wading birds feed tranquilly among the rushes. The romantic beauty of the place – equally breath-taking bathed in sunlight or dappled by wreaths of mist – is further enhanced by the ruins of the ancient Augustinian Monastery of St Molanfide on the islet of Molana, which Grice Smyth linked to the mainland in 1805. In the abbey is the tomb of Raymond le Gros (companion of Strongbow and builder of The Hook) on which Grice Smyth placed a tablet and a stylized Neo-Classical urn. Round the ruins was an eighteenth-century garden with statuary, extending beyond the parterres of the gardens surrounding the house.

It took a considerable amount of money to build a fine house, and more than one over-ambitious gentleman not in the financial class of the Marquess of Abercorn, or even of Grice Smyth, was ruined by reckless enterprises in stone. One of the most drastic instances was Sir Robert Tilson Deane, who in the flush of pleasure at being raised to the peerage as Baron Muskerry in 1781, and emboldened by the fortune of his heiress-wife, Anne Fitzmaurice of Springfield Castle, built Upper Dromore House, Co. Cork, at an outlay of £33,000. He inhabited it for one night, before directing that it be thrown down so that the value of the materials might offset part of the building costs. By 1839 the remains were a total ruin.[5]

Tomb of Raymond le Gros in the gardens of Ballynatray, parish of Templemichael, Co. Waterford

Grice Smyth's brother-in-law, Sir Henry Browne Hayes, thought of a more novel way of raising money, though there is no evidence at all that he actually needed it. In 1783 he married Elizabeth Smyth who (according to the newspapers) was possessed of a considerable fortune. About this time, and certainly before December 1785, he built a small but exquisite house which he called Vernon Mount on a hill-top near Douglas, Co. Cork. Its three-bay front is oval, and both sides have curved bays corresponding with the staircase and one of the reception-rooms. The entrance-hall has an elegant stove in the form of an urn – the height of Neo-Classical conceit – which is still functioning. Three of the ceilings are in the manner of Angelica Kauffmann, and the whole concept of the house is towards entertaining and gracious living. There is even an oval bedroom-hall with a cupola, its ceiling supported by marbleized Corinthian columns; its doors have alternating naïve grisaille paintings of urns and of classical figures. This enchanting house is at variance with everything that is known of Sir Henry's quizzical character. He was knighted while Sheriff of Cork in 1790: his wife, having borne him four children, is said to have left him and gone back to her relations, and she certainly died at Ballynatray in 1794. Three years later – though apparently not financially embarrassed – Sir Henry proceeded to abduct a plain but very rich Quaker heiress, Mary Pike, with whom he was unacquainted, imprisoning her for a night at Vernon Mount and going through a form of marriage ceremony. She, however, threw his ring across the room and resisted when he tried to 'push her towards the bed in the rudest manner', and next morning was retrieved by her enraged uncle. Sir Henry was charged at the Cork Assizes in 1801 and sentenced to transportation to Australia, whither he went on a convict ship, accompanied by his valet and so much luggage that it filled up the cabins of several officers and the vessel's doctor. In time one of his married daughters managed to extract a pardon for him from the Prince Regent, whose fancy she had taken at a Brighton ball. But his troubles were not yet ended, for on the homeward voyage the ship was wrecked due to the Captain's drunkenness. Sir Henry and his ever-present valet immediately seized one of the boats lowered to take off the women and ungallantly rowed themselves away; behaviour that was viewed very unfavourably when they were all rescued by an American ship and landed on Long Island. He did finally get back to Ireland and joined his son and daughter-in-law in his lovely Vernon Mount, where he died in 1832. Poor rich Mary Pike died in Cork the same year, unmarried and having long been insane, and the fortune he had coveted went to her cousins.[6] Vernon Mount remained with his descendants for many years, and is now the headquarters of the Munster Motor Cycle and Car Club Ltd.

The Earl Bishop of Derry was an even more extraordinary and alarming character, for he made off with several married, unmarried and widowed ladies without any intent to espouse them – he having a wife – nor was he in the least deterred if at first they demurred at being swept into bed. This Frederick Augustus Hervey (1730–1803) was already the worldly Bishop of the lucrative Diocese of Derry when his brother died in 1779 and he became 4th Earl of Bristol. The title and additional fortune did nothing to decrease his worldliness. His abiding passions (besides ladies) were Italy – where he spent long years, to the neglect of his episcopal duties in Ireland – paintings, marble and building, all of which expensive tastes he indulged extravagantly.

With the services of Michael Shanahan, a Cork master mason who blossomed into an architect, he erected an extraordinary house at Downhill in Co. Derry. When

The stair and bedroom-hall, Vernon Mount, parish of Frankfield, Co. Cork. Above: stove in the entrance-hall

Beaufort called in 1787 the profligate Earl Bishop was confined to bed with an 'attack in his bowels', but fortunately Shanahan was available to show off the works. The good Mr Beaufort had already been astonished on arrival to be confronted by a Chinese wooden gate manned by a disconcerting porter dressed in tartan plaid. On admittance, he passed through the Doric triumphal arch to the house, which he describes as presenting

> a front of 3 windows between a semi Octagon but the sides are irregular and have the west side 2 and the east side 3 bows now surmounted by as many domes. The whole is now cased with cut stone of no good or even colour and decorated at irregular distances with fluted pilasters of the Corinthian order, which have very little projection and hardly appear at any distance. The entrance is usually by the back door under the staircase which is of portland and gilt iron rails, the Lobby above supported by 4 columns of very fine Derbyshire marble. This door by a few steps leads into a corridor the whole length of the house. The rooms are rather low but magnificently fitted up with much rich decoration of painting and gilding, the furniture is of the same order, the chair frames gilt, the covers and curtains red and white damask with gold lace and fringe. There are pictures and statues innumerable and most of them excellent copies or valuable antiques. The chimney pieces are chiefly Italian and extremely fine. One chimney piece has on one side in Alto Relievo Bachus and Ariadne and on the other Cupid kissing Psyche.[7]

Downhill suffered a fire in 1851 and now only a shell remains, though the gateway, the domed mausoleum built by the Earl Bishop in memory of his brother, and the Mussenden Temple on the cliff can still be seen. The estate is in the care of the National Trust.

Ballyscullion, the Earl Bishop's other great venture in domestic building in Ireland, has entirely vanished. Known as the 'Bishop's Folly', and begun in 1787,

Emsworth, Malahide, Co.
Dublin

it was an extravagant rotunda with outstretched elliptical wings and a dome to vie with that of the Pantheon in Rome, beautifully sited to obtain a view over the hills of Co. Antrim and the woodlands of Co. Derry. Here the Earl Bishop imitated something that had intrigued him – a double-corkscrew staircase, which rendered a grandee on one stair unable to see or be seen by a lesser mortal on the service stair. Such was the Earl Bishop's *folie de grandeur* that it could have been the double-corkscrew stair in the Royal Castle of Chambord in France that inspired him, or possibly the simpler one at Orvieto in Italy. Ballyscullion had an oval lobby, a library and twin drawing- and dining-rooms, lavishly papered and with silk hanging, and everywhere the inevitable galaxy of statues and paintings.

The Earl Bishop was suddenly summoned to his Maker by a 'seizure of gout', and actually passed away in the outhouse of a peasant's cottage near Rome because the owner did not wish a heretic prelate to die beneath his roof. It was indeed a sad anti-climax for this high-liver, as well as being rather unjust, since he had always allowed Catholics the use of the room under his Mussenden Temple at Downhill to celebrate Mass, and his will declared that the practice should continue. He left Ballyscullion and Downhill to his kinsman, Henry Bruce, who decided to live at Downhill and levelled Ballyscullion, selling its materials. The portico is now on St George's Church in Belfast, and an Italian chimney-piece from Downhill – and perhaps originally from Ballyscullion – is installed at Castle Upton, Co. Antrim.

James Gandon (1743–1823), an English-born architect of Huguenot extraction, had been a pupil of Chambers, and settled in Ireland at the instigation of Lord Carlow (later Earl of Portarlington). There he became the leading Neo-Classical architect, though most of his work was in the domain of public buildings, such as the Dublin Custom House (begun in 1781 and completed ten years later), and the Four Courts, which he took over from Thomas Cooley and finished in 1802. He did, however, design a few private houses: the drawings for one of these have survived and the house itself – Emsworth near Malahide – is still a private residence.

It is a pedimented villa and was built about 1790. Near by is another Gandon house, Abbeville, built for the Right Hon. John Beresford, but this has since been enlarged.

For his patron, Lord Portarlington, Gandon first built Coolbanagher Church and then, about 1790, designed a large Neo-Classical mansion, originally called Dawson Court but then renamed Emo Park (p. 122). It was completed about twenty years later by Gandon's pupil, Richard Morrison, and will be described in the next chapter. Indeed Gandon's chief importance in the scheme of Irish domestic building lies in the fact that Morrison was his pupil.

Richard Morrison (1767–1849) was the son of the builder and architect, John Morrison of Midleton, Co. Cork, who died in 1800. Richard had a long and distinguished career, being knighted in 1841, and it was he more than anyone who was responsible for the modified Neo-Classical, Neo-Gothic and Neo-Tudor ideas that influenced the great spate of building in Ireland in the early nineteenth century.

In 1793 he published *Useful and Ornamental Designs in Architecture*, which included plans for various types of houses with estimates 'formed and calculated according to the Medium Rates or Prices as allowed for such Works in the Cities of Dublin, Cork, Limerick, Waterford, Londonderry &c. &c.'. The least expensive of these designs was the small 'Parsonage or Farmhouse', a two-storey three-bay box, with little 12-foot-wide wings, one containing the wash-house, the other the stable, joined to the main house by a cellar and a dairy (each 15 by 8 feet) and hidden behind curtain walls, showing that the old Palladian idea was not yet forgotten. Behind the stable was a cowhouse; behind the wash-house a cart-house. The ground floor of the house contained a narrow hall with a staircase, to the left of which was the 'eating-room' (18 by 15 feet) and to the right the parlour (15 by 14½ feet). Behind the parlour, and sunk 2½ feet below the level of the principal rooms (just to keep everybody in their place) was the kitchen (18 by 14½ feet) off which was a pantry. Access to the kitchen was through a door under the staircase, a much-favoured arrangement. The first floor contained three bedchambers with two dressing-rooms and a house closet, and in the garrets were three bedchambers for servants with closets. The estimate for the whole establishment, including the offices, was a modest £762.

Next up the scale was the three-bay 'Villa or Hunting Lodge' which was larger, and had a basement and a more fancy façade – doorcase with columns, little turrets on the pavilions and a moulded cornice. The corridors that connected with the stable in one pavilion and the coach-house in the other, contained on one side a dog-house and dairy, and on the other a turf-house and harness-room. The ground floor, however, still had a narrow hall with stair and three reception-rooms, a parlour to the left, a study to the right (both 20 by 16 feet) and an eating-room at the back (24 feet square) with a bow overlooking the garden. This house had four bed-chambers and four servants' sleeping-rooms over the outer offices. Kitchen, servants' hall, etc. were in the basement. The cost was estimated at £1,057 with a note that the frontispiece, steps, cornice, etc. were intended for limestone or freestone.

The proposed 'Villa or Country House' cost a mere £43 more, and was the plan that would have suited most small country gentlemen. Indeed, apart from the refinements of Morrison's façade it is the essential arrangement of the mass of box-like Georgian houses that dot the Irish countryside. Kitchen, servants' hall and cellars were in the basement: the ground floor had a square hall with twin rectangular

Knockgraffon Rectory,
Co. Tipperary

Centre: entrance gates,
Mount Desart, parish of
Currykippane, Co. Cork

rooms to left and right: one a study, the other a breakfast-parlour. At the back of the
house were larger twin rooms: one the withdrawing-room, the other the dining-
parlour. Upstairs were seven bedchambers, and above that, for the servants, seven
garret rooms lit by windows in the valleys. For this country-house Morrison suggested that the frontispiece be executed in Bath or Portland stone, the steps, window-
architraves, cornice, etc. in limestone or freestone, the interior walls in brick and
the exterior walls in rough stone masonry, roughcast on the outside. It can be
inferred that a simpler version, without the frontispiece and moulded cornice,
but with a columned door-surround, carved frieze and elliptical fanlight, must have
cost in the region of £1,000.

Morrison illustrated two more expensive villas, the cheaper, at £2,900, having
seven bays and a prostyle Ionic portico with decorated tympanum and a balustrade
ornamented with urns. The principal floor was 15 feet high, the bedroom floor
10½ feet. The ground floor contained a hall, vestibule, drawing-room, dining-
parlour, breakfast-parlour, study and billiard-room. There were eight bedrooms
on the first floor, but no garrets, the sleeping-rooms for the unlucky servants being
in the basement with the kitchen.

The grandest villa of all cost £3,798 18s 0d, and is described as intended for 'A
Temporary Residence for a Nobleman whose Principal Residence is in England.'
The 9-foot-high basement had cellars, kitchen and sleeping-rooms for his staff. The
principal floor, 15 feet in height, had a hall, front and back stair, circular saloon and a
range of reception-rooms – withdrawing-room with a bow towards the garden,
dining-room, breakfast-room, library, billiard-room and gentleman's dressing-
room with water-closet. Upstairs were seven bedrooms and dressing-rooms,
communicating with the gallery running round the saloon which rose the full
height of the house and was lit from above. The roof was to be flat and covered
in copper.

Morrison also offered designs for striking entrance-gateways for the avenues of
the best houses, priced at between £150 and £350, according to the material used.
Mount Desart, Co. Cork, has a fine example of another variety of entrance-gate
popular at the same period, with wrought-iron-work incorporating the arms and
crest of its then owners, the Dunscombes.

The garden front, Mellon, parish of Ardcanny, Co. Limerick

Unless a parson had private means (and many of them had), he might consider himself lucky to have so comfortable a house as that proposed by Morrison at £762. Contemporary reports indicate that many country clergy were then occupying rather squalid houses, a situation rectified in the early 1800s by an intensive building programme. At the end of the eighteenth century the living of Knockgraffon, Co. Tipperary, was held by the Reverend Nicholas Herbert, father of Dorothea Herbert, writer of *Retrospections, 1770–1806*. Herbert was prosperous, married to a peer's daughter, and resided mainly at Carrick-on-Suir, but at his Archbishop's insistence spent three months each year at Knockgraffon. A childish sketch of Dorothea's (published in Volume 2 of her *Retrospections*) shows that in her day the little three-bay rectory had only two storeys; in the nineteenth century another storey was added, as well as the service wing to the right. This house is a good example of how a staircase was sometimes allowed to cross a front window.

Though built about 1780, Mellon, Co. Limerick, with its elliptical fanlight over the front door, is in the range of Morrison's £1,100 country seat, and an archetype of the Georgian box he popularized, and which so perfectly met the needs of the bulk of the Irish country gentry. Within the means of its owner, easy to run and therefore pleasing to his lady, with sufficient accommodation for the customary large family of children, yet suitable for modest entertaining, these houses had much to recommend them. Mellon has the hipped roof and the greatly favoured internal lay-out – a central hall with all the rooms leading off it, though in Mellon's case the hall has a fireplace, a refinement not normally found in later houses of this type and size. The dining-room and the pink drawing-room, still with its mellowed Victorian furnishings, are placed on the garden front to enjoy the view across the Shannon. The house was built by John Westropp and still belongs to his descendants, the Misses Grace and Rose Westropp. It is pervaded by a sense of arrested time – the Shannon still floods periodically over the lower gardens as it has always done; John Westropp's pewter dishes sit in the hall where they have always sat; there is also a pile of calling-cards left on a Vandeleur ancestress of the present owners when she was in Rome about 1820, and including one of *Madame Mère*, mother of Napoleon. Mellon is indeed the distilled essence of gentry life in Late Georgian rural Ireland.

171

The same magical quality of belonging wholly to the past is preserved at Drishane, Co. Cork, a larger and more gracious house, though still compact and comfortable. It was built by Thomas Somerville, the eldest son of a local clergyman of Scottish settler stock, who was originally intended to follow his father's profession. According to one of his daughters, he changed his mind and went into trade, having accidentally lost an eye; it is difficult to follow why it was harder to be a one-eyed cleric watching his flock than a one-eyed merchant watching his stock, but one-eyed or not Tom became highly successful, exporting butter and salted provisions to the West Indies, and bringing back rum, sugar and timber, particularly the prized black mahogany so beloved of the eighteenth-century Cork cabinet-makers. For many years he lived in his father's old converted tower-house at Castlehaven (Castle Townshend) but about 1790, having accumulated a fortune, he built the present house on his inherited lands of Drishane, where he was resident at least by 1792. Always with his remaining eye to a lucrative deal, he leased the old castle to the Rector, whose successor in the course of a quarrel ripped off its roof and thus let it fall into ruin. Drishane has a geometrically leaded version of the elliptical fanlight which became popular in the 1790s, remained the rage for over half a century and is ubiquitous in Ireland (p. 104). Like Landsdown the house is weather-slated, and when it glistens with dew in the early morning sunlight is nothing short of beautiful. Its interior doors are made of Tom the Merchant's imported timber, and there are also several pieces of furniture in the valued black mahogany. For eighty years Drishane was the home of Tom's great-great-grand-daughter, the writer Edith Somerville, and its atmosphere pervades her books. Her nephew, Brigadier Desmond Somerville and his wife, the present owners, have lovingly kept her rooms and their contents intact, as well as her many manuscripts and paintings. In addition to being a very successful author she was also an able artist, and some of her best work is still in the house. Like Mellon, Drishane is scarcely touched by time and seems impregnated with memories: it is impossible not to respond to its wonderful, gentle atmosphere.

The descendants of John Odell, builder of The Turret at Ballingarry, Co. Limerick (discussed in Chapter 3), remained in the district into the present century, marrying their neighbours who were usually their cousins, and in their general habits being fairly typical of the provincial gentry. From 1751 until his death in 1763 the head of the family, Thomas Odell – evidently considering The Turret a bit inadequate – leased Shannongrove as a residence. However one or another branch of the Odells remained at The Turret until the 1840s when Major Thomas Odell emigrated to Ontario. Others of John Odell's descendants lived in the old tower-house and its additions at Bealdurogy, the ruins of which with its stout bawn and stables still stand beside the house named Fortwilliam. William Odell was born at Bealdurogy in 1752, became a Colonel in the Limerick Militia and served as Member of Parliament for Limerick for twenty-six years, in both the Irish and Imperial Parliaments, becoming a Lord of the Treasury. As he rose in office, and after being High Sheriff for the county, he deemed it advisable to move into something rather more imposing than his converted tower-house. He therefore leased the old premises to the Rector and built himself a fine Neo-Classical mansion called The Grove, near Ballingarry. In 1773 his bride had brought him a dowry of £2,000 and in 1790 – most opportunely, when the Colonel wanted to build – her father died, bequeathing her a further inheritance. In good eighteenth-century tradition the Colonel expended her money (as well as the legacies left to his minor

children) in building, decorating and furnishing his new mansion, which was apparently in the class priced by Morrison at about £2,900. Only its foundations and the enormous stables now remain. It was ransacked during the Famine and quarried for local building: the portico with its Greek-fret frieze is now on the Convent in Ballingarry village, and on several occasions during the last century the local doctor, making his rounds in the cottages, recovered Hepplewhite dining-chairs that had once been at The Grove.

Detail of fanlight over the front door, Ballyknockane, parish of Ballingarry, Co. Limerick (see also p. 206)

Colonel William is said to have been offered a title and to have refused it, but much of his correspondence with the Prime Minister includes requests for one, besides begging favours for his numerous progeny. In the hope of further advancement he voted for the Union, but all ended in disaster, for he was sued by some of his children concerning the missing legacies from their grandfather, and after engaging in appalling litigation with his daughters over their dowries, he spent his latter years in the Debtors' Prison in Dublin. His relations with his family had not been improved by his second marriage, at the age of sixty-six, to the young heiress-niece of the parish priest of Kilfarboy, Co. Clare. She kept him company in the Marshalsea, gave birth there to some still-born children, and died before he himself succumbed in 1831.

In January 1794 his eldest daughter Frances married Captain Michael Scanlan, who was then living in the simple old house at Ballinaha. That same year Scanlan started to build a new and more fitting residence on his adjoining property, the townland of Ballyknockane. This is of the box-villa type, relieved by naïve one-storey-high bows at the sides and another breaking the centre bay at the front. Based on Morrison's figures, this must have cost in the region of £1,000. The severity of the house is diminished by the extremely pretty leaded fanlight incorporating a group of a reclining classical figure with two cupids (a very rare device) as well as by the fine carving on the Ionic columns of the doorway (p. 206). Inside, the entrance-hall is divided from the staircase by an elliptical arch with an attractive timber fanlight. These refinements are undoubtedly the work of local craftsmen from Rathkeale, then a small but flourishing town. Ballyknockane remained in Scanlan hands until it was sold in 1920, and is now the property of Mrs E. A. S. Murray.

Glenwilliam, parish of
Ballingarry, Co. Limerick

Above right: Greenhouse,
parish of
Tullowmagimma, Co.
Carlow

XXI Right: the Library,
Donacomper, Co. Kildare
(p. 215)

Mrs Scanlan's sister, Colonel Odell's fourth daughter, married George Massy of Glenwilliam, Co. Limerick, whose father built that house in 1797. Glenwilliam is a simple box in Morrison's £1,000 category, relieved by semicircular bows at the centre front and back, whose windows light the hall and drawing-room. It looks rather as if the Massys, having seen the newly finished Ballyknockane, decided to improve on the bow effect: the result is certainly more harmonious, though they abandoned the good door-surround and elaborate fanlight in favour of rather naïve rustication. The Massys had the reputation of being wild and inveterate gamblers and, having survived one nineteenth-century fiasco when Mr Massy shot dead a gaming opponent in the little card-room, they one night staked the entire Glenwilliam property and lost it. It was then bought by Dr Atkinson, who added the fake castle and whose grand-daughter, Sybil Worlledge, is its present owner.

Houses of this type were just what the gentry needed, and all over the country there was a sudden frenzy of building these good, solid box-houses, the bulk of which survive to this day and form the backbone of what is generically known as 'Georgian Ireland'. The style, which persisted with little change almost up to 1850, was enormously despised by the Late Victorians, quite unfairly as most of these houses are not only easy on the eye but convenient to live in. The gentry liked them so much that they even introduced them to their tenantry, and estates sprouted small versions for stewards and bailiffs, and still smaller versions for tenant farmers. In Co. Carlow, directly opposite the entrance-gate to Castletown, is a little pedimented farm known as Greenhouse, with a pretty fanlight to its front door and curved cut-stone front steps. This was built by the owners of Castletown for a tenant named McDarby in the late eighteenth-century. Its pretensions are all to the front: the back of the single-pile house has only a door and one window, though there is a commodious farmyard with dressed-stone surrounds to its doorways. Two other similar houses were also built on the Castletown estate, apparently with the idea of rendering the tenant farmers' dwellings an ornament to the landscape – an idea which certainly succeeded.

The late eighteenth century was a great era of eccentrics in Ireland – the Earl Bishop, Sir Henry Browne Hayes, Peter Walsh and Richard Edgeworth, father of Maria, the novelist. The latter designed his own remarkable house at Edgeworthstown, Co. Longford, which was full of his ingenious inventions, including leather straps to prevent the spring doors from clapping. Each chimney emitted warm air from above the mantelpiece, and in the dining-room, as the warm air coursed from the kitchen, it passed through a pedestal where plates were put to heat.

Peter Walsh was the eldest son of John of Fanningstown, Co. Kilkenny, and was born about 1740; his obituary in 1819 mentions that he died at an advanced age.[8] At Belline, in his home county, he built a house of no particular interest save for two quite unusual detached three-storey circular pavilions (p. 121), perhaps intended to be linked to the house in the conventional manner, though there is no trace of any curtain walls. Both pavilions have chimneys, and that illustrated had its ground floor fitted up as a kitchen. It is rather too close to the house to make a desirable summer-house, and it has been suggested that the eccentric owner and his wife (who were childless) each occupied a pavilion and entertained jointly in the main house. In the grounds he later built a rustic temple, which has been mistaken for a summer-house, but which was clearly a gate-lodge. The double row of columns at the front of this picturesque little house are actually tree-trunks and their capitals are made of whitewashed rope. It contains three rooms: across the front a small living-room with fireplace and sink, and behind it two bedrooms. It is still inhabited.

The rustic lodge, Belline, parish of Fiddown, Co. Kilkenny

XXII Left: the 'Pack of Cards', Barrack Street, Cobh, Co. Cork (p. 229). In the background is the Roman Catholic Cathedral

177

In England, John Soane – who worked on Baronscourt – was responsible for popularizing this sort of romantic construction. His *Plans of Buildings executed in Several Counties, 1788* included a dairy which was a prototypal temple in timber, and his *Sketches* of 1793 contained porticoes made of 'trunks of trees decorated with woodbines and honeysuckle'. Queen Marie-Antoinette and her coterie were enchanted to romanticize the rustic life, playing at shepherds and shepherdesses in mock-pastoral settings at Versailles. Such fantasies did not meet with favour in Ireland until some years later, when it became fashionable for young ladies to design cottages and arbours and the *cottage orné* emerged. Derrymore, Co. Armagh, built in 1766, is really a thatched manor-house, and it is likely that its present appearance of a *cottage orné* was given to it later when the Picturesque genre was really in vogue. It is now in the care of the National Trust.

Most Irish gentry lived too close to the land and saw too much of the miseries of rural life to want to play at it: for example when the fashion for an ornamental apron worn over ladies' dresses was introduced into England it failed to find favour in Ireland.

Life in a cabin, which was the life of the bulk of the population, was far from rustic bliss, and remained much as it had been for centuries. Connaught still had many improvised cabins, and travellers in Co. Galway about 1790 even noted a number of marble cabins, made from lumps of outcrop marble gathered by the cottagers and fitted together to make walls in the old dry-stone manner.

Since the middle of the century improvements had been made in a number of towns and villages, so that by 1790 the general aspect was better, if not yet good. Some improving landlords had laid out small model towns, such as Thomas Vesey's Abbeyleix or the Earl of Aldborough's village for weavers, Stratford-on-Slaney in Co. Wicklow. This had regular streets and 400 stone houses; it was begun in 1775, but when the linen industry collapsed after the Act of Union it fell into decay and now has only a few inhabitants. Gandon was engaged to design a lay-out for New Geneva, Co. Waterford, a project later abandoned. The village of Slane, Co. Meath, was also laid out formally with four matching houses facing each other diagonally at the cross-roads. The Moravian community at Gracehill, Co. Antrim had neat, two-storey houses and shops built round a square with a very tidy appearance. Even Connaught benefited, the new Westport being neatly planned; and at Oughterard in Co. Galway the village was colonized with weavers from the north who were provided with small, well-built houses; this village also vanished when the bottom fell out of the linen industry.

Mrs Montagu was impressed with the Archbishop of Armagh's projected improvements for his tenantry when she visited him at Clifton in 1793 and wrote:

> His Grace shew'd me the plans of Farm Houses and Cottages he had erected on his estate near Rokeby in such a manner as will give prosperity to his tenants and comfort and subsistence to the cottagers; to all these he has restricted the Rent, that the avarice of a future Landlord and the extortions of stewards may not encroach on his benevolent institutions. As the Irish derive a great part of their subsistence from the linen manufacture his Grace has built large rooms for the purpose of spinning and weaving and has allotted garden and field to each cottage.[9]

Unfortunately such well-designed and attractive places were vastly outnumbered by the plethora of wretched ones, and travellers of the day rarely failed to remark on the miserable appearance of most villages. For instance, Adare, Co. Limerick – now a tidy model village – was then a poverty-stricken place, full of tumble-down

Old shop front, Kilkenny

Left: doorways,
Parliament Street,
Kilkenny

cabins in such appalling state that early in the next century they had to be demolished. The inn near the gateway to the Manor House was one of the most wretched in Ireland, a filthy one-roomed cabin. On its site today stands a different sort of establishment, still a hotel, but catering for the more affluent tourist. Omagh, too, had an awful appearance, and Antrim, which once had had good houses, had become very shabby. Enniskillen, however, was praised as one of the most respectable-looking Irish towns, and Derry, Coleraine and Magherafelt all made a good impression and were still improving, while other towns mentioned by travellers as neat, pleasant or decent were Drumsna, Ballina, Ballinrobe, Loughrea, Hillsborough, Carrickmacross, Moate and Tullamore.

There is a numerical census for the town of Carrick-on-Suir, Co. Tipperary, in 1799,[10] from which some interesting facts can be deduced concerning small towns. It had 802 dwellings, plus 370 in the suburb of Carrickmore and 566 in the suburb of Carrickbeg, with a total 10,907 inhabitants (all of whom except 298 were Catholics). There was an average of just over 6 persons per house in the town and 5 per cabin in the suburbs. Nearly 500 of the adult males were agricultural workers, but the next largest field of occupation was the weaving industry, in which over 400 males were employed, in addition to the womenfolk spinning at home. Carrick was then a substantial little town with relatively good living conditions, but being so dependent on the textile trade its situation soon changed radically. In 1799 it had the following persons engaged in the building and allied trades: 1 architect, 32 masons, 5 stone-cutters, 3 'paviers', 77 carpenters, 7 turners, 1 cabinet-maker, 25 nailers, 20 sawyers, 5 glaziers, 2 lime-burners, 2 wire-workers, 1 painter, 18 slaters and only 3 thatchers.

At Kilkenny, where there was a flourishing social life, a number of Georgian terraces, such as those in Parliament Street and the Parade, had been built; there

179

Houses on south side,
Merrion Square, Dublin

were also good cut-stone town-houses and a hotel in Patrick Street. Some of the shops even began to sport elegant display windows, although the town still retained a predominantly medieval aspect, particularly in the old stepped alleys. An unusual feature of a number of the new houses was a large elliptical fanlight shared by two hall doors. Most of these have now disappeared, but at one time they were fairly numerous in the town, though rare to unknown elsewhere.

The city of Limerick was greatly improved; the new development of Newtown Pery was in progress and many fine terrace-houses had been built. Likewise in Cork, whose best districts were quite beautiful, a contrast to the terrible slums. Belfast had blossomed under the patronage of the 5th Earl of Donegall: the town was surveyed, leases were reviewed and most of the old ones cancelled and re-granted under new terms, such as obligation to build with sound materials (brick or stone and lime) with slated roofs. Fines were imposed for casting cinders, dung or other filth into the streets and letting it lie, though it was apparently permissible to dump it in the street provided it was removed the same day. The better houses had to be 28 feet high, the medium ones 15 or 18 feet, and the cabins 10 feet. When Beaufort visited Belfast in 1787 he noted that most of the houses were brick and the town had a nice 'neat English appearance'.

Dublin, with Grattan's Parliament and all it entailed, was at its peak of importance.

In the 1790s there were a hundred peers living in the capital, in addition to dowagers, younger sons, baronets and knights. In these palmy days – palmy at least for them – they jockeyed for sinecures and higher titles in the vortex of vice, wit, pleasantry, high living, corruption and selfishness which was fashionable Dublin. There were many layers in Dublin society. At the top were the rich and powerful peers, who had their great mansions, some built in the previous generation and inherited from their fathers, some newly built, like Belvedere House in Great Denmark Street, a huge five-bay mansion with an imposing façade constructed in 1786. It was lavishly decorated in the Classical manner by Michael Stapleton, whose Diana Room, with its original mahogany bookcases and organ, and Apollo Room, can still be seen – though when the house became a school for boys in 1841 the Jesuits deemed it best to dismantle the Venus Room. The last great Dublin mansion was Aldborough House, begun in 1792, dated 1796 and completed soon after 1798. Built for the Earl of Aldborough (1736–1801), it has a forbidding aspect, mainly due to its dark grey stone. It included a music-room, a private theatre and a cold bath; the reception-rooms on the first floor are arranged *en suite* and once contained splendid Bossi mantelpieces. Its career as a private residence was brief; on the Earl's death it passed to his widow who soon remarried and then died, after which it went to his nephew. He did not live there, having other properties, and it was leased to Professor von Feinagle, whose successful teaching institute was conducted there, and in Rossmore House in Kildare Street, until closed by his widow in 1830. During the Crimean War the house was used as a barracks; it is now a department of the Post Office.

Beneath such strong peers were the middling peers, and beneath these the numerous weak peers. Then there were the relations and connections of the peers, not always in the strata of society one might expect – for example the Viscounts Doneraile had fairly close relatives on the farm, not to mention some in domestic service. Many of the new peers had come from rich merchant families – brewers, chandlers and linen-factors – and they naturally had cousins who were shopkeepers, a fact about which they tended to be sensitive. Sir Jonah Barrington divided gentlemen into three categories: half-mounted gents, every-inch gents and gents-to-the-backbone. It is hard to know to which category he himself belonged, considering that he blocked up the window at the side of his house when a malicious neighbour, Lady Clonmell, put it about that Lady Barrington (*née* Grogan, a silk-mercer's daughter) sat there because she was accustomed to being in the front of her father's shop. Lady Clonmell might be expected to know, being newly removed from trade herself. There were also quite a number of charlatans hanging around the nobility, such as the extraordinary Dr Achmet, supposedly a Turk, who obtained several grants from the Government to establish his 'Hot and Cold Sea-Baths', but who turned out to be one Patrick Joyce from Kilkenny.

Thus the top level consisted of nobles and politicians, conducting their lives with great panache and little foresight, and trailing in their wake their indigent relatives and hangers-on. Beneath them came the businessmen who were accumulating fortunes, and then the small tradespeople and artisans who were fully occupied earning enough to support themselves and their large families. At the bottom came a veritable army of beggars and a boisterous rabble, ready to pelt funeral processions with dead cats, and easily procured with whiskey and gingerbread to disrupt elections. The strong peers had their great mansions, the middling peers occupied elegant terrace-houses such as those in Merrion Square, the east and south sides of which were laid out in the 1780s and 1790s, and the weak peers lived in decent lodgings along with ladies of the stage, superannuated dowagers and country Members of Parliament. Doctors, lawyers and successful merchants lived in the second-class streets, which were increasing rapidly on the north side of the city. Such houses were usually put up by builders and speculators who often took leases of three or four plots, which explains the uniformity of blocks of houses in some streets, whereas when a street was entirely developed by one contractor all the houses tended to be uniform. Speculative building continued at a heady pace: squares and streets of terrace-houses of varying sizes and standards going up on both sides of the Liffey. To the north the city was spreading across the River Tolka, though temporarily halted by the 1798 Rising, when the 2nd Lord Mountjoy, owner of the Gardiner estates (who had had a scheme for building a grandiose circle of fine houses to be called the Royal Circus) was killed at the Battle of New Ross.

The United Irish movement was an uneasy amalgamation of Jacobin-Republicanism, fired by the French Revolution, Irish Nationalism, Catholic Emancipationism and Protestant religious liberalism. It culminated in the insurrection generally called the 1798 Rising. Fighting – and consequent damage to property – occurred in various parts of the country, Wexford, Antrim, Armagh and Mayo being particularly affected. One French expeditionary force landed at Killala, Co. Mayo; another was prevented from landing at Bantry Bay. Marauding bands called 'Whiteboys' joined the insurrectionists and there was a short reign of terror, with murders, arson, pillage, torture and the inevitable vicious retributions. By this time many of the Penal Laws had been repealed, but the country as a whole suffered from the iniquitous tithe system, lack of franchise and representation for the Catholic majority and – in parts of the country – from the excesses or uninterest of bad or absentee landlords. The bulk of the Protestant gentry was against the proposed Union with Great Britain, but the politicians used bribery and the Rising as tools to ram the measure through, supported by the Catholic hierarchy who were promised a better deal in return for co-operation. The masses, who were not consulted, merely hoped that their lot would somehow be improved.

As an indirect result of the Rising and a direct result of the Act of Union, which came into effect on 1 January 1801, the close of the century was also the end of an epoch in Dublin, which continued to grow but lost its importance as a capital city. Many of the peers moved to London; some even went to sulk on the Continent, mourning the good old days, and the brilliance of Dublin society was dimmed. The up-and-coming middle class took over their houses – they were doing well, for the Napoleonic Wars prevented any slump. Many country gentlemen who had sat in the Dublin Parliament decided not to seek re-election, being unable to afford constant travel back and forth to London, and withdrew to their estates, turning their attention once more to their county town, to their local affairs and – presently – to building themselves new houses.

CHAPTER 7

From the Union to the Famine

1801–1846

IT HAS FREQUENTLY BEEN IMPLIED that the first chime of the clock at midnight on 31 December 1800 sounded the death-knell of a flourishing Ireland, thus creating an impression that the Act of Union, like a wicked fairy, touched the glass coach and its horses, transforming them in a twinkling into a pumpkin and mice. The Union's ultimate effect was indeed deleterious, but for a time the inevitable slump in the Irish economy was staved off by the Napoleonic Wars, and the void created by the departure of the leaders of society was partly filled by the presence of a large military establishment with its attendant swashbuckling gaiety. There is no doubt the Napoleonic Wars benefited Ireland. Merchants and tradesmen, who were not only provisioning Army and Navy but also supplying corn to blockaded England, basked in an unaccustomed period of free spending. Numerous young men, who otherwise would have been unemployed or forced to emigrate, were receiving a regular wage in the ranks of Army, Navy or the local militias which had been raised in every county. A number of impecunious gentry also became commissioned officers, particularly in the Militia, and were paid hard cash – always scarce in Ireland – in return for duties which can hardly be described as arduous. Other young men joined the ever-swelling ranks of the East India Company, where there were valuable pickings available in a short time for bright lads, and even for honest ones. Money and Nankin dinner-services both returned to Ireland in some quantity, and the former not infrequently found its way into house-building. In short, there was a typical war boom, which provided work for many, enriched some and beguiled all but the most far-sighted into believing that everything would continue to go well.

The millers were among those who did good business supplying war needs; most of the big water-mills were built (or enlarged) about this time, and many a miller moved from his cottage into something more akin to a gentleman's villa. In Co. Kildare, a number of these mills were castellated, such as that at Levitstown on the River Barrow, beside which the miller had a comfortable residence. Castellation is also to be found on the mills at Moone and at the Quaker settlement at Ballitore. At Lismore, Co. Waterford (where in 1812 the Duke of Devonshire restored the Great Earl of Cork's now-ruined castle and much improved the town) the flour-miller leased his premises from the estate: he prospered so much that he was able to add on to the simple old house a brand-new one with a fancy façade, so that by 1837 it was described as 'Ballyinn, the *residence* of P. Foley *Esq.*'. The new house – with the old miller's house still behind – has been little changed since the early nineteenth century, and is now the residence of Miss Clodagh Anson.

Levitstown Mill, parish of
Castledermot, Co.
Kildare

Ballyin, parish of
Lismore, Co. Waterford

At Cadamstown, Co. Offaly, can be seen an example of a miller's small house, unaffected by prosperity. In 1821 the corn-mill was held, with one acre, by a miller called William Morough, and though the little house has only two rooms on the ground floor and a loft above, he and his wife were able to afford a resident servant-girl. In 1837 the mill was in use and described as a 'bolting-mill', but it is now derelict, although the house is still occupied.

The canal system, which had been undergoing steady expansion since the 1750s, also flourished greatly in the early nineteenth century, and until it was superseded by the railways conveyed a stream of passengers as well as much goods-traffic. Handsome hotels were built for the overnight reception of travellers, and the banks were dotted with the little houses of the lock-keepers, such as that at the Twelfth Lock on the Grand Canal, between Lucan and Milltown, Co. Dublin (p. 139).

The great landlords had no immediate cause for complaint after the Union, at least so long as the war lasted. Many of their tenants, who had never had a steady source of hard cash, now had a boy or two who had taken the King's Shilling, which meant that rents could be paid-up regularly. The Irish rentals of the greatest landowners were certainly impressive. In 1799, headed by Mr Conolly of Castletown with £25,000 a year, there were four others with £20,000 or more, and a further eighteen with £10,000 or more, all but five of whom were peers. One of the richer commoners was Joshua Cooper, Member of Parliament for Co. Sligo, whose rental was £10,000 per annum from forty thousand acres. Wealthy as he was, he remained content with the rather modest old house on his family estate at Markree (sometimes called Mercury) in Co. Sligo, but, when he died in 1801, his son Joshua (1761–1837), in the first flush of his new affluence, employed Francis Johnston to provide him with a more fitting seat.

The miller's house, Cadamstown, parish of Letterluna, Co. Offaly

185

The blue and gilt drawing-room, Markree Castle, parish of Ballysadare, Co. Sligo, and right: the gallery

Johnston was versatile, as proficient in the Classical idiom (wherein he excelled at Townley Hall) as in the castellated style, which he proceeded to use at Markree. At this period, these did not represent distinct schools and were, in fact, different expressions of parallel and unopposed movements. Johnston was, however, a disciple of Wyatt, and in the opening years of the nineteenth century was busily engaged in building or rebuilding in the castellated manner in various parts of the country. In 1801 he began the huge Charleville Forest in Co. Offaly for the Earl of Charleville, and in 1802 received his commission from Joshua Cooper.

His drawings for Markree, dated 1802–04, are in the National Library of Ireland, and from these it can be seen how he repeated Gandon's basic scheme in the original designs for Slane Castle. There is a pencil sketch, dated 1827 and signed 'S. Bossi', showing the exterior of the house after Johnston completed it, with its massive castle effect and Irish battlements. However, the Gothic treatment of the interior, as seen in the gallery where the corbels below the wall posts are embellished with angels, does not seem to have satisfied Joshua's nephew and heir, Edward Joshua Cooper. Though the Gothic style was retained for the gates and lodges built as late as 1832 or thereabouts, the new owner decorated the drawing-rooms in a very florid manner: the decadent *putti* in the gilded and mirrored rooms would look much more at home on the Continent than in this huge castle in Connaught. On Edward Joshua's death in 1863 he left only five daughters who, piqued at not inheriting Markree, took most of its furniture away with them. The castle passed to their cousin, Colonel Edward Henry Cooper, who married a rich English wife and surrounded the estate with battlemented walls like the outworks of a fortress, also adding several excrescences to the castle. His great-grandson, Lieutenant-Commander Edward F. P. Cooper, is the present owner and has struggled bravely to arrest the dry-rot in parts of the building, though, in order to keep the roof on at all, he and his family have had to withdraw to one wing of the vast place, which was intended to be manned by a host of servants.

Johnston and Morrison – both Irish born – shared the country-house practice at the beginning of the nineteenth century, having become Ireland's leading architects. By this time Gandon was ageing, gout-ridden and wholly preoccupied with finishing his last public work, the King's Inns. The building of Emo Park, Co. Leix (p. 122), had been interrupted by the death of the Earl of Portarlington in 1798 when his heir was only seventeen. The 2nd Earl presently engaged Morrison to complete the domed Neo-Classical mansion. Inside the dome (whose exterior dates from about 1850) is a lavish blue and gilt ceiling over a richly decorated saloon, designed as the principal feature of the interior. The Ionic portico is repeated on the garden front but without a pediment, and the unusual bas-relief panels of *putti* in the frieze are also repeated on the garden front. For a period the house became a Jesuit College, but it has now been bought by Mr Cholmeley Harris as a private residence and is being restored internally at great expense.

Chidley Coote of Ash Hill, Co. Limerick, died in 1799 leaving his heir, Charles Henry, aged only five. Three years later, on the death of a distant kinsman, the boy succeeded to the premier Baronetcy of Ireland as 9th Baronet. In January 1813 he purchased the house and demesne of Ballyfin, Co. Leix, from William Wellesley Pole, which house appears in a 1787 engraving of Milton's. Sir Charles Henry at once proceeded to replace it by a great classical mansion of the local sandstone, which was completed at a cost of £20,000; a drawing by J. P. Neale of 1828 shows it just as it now is, save that there were then three statues on the pediment over the portico. The arms of the 9th Baronet, impaling those of his wife Caroline Whaley, are set in the entablature over the Ionic portico. This portico leads into a vestibule whose floor is a copy of a Roman mosaic, and which communicates with an ornate saloon with a patterned parquet floor and green marble columns. The stained-glass lantern – a later addition – shows the Coote arms, while the family crest, a coot, is used throughout the house as a continuous and finally monotonous motif. The saloon communicates on one side with the staircase-hall, whose handsome stair

Ballyfin, parish of Clonenagh and Clonagheen, Co. Leix

187

Marble mantelpiece in the green and gilt music-room, Ballyfin, and right: the library-ballroom

Stone sofa, Lyons House, parish of Lyons, Co. Kildare

with brass balusters rises to a columned gallery, and on the other side with the drawing-room, with a rotunda whose blue cupola is spattered with stars, and with a music-room. The last is a most elegant apartment, with carved and gilded musical instruments in panels on the walls and the stucco-work of frieze and ceiling depicting musical instruments, archery and doves. It also has a particularly fine marble mantelpiece. The rotunda and the two principal reception-rooms communicate with the library (or ballroom) which runs the full length of the house. It too has a patterned parquet floor, and its pairs of green marble Ionic columns have gilded capitals; the classical frieze is ornamented with lyres, wreaths and Vitruvian scrolls. The care with which Morrison designed Ballyfin was extended to the classical gate-lodge beside the fine architectural gate-piers with stone figures of the ever-present coot. In 1929 Sir Ralph Coote sold the house and six hundred acres for £10,000 to the Patrician Brothers, the present owners, who have a College there and maintain the house and its grounds with care and attention.

Morrison also worked at Lyons House, Co. Kildare, for Valentine Lawless, who succeeded his father as 2nd Baron Cloncurry in 1799. Colonnades and wings were added under his supervision about 1810. The concept is severely Neo-Classical, with a high standard of interior decoration. Outside there are not only urns on plinths in the niches of the colonnades, but also a deceptively comfortable-looking stone sofa with stone bolsters and in the height of Regency fashion.

In the eighteenth century the term 'villa' was used to denote the secondary seat of a gentleman, and was usually applied to a compact house of five bays. As this size and style suited many Irish country gentry for their primary (or only) residence, the term came into use more loosely and was finally applied to a middle-class

suburban dwelling. Bearforest, a mile from the town of Mallow, designed by
Morrison and built for Robert Delacour in 1807–08, would have been termed a
villa by its architect. An account of the house, published in 1821,[1] mentions that
the work was executed under Morrison's 'special directions and frequent superintendence', and that his object was to prove his ability to design 'a residence that should
combine simplicity and purpose of a large family, or of affluent fortune, while it
retained the modest character becoming the habitation of an unostentatious private
gentleman'. He succeeded in his aim, for the house is judiciously planned, well
proportioned, well built and very pretty. The curved portico contains a part of the
hall floored in Portland stone, and has two pairs of Ionic columns flanking the
entrances to the principal rooms on either side of the hall. So that the house's
Classical ancestry should not be overlooked, a motto from Horace was set in the
entablature over the entrance. The basement, which is at the back only, is vaulted
and was floored with flagstones. A cistern was placed on top of the house, supplying
water from a spring on the hill above to all parts of the premises – very advanced
plumbing for those days.

Another of Morrison's villa-style houses is St Cleran's, Co. Galway, built about
1810, larger and more imposing than Bearforest, and less successful in avoiding
ostentation. Until recently it was the property of Mr John Huston, by whom it was
carefully restored.

Provincial architects and masons tried to emulate the villa style but often without
marked success, the result usually being a variant of the box-house, sometimes with
the addition of a grandiose portico out of proportion to the house itself. Undoubtedly the prize for porticoes must go to Annesbrook, Co. Meath. In 1821

Annesbrook, parish of
Duleek, Co. Meath, and
right: a corner of the
'banqueting-room'

George IV visited Ireland – the first British monarch to do so since James II and
William III fought for the crown at the Boyne – and was generally acclaimed by the
populace, his progress seemingly unmarred either by the inefficiency of the organization or the acute diarrhoea which assailed the King throughout. His engagements
included spending a few nights at Slane Castle, and it was planned that during this
he should dine with his subject, Mr Henry Smith, at Annesbrook near Duleek.
Smith was an insignificant gentleman with fourteen children, and one can only
suppose he was singled out for this attention because his name rendered him
representative of many. Flurried by the impending honour, he decided that his
little house must be improved before it received a sovereign accustomed to the
glories of the Royal Pavilion at Brighton. He therefore hastily added a huge Ionic
portico rising the full height of his house and a Gothic banqueting-room linked to
the main building by a corridor. When the diarrhoetic King finally arrived, the
August sun shone brightly, and whether from a sudden whim or a feeling of
claustrophobia at entering Annesbrook with all his retinue, he requested to dine
al fresco, and thus never saw the new dining-room, though he can hardly have
missed seeing the new portico.

The Hindu-Gothic gateway at Dromana, Co. Waterford (p. 158), is a direct result
of the excitement aroused by the King's extravaganza at Brighton. Some building
ventures in Eastern styles had already been made in England in the eighteenth
century – a Moorish 'Alhambra', a Turkish mosque and a Chinese pagoda had all
been devised as follies, and in 1803 Sir Charles Cockerell, after years with the East
India Company, asked Repton to make designs for an 'Indian' house at Sezincote in
Gloucestershire, which resulted in a house with multi-foil arches and onion domes
inspired by drawings of the Taj Mahal. Shortly afterwards the Prince Regent
'indianized' his stables at Brighton, and in 1815 Nash began orientalizing the whole
Pavilion. Since the style never became popular – perhaps due to its inability to live
down the comment that the Royal Pavilion looked as if St Paul's Cathedral had gone
to the sea and pupped – it is remarkable that Ireland can boast one of its very few
examples. Henry Villiers-Stuart (1803–74) inherited Dromana from his mother, and

in 1826 married Theresia Pauline Ott of Vienna. To greet and surprise the returning bridal pair a Hindu-Gothic gateway was erected in some temporary materials, perhaps wood and papier mâché. The young couple were so enchanted with this close replica of one of the Brighton gateways that they had it reconstructed in durable materials and turned into a gate-lodge. It stands on that part of the estate which was acquired by the Forestry Commission, and once uninhabited it quickly fell into serious disrepair. But for the salvage operation carried out in 1967–68 by the Irish Georgian Society the lodge would no longer exist. Fortunately the operation has been most successful, and in 1971 the County Council opened a new bridge across the Finisk River, in whose waters the dome and minarets cast their graceful reflection, to astonish and delight the traveller (p. 158).

The entrance gateway at Portumna Castle, Co. Galway (p. 140), is older than that at Dromana. When Beaufort saw it in 1808 he described it as 'a handsome modern gate in the Gothick style'. Further up the avenue is an arched Gothic gateway in a castellated wall, which in turn gives access to a courtyard divided from the forecourt by yet a third stone arch of much earlier date.

The Gothic gateway at Creagh Castle, Co. Cork, is contemporary with that at Dromana. It was built, according to a date-stone, in 1827, and was local work, the masons being the Regans of Doneraile and the stone-cutters two men named Flynn from Dromore Cross beyond Mallow. While the Hindu-Gothic gates at Dromana led to an eighteenth-century mansion (now demolished), and the Gothic gates at Portumna to a Jacobean castle, the Gothic gates at Creagh lead to a formal, Late Georgian house, dated 1816 on a medallion on its front steps, built by Captain William Johnson Brazier-Creagh. He died in 1827 and the gates were built for his brother, underlining their difference in taste. The house of 1816, which stands beside the sixteenth-century tower-house, is itself on the site of a former house called Castle Saffron, mentioned by Charles Smith in 1750 as owned by John Love and having Francini stucco-work.[2] Dr John Creagh, who was living in Doneraile in 1779, acquired the property and changed its name to Creagh Castle, and died there in 1792. As his grandson was married from Creagh Castle in 1801 it is clear that the

Gothic entrance gates, Creagh Castle, parish of Doneraile, Co. Cork

Frontispiece, Creagh Castle

Detail of cantilevered stair, Castle Hyde, parish of Litter, Co. Cork, and right: the entrance-saloon

remains of old Castle Saffron must have been made habitable after a disastrous fire in Love's time. It is probable that the present (1816) house is largely a rebuild, which would account for its eighteenth-century appearance. It is now the property of Squadron-Leader R. B. Black.

The appearance of Castle Hyde is also anachronistic, being in a style already out of fashion by 1800, and because of this it has been wrongly considered an eighteenth-century house. It was designed by the Cork architect, Abraham Hargrave (1755–1808), and when it was sold by the Incumbered Estates Court for £18,000, the then owner stated in his appeal that his father, John Hyde, had built the house and on it alone had spent £40,000. John Hyde had married the daughter of the 1st Lord Lismore in 1801, and built or rebuilt his house about that time. Hargrave, though essentially a provincial architect, was competent: he was much influenced by Ducart, for whom he may have worked in his early years. Thus Castle Hyde could derive either from his wish to continue in a traditional style, which he managed well, or from John Hyde's wish to imitate a house he admired: his mother was a daughter of the Earl of Bessborough and he may have desired to emulate his grandfather's Palladian lay-out. On the other hand, there was certainly an earlier house on this site on the banks of the Blackwater, and judging from the prosperity and social consequence of the Hydes it must have been an important one, and it may be that the main body of the house is more an adaptation than a total reconstruction. When the present owners, Mr and Mrs Henry A. Laughlin, had work done on the staircase walls they discovered bricked-up doors, indicating clearly that this part at least was the remains of an earlier building. The staircase is particularly fine; its curved steps are beautifully cantilevered giving the effect of ripples of water, in much the same manner as the stair at Lotabeg, also by Hargrave. The entrance-saloon communicates with the fine dining-room and drawing-room at the front, and at the back from a columned arcade with the staircase-hall and two long radial corridors leading to the wings. The saloon has good plaster-work and handsome twin mantelpieces, but the really superb mantelpiece is that in the drawing-room.

Behind the house a wrought-iron bridge has been added, leading from an upper floor to the top of the cliff which has been cut away to accommodate the yard. On this higher level is a large seventeenth-century garden – one of the very few remaining in Ireland – with ancient beech hedges, long lines of yews and radial walks.

In Ireland, where there were so many ruined castles, castellation was to reach almost the proportions of a mania extending, as previously mentioned, to such utilitarian buildings as mills, and reaching the *nec plus ultra* of absurdity later in the century in semi-detached castles at Killiney. The gentleman who envisaged building a new house in the first decades of the nineteenth century was faced with a choice between a Neo-Classical house or a Neo-Gothic or Neo-Tudor castle. Richard Morrison's son, William Vitruvius, submitted both Classical and Neo-Tudor designs to John Smith-Barry of Fota, Co. Cork. He opted for the former, but most of the Irish gentry, when faced with the choice, selected the castle, like Sir Edward O'Brien of Dromoland, Co. Clare, for whom the Pains likewise prepared alternative plans.

There were several good reasons for this preference. In Ireland a castle of one sort or another had always been synonymous with authority and position, and even in the nineteenth century ownership of a castle still imparted a sense of connection with the Norman lords, from whom many were now anxious to claim descent. This was the period when the Mullinses (Lords Ventry) suddenly became de Moleyns, the Morreses became de Montmorency and the Burkes reverted to de Burgh and finally to de Burgho. Coronets were prized above kind hearts, and castles accorded well with coronets. Moreover, in case of a bit of trouble it was desirable to have a fairly impregnable place – and there was often a bit of trouble, starting again with the Emmet Rising in 1803, followed by local unrest, the Tithe War of the 1820s and the Cabbage Patch Rebellion in 1848.

John Nash (1752–1835) already had a great reputation in England when he designed a castle of local stone at Killymoon, Co. Tyrone, for the Stewarts. Here he followed the Gothic style, which he is said not to have liked personally, but at which he excelled. The Beauforts visited Killymoon in 1807, so soon after its completion that stuccodores were still working on some of the reception-rooms. They were full of admiration, Mr Beaufort describing it as 'semi Gothick and Saxon style but very light', being particularly impressed by the high portico under which carriages could drive to the door. They also admired the Portland stone staircase and extolled the lighting effect from a lantern formed by four Gothic windows of ground glass. These windows had painted yellow and violet borders which Miss Beaufort declared had 'the happiest effect'.

In 1811 work commenced on a sham castle at Lough Cutra, Co. Galway, also designed by Nash and based on his own castle in England. It was commissioned by Colonel Charles Vereker, who in 1810 had been created Baron Kiltarton and later became 2nd Viscount Gort. Here again Nash employed his well-tried arrangement of towers linked by castellated blocks. To supervise the work he sent his assistants, the brothers James Pain (1779–1877) and George Richard Pain (1793–1838). These young men, realizing the lucrative possibilities of a practice in Ireland, soon set up on their own. Strancally Castle, Co. Waterford, now a guest-house, was built by them on the banks of the Blackwater, on the site of an earlier Desmond Castle, from which much of the stone was quarried. Strancally had had a gruesome history, and the nineteenth-century castle built for John Keily has a strong and forbidding appearance. On the garden side it stands on an artificial outcrop of rock, and its

Ballysaggartmore, parish of Lismore, Co. Waterford: the entrance gates to the house that was never built.

Right: Castle Garde, parish of Doon, Co. Limerick

defensible aspect is enhanced by a false moat with a drive-in to the kitchens at basement-level. The interior has some fine features – a delicate stair in light oak, skilfully cantilevered, and handsome light oak doorways. The dining-room possesses a handsome black Kilkenny marble mantelpiece in the form of a crenellated castle, complete with a battlemented grate. The castle is very large, but so far from being displeased by the inconvenience, John Keily was delighted that it necessitated four and a half minutes fast walking to reach his dining-room from the basement kitchen.

His younger brother, Arthur Keily, inherited some of the family estates at Ballysaggartmore in 1808, and in 1824 married a Miss Martin of Ross. It is said that she – who considered she had greatly honoured the Keilys by marrying one of them – was very jealous of her sister-in-law, Mrs John, and urged her husband to build a castle which would quite outshine Strancally. Work began with the long winding avenue, but after completion of the magnificent main gateway and inner gateway further up the drive, both with lodges, funds ran out completely and the Arthur Keilys were compelled to remain for life in their insignificant house. Whether they experienced satisfaction or disillusion while passing along their lengthy avenue and through their fabulous gates is hard to know.

One of the largest castles built by the Pains, Mitchelstown, has been burned, but others can still be seen, such as the vast Dromoland, Co. Clare of 1826, now a hotel, Castle Bernard, Co. Offaly of 1833, Blackrock Castle on Cork Harbour, built by the Corporation for £1,000, or the Tudor Revival Adare Manor of 1832, which is open to the public. James Pain settled in Limerick, and Castle Garde in that county is probably also his work. Here skilful additions were made in the 1820s to an old tower-house. The bawn wall was repaired and crenellated and given a castellated gateway with a lodge in the form of a circular keep. On the forecourt side of the gateway are three curious stone figures of obscure origin, representing Bacchus, Mars and a goddess entwined with a fish. It is interesting that when this work was done for the Hon. Waller O'Grady, who married in 1823, he and his wife wished to retain the use of the rooms in the tower-house, which were carefully renovated so as not to spoil the external appearance, although the windows were enlarged and fitted with Gothic glazing bars. It is now the property of Mr Hugh Thompson, who still uses the rooms in the tower-house.

Early in the nineteenth century the old Talbot Castle at Trim, Co. Meath (mentioned in Chapter 3) was also given a Gothic dress when further additions were made. The interior has panelling in the Neo-Gothic manner, and not only were the old windows given Gothic glazing bars but new windows were cut in traditional Gothic shape. In 1821 the castle served as the Diocesan School and was occupied by the Reverend James Hamilton, curate and diocesan schoolmaster, his wife, family, servants and three boarders. It must have been the Diocesan School in the eighteenth century also, for the great Duke of Wellington is said to have been educated there, which would have been about 1780; though in 1799 the Rector reported to his Bishop that they had 'no Protestant school kept here nor have had for some years past. . . .' James Hamilton taught at Trim until his death in 1847, and in 1855 the house ceased to be a school. It is now in private occupation and known as 'the Abbey'.

Talbot Castle, Trim, Co. Meath

Another renovation was undertaken at Glin, Co. Limerick, the seat of the Fitz-Geralds, Knights of Glin. Soon after his marriage in 1812 John Fraunceis, the 25th Knight, added battlements to the eighteenth-century house, Gothicized a wing and adorned the farm-buildings with loops and crenellations. A few years later he built three pepper-pot Gothic lodges. These and the castle itself are now painted white, and the whole complex is fanciful and decorative, quite unlike anything else in the country.

Modernization of eighteenth-century houses by means of Gothic additions was not uncommon. Lisnabin, Co. Westmeath, was a plain, mid-eighteenth-century house subjected to this treatment, its old roof and dormer-windows being partly masked by fake battlements and tall narrow towers superimposed on the frontis-piece and angles. The Georgian windows were dressed up with hood-mouldings and arched glazing bars in their upper sashes. This transformation was effected for Edward Purdon, who married in 1810, and whose descendant, Captain Denis J. D. Purdon, now lives there.

Frontispiece, Lisnabin, parish of Killacan, Co. Westmeath

That the core of Shankill Castle, Co. Kilkenny, is an early eighteenth-century house can be seen on the garden front. It too was castellated in the nineteenth century, its exterior refaced and its windows adorned with hood-mouldings. A new wing was added, with fake flanking towers, fake loops and a quatrefoil window in the stylized crow-stepped gable – to balance which at the other end of the house

Above left: Shankill Castle, parish of Shankill, Co. Kilkenny. The entrance gateway and lodge (above)

Left: Castletown, parish of Tullowmagimma, Co. Carlow

Below left: Thomastown Castle, parish of Relickmurry, Co. Tipperary. The chimney-piece in the hall (below)

were perched rather infantile imitations of bartizans. With the gateway and lodge the architect had complete freedom, since he started from scratch, and these would more fittingly belong to a full-scale castle. Shankill is still in possession of the Toler-Aylward family, and is the residence of Major H.J. Toler-Aylward.

A much bigger job was done on Kilkenny Castle, which William Robertson of Kilkenny reconstructed in 1826 for the 19th Earl of Ormonde, who in the preceding year had been advanced to the dignity of Marquess. The grounds are now open to the public and it is intended to open the castle also. Another large work of Robertson's is the Norman and Gothic Revival Johnstown Castle in Co. Wexford (now an agricultural college) which even has a battlemented boat-house by the lake. An example of one of his small works is Castletown, Co. Carlow, where he neatly incorporated a truncated tower-house in a sturdy castellated block which, however, hardly even pretends to be fortified.

The first house at Thomastown, Co. Tipperary, was the Classical pink brick two-storey residence of George Mathew, put up during the building activities in the Ormond Palatinate in the reign of Charles II. Early in the eighteenth century, additions and improvements were made to this house by another George Mathew, grandson of the first, who also laid out the large formal garden with terraces and ponds, remains of which can still be traced. By 1812 it had become the property of Francis Mathew, 2nd Earl of Llandaff, a descendant of the first George, who commissioned Morrison to enlarge and beautify the premises. Vast changes were made, and the old house all but disappeared behind the great castle-style mansion that Morrison created. The open arcade of the seventeenth-century house was glazed and transformed into a Gothic hall with a fancy plaster chimney-piece. Most of the rooms were Gothicized, with the notable exception of the drawing-room which was allowed to retain its original aspect apart from the addition of scagliola columns. Tall narrow turrets, grander versions of those at Lisnabin, were set on the front of the house and crowned with still smaller turrets with conical roofs. A large service wing and an immense kitchen court were among other improvements, but the round tower originally planned by Morrison was never built. There is a fine brick entrance-gateway with a crenellated turret. The Llandaff title became extinct in 1841, and on the death of the last Earl's sister the estate passed to cousins in France. After Comte de Jarnac's death in 1872 the house slowly fell into decay. To save it from total demolition the ivy-hung ruin and twenty acres were bought by Archbishop David Mathew in 1938, he being a descendant of the first George and of the same branch as Father Theobald Mathew, the Apostle of Temperance.

At Kilruddery, Co. Wicklow, Morrison also had the task of rebuilding and enlarging a seventeenth-century house, which can still just be discerned behind his Tudor Revival mansion overlooking the seventeenth-century twin canals and knot-garden. Morrison's additions were vast, and included a Great Hall 40 feet high. In order to preserve at least part of this attractive house in good condition, the present Earl of Meath has successfully reduced its size (p. 140).

At the express request of Evelyn John Shirley, who wished to commemorate the grant of lands to his ancestor by Queen Elizabeth, Thomas Rickman used the Tudor Revival style when he designed Lough Fea, Co. Monaghan, built in 1825–27. Though the Shirleys had held the Irish property for so long, they had lived in England until Evelyn John (1788–1856), who was successively Member of Parliament for Co. Monaghan and South Warwickshire. Here, as at Kilruddery, there is a Great Hall, and the lay-out of the house is rambling, sacrificing convenience to effect.

The garden front, Lough Fea, parish of Magheracloone, Co. Monaghan. Right: a corner of the house

Morrison built Kilruddery in grey stone, undoubtedly to match the old house, but Rickman, having no such problem at Lough Fea, used warm pinkish stone that exhibits gradations of shade from ashlar to ashlar with pleasing effect. Lough Fea is now the residence of Major J. E. Shirley, a descendant of its first owner.

Rossmore Park, in the same county, is another vast Tudor Revival castle in grey stone; it stands in a commanding position, and though now only a shell, its outline remains most impressive.

The Tudor Revival style met with great favour throughout Ireland and was widely used. One of its most successful examples is Muckross House, beside the Lower Lake at Killarney, now open to the public. It was built in 1843 for Henry Arthur Herbert, MP, by the Scottish architect, William Burn. Another Scottish architect, William Playfair of Edinburgh, designed Brownlow House, Lurgan, Co. Armagh (which now belongs to the Orange Institution), also in Neo-Tudor style. Begun in 1836, it was built of golden sandstone with a dome tower and numerous spiralled chimney-pots rising from the gables and the roof-ridge. There were, however, exceptions in taste. When Henry Kyle asked Charles Lanyon of Belfast to design Laurelhill House for him in Co. Armagh, Lanyon advised him that 'the Elizabethan style is better adapted to the character of your plan than any other. Its pointed gables and irregular outline would harmonize better with the abrupt features of the ground than any plain Classical building.' Kyle was unconvinced and determined on a plain, regular classical house, which he started in 1841 and which is still there.

In the late 1820s a style then known as 'New English' evolved, derived rather haphazardly from domestic Tudor. Its propagandists aimed at the Elizabethan touch without any castle effect. Carriglea, Co. Waterford (now the Bon Sauveur Convent), is in this manner. It was built of local stone for John Odell soon after his marriage in 1827: the stone has a pinkish hue and the ashlars are set to show off the variations of colour so that it resembles the polychrome effect that became so popular for brick later in the century. The architect eschewed castellation, but slender polygonal turrets flank the gabled frontispiece. The house is well appointed and well finished internally, and has a good cantilevered staircase with brass

balusters. The cornices were in the height of fashion, breaking completely with traditional stucco-work. The hall is fitted with a handsome cast-iron stove, specially ordered from Baileys' of Holborn, London, and with the Odell crest and motto incorporated into the Gothic decoration.

Ballygiblin, Co. Cork, was built about the same time for Sir William Wrixon-Becher, who was created a Baronet in 1831. Here too the style was described as 'New English', and in 1837 was considered 'modern, elegant and beautiful'. It shows a total lack of serious historicism: the architect merely assembled a random collection of vaguely Tudor elements – tall chimney-stacks, gables, oriels and a turret with loops and a conical roof.

Thomas Cobden, an accomplished architect who worked mostly in Co. Carlow, was more successful when about 1830 he built Ballykealy in that county for John James Lecky, who had married in 1825. While Ballykealy cannot pretend to historical accuracy in its design, the elements used are harmonious and consequently its appearance is pleasant. It is now a Patrician Novitiate.

Not all gentlemen who built in the 1820s and 1830s were attracted by the Gothic, Tudor or New English styles. The architect Joseph Michael Gandy, a protégé of Soane, had already published two books wherein the primitive idea was pushed beyond the Picturesque to the Grotesque, when, in 1819, he built a seat in Co. Galway for the 2nd Earl of Clancarty. Here, perhaps from fear of his client's displeasure, he was most restrained, and Garbally is a rather dull mansion in the Neo-Classical tradition, lacking any of its best features. The 3rd Earl allowed the public free access not only to his gardens (where there is a fluted obelisk folly, Grotesque stone seats, undoubtedly designed by Gandy, and splendid stone urns), but also to the mansion itself, which housed a good collection of paintings. This generous practice, so early as the 1830s, may distinguish Garbally, now a school, as the first house in Ireland to be opened to the public. It was, however, customary for respectable-looking visitors to be shown round large country-houses on request, the housekeeper usually acting as guide.

John Benjamin McNeill, FRS (1793–1880), was a self-taught civil engineer who rose to the top of his profession, becoming the first Professor of Engineering at

Ballykealy House, parish of Kellistown, Co. Carlow

Stove in the staircase-hall, Carriglea, parish of Whitechurch, Co. Waterford

Mount Pleasant, parish of Ballymascanlan, Co. Louth

Right: the gallery-hall, Lissadell, parish of Drumcliff, Co. Sligo

Trinity College, Dublin, in 1842 and a Knight in 1844. During the 1830s he added a new house on to his old family home at Mount Pleasant, Co. Louth. This new house was to his own design, an adaptation of an established Neo-Classical pattern. The portico is redolent of success, and McNeill may have thought that in eschewing all current trends he would both avoid any possible vulgarity and also display discernment and discretion. The house, now called Mount Oliver, is a Catechetical and Pastoral Centre.

One of the last in Ireland to select the Neo-Classical style for a large country house was Sir Robert Gore-Booth (1805–76), who was an artist, a traveller and an individualist, resistant to new modes. For his house at Lissadell, Co. Sligo, he chose an experienced London architect, Francis Goodwin (1784–1835), who was proficient in both Greek Revival and Gothic Revival design, and whose outstanding work was the old Town Hall in Manchester. The effect achieved at Lissadell is one of chaste grandeur. The lofty rooms lit by their tall windows are commemorated by Yeats in his poem to the memory of the famous sisters, the poet Eva Gore-Booth and the patriot Constance, Countess Markievicz:

The light of evening, Lissadell,
Great windows open to the south.

The entrance-hall communicates with the reception-rooms by a long gallery rising to the roof and lit from above. The house commands a magnificent view across Sligo Bay, and the bright light pervades all the rooms, illuminating their faded charm, steeped in remembrance of the brilliant people who have lived there. Lissadell is still the property of the Gore-Booths who have opened it to the public.

Newport, Co. Mayo, the old seat of the O'Donels and now a hotel, is basically an eighteenth-century house which has undergone a number of changes and

additions. Its finest room is the staircase-hall, whose arches and plaster-work date from the 1820s.

The Reverend Percy Smyth of Headborough, Co. Waterford, married Catherine Odell of Carriglea in 1827. About the time her brother was building his new seat in a quasi-antique manner, the Smyths simultaneously renovated their old house at Headborough (parts of which dated back to the late seventeenth century) and built a summer residence a few miles away on the sea-shore at Monatrea. Monatrea (now a hotel) and the new parts of Headborough have several features in common, such as the clustered columns round the arch which divides the staircase from the hall. Before her marriage Mrs Smyth had travelled extensively on the Continent, spending some years in Germany, Italy and France, and to decorate the Headborough hall she procured a scenic wallpaper, *Rêve d'Amour*, first issued by Desfossé and Karth of Paris in 1825 and thus so abreast of fashion as to have caused quite a sensation in Co. Waterford. Headborough is now the residence of Mr and Mrs P. A. Cornell.

There may once have been a fair number of French wallpapers in Irish houses, though few have survived. *Rives du Bosphore*, from the factory of Dufour in Paris, was first issued in 1816, and some of its strips, depicting trousered ladies among turbanned Turks smoking hookahs against an imaginative background of minarets and domes, still hang in the living-room of the so-called Swiss Cottage in Cahir Park, Co. Tipperary, along with another Dufour paper, *Monuments de Paris*, first issued in 1814–15. The Swiss Cottage is a *cottage orné*, one of the finest examples surviving in England or Ireland, possibly designed by Nash and built about 1817–20 (*not* 1785 as proclaimed by a notice now on the premises). The *cottage orné*, originally an architectural toy, epitomized the Picturesque movement led by Nash who, in partnership with the landscape-designer Humphry Repton, produced a number of

The staircase-hall, Newport House, parish of Burrishoole, Co. Mayo

Left: *Rêve d'Amour* wallpaper in the entrance-hall, Headborough, parish of Kilwatermoy, Co. Waterford

ornamental cottages for the grounds of country houses between 1795 and 1802. The 1st Earl of Glengall died in 1819 and the Swiss Cottage was probably built by his son, a fashionable young man, on succeeding to the title. It has verandas decorated with elaborate rustic stick-work, and the fantasy is extended to other small details such as the rural scenes engraved on the living-room window-panes and the cobweb pattern in the hall parquet. It is now run as a fishing-lodge and is open to the public.

Verandas were an idea brought back from India by the Nabobs, and Repton combined them with French *treillage* as an architectural feature. They did not become very popular in Ireland but there is a good example at Ashley Park, Co. Tipperary, erected when the old home of the Head family was enlarged and renovated by the next owners, the Atkinsons.

Malahide, Co. Dublin, had many handsome cottages, mostly for occupation by visitors during the bathing season, but in some cases used by permanent residents. Casino is a small gentleman's house, built as a decorative cottage with curved bays, thatched roof and Georgian-type hall door. Cottages, summer pavilions and ornamental lodges were all products of the Picturesque movement, some being designed by young ladies.[3] On Dinis Island in the Lakes of Killarney Mr Herbert of Muckross built a cottage for the gratuitous use of visitors, which was described as 'exceedingly pretty, picturesque and commodious . . . furnished with every requisite'.[4]

Early in the nineteenth century a vernacular style in the form of one-storey gentlemen's residences came into being. The oldest example is probably Delaford, Co. Dublin, where a single-pile five-bay one-storey house was built on to an old inn. Unfortunately in the last few years this elegant house, with its tall windows and graceful doorway in the tradition of Merrion Square (p. 180), has fallen into decay, inhabited only by squatters. Terrace-houses of this kind were built several decades later in such Dublin suburbs as Sandymount and Merrion; there are also numerous examples of the style used for country houses, such as that at Haggardstown, Co. Louth, once the residence of the parish priest, or Fortwilliam, Co. Limerick, built just outside the bawn when the converted tower-house of Bealdurogy was finally abandoned. Such one-storey houses were never considered cottages. One such house, Hermitage, built about 1820 by the Reverend John Bagwell Creagh on the townland of Ballyandrew, Co. Cork, was described in the *Field Book* of 1840 as a 'gentleman's residence with a small demesne'. Another house of this type near Kilcullen, Co. Kildare, and also called Hermitage, certainly has all the external appearance of a cottage; the illustration shows it being re-thatched in 1972. Inside, however, the lay-out is entirely that of a gentleman's residence, it having three sitting-rooms and four bedrooms.

True cottages of this period, such as that on the townland of Mount Temple, Co. Sligo, were still being built in the traditional manner. A superior example (p. 157) has three windows in front but none at the back or sides. It is built of big blocks of stone with huge rocks as foundations, a not uncommon practice in Connaught where stone was plentiful.

Among the country gentry the box-house maintained its favour, often in a very economical form with few decorative effects; it was much patronized by the Church of Ireland during the wave of rectory-building financed by the Board of First Fruits. Oldcourt, Co. Cork, whose foundation-stone was laid in May 1814, has geometrical architraves on only two of its windows, while Bushmount, Co. Kerry, of about the same date, has no external decorative features except its steps which

The 'Swiss Cottage' in Cahir Park,
parish of Cahir, Co. Tipperary

Below: Hermitage, Kilcullen, Co.
Kildare

Above left: Casino, Malahide, Co.
Dublin

Left: Bushmount, parish of Molahiffe,
Co. Kerry

203

Above left: the gate-lodge,
Maryborough, parish of Carrigaline,
Co. Cork

Left: the gate-lodge, Fota, parish of
Clonmel, Co. Cork

Former estate houses. Above:
Villierstown, parish of Aglish, Co.
Waterford. Below left: Thomastown,
parish of Relickmurry, Co. Tipperary.
Below: Castle Bellingham, parish of
Gernonstown, Co. Louth

rise to the front door above the basement: these were, of course, a practical necessity, but serve to relieve the starkness of the façade.

Some of these plain houses had decorative stables, such as those at Gibbingsgrove, Co. Cork, which bear a date-stone, 1835, beneath the clock, or a decorative gate-lodge like that at Maryborough near Douglas, which is indeed a Gothic toy, and has nothing in common with the house.

This was a time when many gate-lodges were built, some in keeping with their house and some not. The large Neo-Classical house at Fota, designed by Richard Morrison and his son William Vitruvius, has handsome gate-piers resembling those at Ballyfin and Kilruddery, and an equally handsome Classical gate-lodge. Gurteen-le-Poer, Co. Waterford, has Neo-Classical gate-lodges to both its back and front avenues: these were built in the 1830s, and one has a temple-front. Other styles were used too. In 1849 when Alderman Robert Cane was Mayor of Kilkenny he devoted the year's salary to building the little lodge in the form of a miniature castle beside the bridge over the Nore.

In various parts of the country improving landlords were building attractive estate houses and almshouses. The comfortable double-fronted estate house at Thomastown, Co. Tipperary, was probably designed by Morrison: it has quatre-foils and Gothic windows in keeping with the style of the castle. The double-fronted two-storey estate house at Villierstown, Co. Waterford, is probably a renovation of one of the first houses built when the village was laid out about 1750. The antique effects, such as the hood-mouldings, must have been the deliberate choice of Henry Villiers-Stuart, who might have left a unique heritage had he only chosen a Hindu-Gothic village green to match his newly built gates (p. 158).

The almshouses for aged couples built and endowed in 1830 by John Boyce at Tallow in the same county form a terrace of six dwellings, each with two rooms and a kitchen. They still have no internal plumbing, but their appearance retains its charm and the little Gothic windows show that the builder considered aesthetics as well as charity.

The Widows House, later called the Widow Houses, consists of apartments in a single two-storey building beside the church at Castle Bellingham, Co. Louth, built in 1827 and endowed by Sir William Bellingham. The Gothic windows have arched hood-mouldings, stylish latticing and arched glazing bars. Across the road, and built a few years later, are detached stone estate houses with tall chimney-stacks in polychrome brick. One has particularly fancy frilly bargeboards and another a latticed oriel-window. These elaborate bargeboards were popularized by Pugin's *Ornamental Timber Gables from Existing Examples in England and France*, published in 1839, and can be found elsewhere in Ireland, as for instance on the house beside the Police Station in Randalstown, Co. Antrim, and, graceful but less ornate, on the picturesque gate-lodge at Walterstown, Co. Meath.

By the 1820s and 1830s the appearance of many Irish towns had been improved by the building of smart little town-houses, often in terraces, and suitable for the nascent middle class. A universal feature of such houses was a handsome doorway with a leaded fanlight. Pages 206 and 207 show a selection of these. The houses in the Mall, Waterford, are important ones, provincial rivals of Merrion Square. Charlemont Place is a terrace of superior houses in the Mall at Armagh, built of local limestone ashlar and having pretty wrought-iron balconies. The low two-storey house at Cloghan, Co. Offaly, which belonged to the Lestrange family, is much simpler, its only pretension to refinement being the doorway. Ballyknockane,

Six provincial doorways, left to right, above: the Mall, Waterford; Cloghan, Co. Offaly; the Mall, Waterford; below: Ballyknockane, Co. Limerick; Charlemont Place, Armagh; Harmony Hall, Benown, Co. Westmeath

Six Dublin doorways, left to right, above: 3–4 Upper Pembroke Street; 25 Mountjoy Square; 10 Ely Place; below: 38 North Saint George's Street; 9 Hume Street; 71 Merrion Square

No. 9 College Street, Armagh

Centre: houses in Oxmantown Mall, Birr, Co. Offaly

Co. Limerick, and Harmony Hall, Co. Westmeath, are both country houses but have been included to show the widespread use of fancy fanlights and sidelights.

Dublin has a vast number of these doorways and lights in a variety of shapes and sizes, to such an extent that they have almost become the city's trade mark. Those illustrated are an arbitrary selection from some of the best, and indicate the skill of both designer and artisans. Smith's Buildings, Nos 1–5 Upper Ely Place, dated 1825, are representative of the average quality.

Disgusted by the Act of Union, of which he had been a most consistent and vigorous opponent, Sir Laurence Parsons (later 2nd Earl of Rosse) retired to his estate at Birr. There he remodelled his house in the castle manner with the aid of an architect named John Johnston, built a new Protestant church and laid out Malls in the town. One of these, Oxmantown Mall, which extends from the castle gate to the church, has excellent stone terrace-houses built about 1822.

A house somewhat similar to these, but detached, is to be found next to the Bank of Ireland in Monaghan, built of stone with brick dressings, and of the same date as Oxmantown Mall. Tralee, Co. Kerry, was also improved about this time, with a number of elegant terrace-houses, the best being those of the Mall in Denny Street. Indeed, improvements of this kind were so general that even a small town like Clonakilty, Co. Cork, could acquire a respectable square of tall weather-slated houses set round a green, and with coach-houses behind them. Belfast and Armagh also benefited. The four-storey-over-basement terrace-houses in Chichester Street are a surviving example in Belfast, and date from 1804. Armagh has Leonard Dobbin's splendid house (p. 204, now the Bank of Ireland), built in 1813, whose front doorway vies with the best in Dublin. Armagh's smartest terraces – Beresford and Charlemont – were in the Mall, but there are plenty of neatly built lesser ones, such as Melbourne Terrace. No. 9 College Street, dated 1820, is a stone house with a carriage-entrance to the stable-yard behind, the acme of respectability.

Among the smaller towns and villages to benefit from such improvements was Caledon, Co. Tyrone. In 1816 it was a mean place, but by 1837 it contained 225 neat stone houses and had become a model estate village. Its character has since changed little, and the houses to be seen today show what could be done by a good landlord.

Another landlord-village was Tyrrellspass, Co. Westmeath, laid out by the Rochforts round a semicircular green. Jane, Countess of Belvedere, enclosed the market area, and her other benevolent improvements included a dispensary, a savings bank and a schoolhouse, built in 1823 with the aid of a Parliamentary grant, and which was also the residence of the master.

The schoolhouse, Tyrrellspass, parish of Clonfad, Co. Westmeath

At Portlaw, Co. Waterford, the Quaker firm of Malcolmson, who had introduced a thriving cotton industry employing four thousand persons in 1837, built a model village, later copied at Bessbrook, Co. Armagh and at Bourneville in England. Solicitous for the health and education of their workers, they built not only a dispensary and school but also a hall for the local temperance society. It is indeed sad that these once-handsome little houses, with their low, rounded gables and picturesque chimney-stacks, situated on the confines of the Marquess of Waterford's demesne, keep little trace of their former distinctive appearance, so that it is hard to imagine that Portlaw was once a pioneer in model villages.

The Mahon family's market town, Strokestown, Co. Roscommon, is one of the best examples of spacious town-planning in the early nineteenth century. Lord Hartland, then head of the family, wished his main street to rival Sackville (now O'Connell) Street in Dublin and the Ringstrasse in Vienna, which he had seen. He therefore laid it out 147 feet wide with the intersecting street 63 feet wide. The main street was lined with trees, and in the 1820s and 1830s a hundred good stone houses were built along it, roofed with Welsh slate.

Tenants who lived in such improvements were a lucky minority. In 1822, when Dr Thomas Reid was preparing his *Travels in Ireland*, he inquired of the inhabitants of the lanes of Cork how many persons lived in each cabin. He ascertained that the average content was 18·5 persons per house of two to four rooms. At the very same time there was almost frantic public building in progress in Cork, including the Commercial Buildings, the Custom House, Savings Bank, temple-fronted Gaol and both Catholic and Protestant churches. The population of Ireland was approaching seven million and growing with alarming rapidity, only to be checked slightly by the cholera epidemic of 1832, and then permanently by the horrors of the Potato Famine which struck in 1846.

Houses and locations in Chapters 7 and 8

CHAPTER 8

Victorian and Edwardian building in Ireland

1846–1914

The rich man in his castle,
The poor man at his gate,
God made them high or lowly
And order'd their estate.

THUS IN 1848 WROTE THE HYMNIST Cecil Frances Alexander (1818–95), wife of the Bishop of Derry (later Primate of All Ireland), and thus sang the congregations until this particular verse was expurged from the Irish Hymnal in the present century, by which time the ecclesiastical authorities had decided that God's intentions are not to preclude movement within the social system. However, few of her contemporaries doubted that Mrs Alexander's interpretation was correct. In his *Secular and Domestic Architecture*, published in 1857, Sir Gilbert Scott wrote, 'Providence has ordained the different orders and gradations into which the human family is divided, and it is right and neccessary that it should be maintained.' Having pontificated on the role and responsibilities of the landed proprietor, he remarked that 'he has been placed by Providence in a position of authority and dignity, and no false modesty should deter him from expressing this, quietly and gravely, in the character of his house.' Sir Gilbert's sentiments certainly found an echo in Ireland.

During the Famine years, beginning in 1846, a million people died of malnutrition and the ailment called 'Famine Fever', and as a direct consequence of the Famine a further million left for the United States, Canada, Australia, New Zealand and Great Britain, a sizeable number of whom perished before reaching their destination. This horde of emigrants was composed not only of desperately hungry cabin-dwellers, who struggled to the ports hoping to find a ship to take them away, but also of farmers, ruined by the Famine and unable to meet their obligations or feed their families, and a number of lesser gentry, now incapable of redeeming their mortgages or obtaining their rents. Mortgages were the bane of Ireland, and often amounted to as much as ten years' income from the borrower's rents. After the Famine the situation was so bad that the Incumbered Estates Court had to be set up, to sort out the entanglements created by a welter of charges on landed property, and many an overcharged estate was sold by its direction. One such was that of the Marquess of Donegall, whose sale in 1850 changed Belfast from a landlord's town into a city of freeholders, and gave impetus to the great building and expansion that took place there in the second half of the nineteenth century.

Killyleagh Castle, parish of Killyleagh, Co. Down

The Famine drastically reduced the landlords' incomes from the rents of their tenant farmers. Archibald Hamilton of Killyleagh, Co. Down, held lands scattered through seven counties in three provinces: in 1844 these produced a total rent of £3,147 12s 1½d. By 1847 this had dropped by nearly a quarter; in 1849 by one-third and by 1850 was down to half of what it had been only seven years before. Nevertheless, due to his English heiress wife, who inherited £26,000 in 1849, Mr Hamilton was able to begin work on his house in that year. This consisted mainly of pulling down and rebuilding some of the walls of the old castle (discussed in Chapter 2) and adding on to the more solid parts of the keep. New plumbing was installed and the interior was generally renovated, somewhat in the Tudor manner with lavish oak panelling and an impressive, if unimaginative, oak staircase and an arcaded gallery. All this work, which must have provided welcome employment, was completed by the winter of 1850 at the modest cost of £7,325. The architect was Charles Lanyon (born in England in 1813), whose future partner in the Belfast firm of Lanyon and Lynn, Henry Lynn, had just joined him as an apprentice. Lanyon retained the old Scots Baronial features of the castle, even duplicating the conical turrets on his new wings. This was a style his firm was to render popular; it found considerable favour in Ulster, conscious of its Scottish heritage. As late as 1870 Lanyon, Lynn and Lanyon used this style for Belfast Castle: the six-storey square tower is borrowed from Balmoral, and here again are the corbelled machicolations with conical candle-snuffer roofs. The extraordinary Baroque exterior staircase on the garden front was, however, added in 1894.

Craigdun Castle in the same county (now Peter Stott Martin House) is a duller example of this Scots Baronial style, with a five-storey tower topped by bartizans and machicolations with conical roofs. All its gables are crow-stepped and the spouts on the front of the house are adorned with griffins and other beasts.

By 1851 the population of Ireland had declined to five million, and it continued to fall steadily for the remainder of the century, reaching only three million in 1901. If it seems strange that any landlord should have built a conspicuously expensive house in the years of distress and poverty that followed the Famine, it may be that

212

he was only heeding Sir Gilbert Scott's injunction. Such piety was in fashion. When the Moores built their large house at Killashee, Co. Kildare (now a convent), they not only had their initial M carved extensively in the strapwork with their coat of arms, and medallions sculpted with portraits of two of their favourite gun-dogs, but also sanctimoniously placed the text 'Except The Lord Build The House Their Labour Is But Lost That Built It' over the door. The building of a great house in a country so depleted by death and disease may at first seem shocking, but it should not be forgotten that directly and indirectly such ventures provided much-needed employment.

At this time the middle and upper classes in Victorian England were enjoying a period of prosperity and expansion. Many new fortunes were made, both in the booming home industries and in the colonies. Ireland was largely excluded from this wave of prosperity, her chief participation being to supply cheap labour for English factories and building sites. In Ireland, as usual, money was short: natural resources were few and those that did exist were barely exploited. Whereas in England the great *nouveau-riche* class was building massive houses both in the city suburbs and in the country, there were few manufacturing fortunes in Ireland, with the partial exception of Ulster, where linen, iron-founding and shipbuilding created several magnates. In the other three provinces new fortunes could be quickly counted – brewing and whiskey-distilling accounting for some of them, and the others stemming from no heavier industries than biscuits and bacon.

Due to depleted coffers there was relatively little building of any consequence from 1846 until almost the end of the 1850s. Oak Park, Co. Kerry, begun for Maurice FitzGerald Sandes in 1857, the year of his marriage, was finished in 1860. The arms of Sandes impaling Dennis and the date of completion are over the front porch. Externally the house, which has the polychrome brickwork so beloved of Victorians, is rather unprepossessing: the unusual shape of its window-heads derives from those in the thirteenth-century Cistercian Abbey at Graiguenamanagh, Co. Kilkenny, and the east window of St Canice's Cathedral, where alone they are found. The same manner of arch was used for the arcade with marble columns which separates the entrance-hall from the staircase-hall. The decoration here is expensive, the walls of the entrance-hall being marbleized, the timber stair ornamented with brass flowers between the baluster rails and the high-quality doors being sur-mounted by tall floral carvings. Nor was the cost counted in such matters as plumbing or minor fittings, like the fine brass lock on the front door, to which details the

Oak Park, Tralee, Co. Kerry. Below: the entrance-hall

Old Conna House, Bray,
Co. Wicklow

Right: the £2,500 house,
1870. Advertised as a
villa 'without any
expensive or elaborate
detail'

architect, J. P. McCurdie, devoted considerable attention. The disposition of the rooms is convenient; these included the usual Victorian smoking-room, butler's pantry, housekeeper's room and boot-room. The house became a Presentation Convent but was offered for sale in 1973.

In 1865 the editors of the *Dublin Builder* selected the beautifully situated Old Conna House as one of the most important of those which had sprung up in the early 1860s in the neighbourhood of Bray, Co. Wicklow. Designed by Lanyon, Lynn and Lanyon and built by Messrs Cockburn, the whole horrid house cost under £12,000. The pride of all concerned, its style was described as 'Tudor . . . carried out with great fidelity in point of detail and with great judgement.' Such a comment in a serious architectural journal demonstrates the total lack of serious historicism that then prevailed. Old Conna had an ante-hall divided by a carved wooden screen from the hall proper, which had a timber ceiling, panelled walls and that much-prized feature, stained-glass windows. The ceilings in the main reception-rooms were elaborately panelled with moulded ribs and had bosses of foliage at the intersections and in the centre of each panel. Most of the floors were laid in Arrow-smith's Patent Parquetry, imported from England. Other floors, doors and panelling were stained with Swinburn's dye and varnish, producing that funereal gloom that the Victorians believed to convey indestructible opulence, and which was described by the *Dublin Builder* as having 'a remarkably good effect'. Old Conna has passed through several ownerships and seen various changes, but no real improvement has been effected, either by them or by the hand of time.

Astonishing exterior effects could be had for a considerably lower price than Old Conna's £12,000. In 1870 the *Irish Builder* offered a design for a villa, allegedly in the 'Early Gothic style', and having several features better suited to a Non-conformist chapel. Its purveyors claimed that it was 'an endeavour to obtain a good effect in honest material without any expensive or elaborate detail', and priced it at £2,500. The thought of what they might have produced given unlimited funds and asked for something elaborate is terrifying. Internally the arrangements were quite normal; three reception rooms and a billiard-room on the ground floor, with four bedrooms, a dressing-room, bathroom and separate water-closet upstairs. The service quarters were detached from the main house, and consisted of a kitchen, scullery, larder, pantry, water-closet and fuel-store, with two servants' bedrooms and a nursery above. The *pièce de résistance* of the establishment, and included in the amazingly low price, was an octagonal conservatory with a high-pitched roof, its interior decorated with carved figures, and joined to the drawing-room by a glazed cloister. Unfortunately it is not known whether this 'villa' was ever actually built.

By 1860 most substantial houses were designed complete with a conservatory, usually adjoining the drawing-room. The idea had begun early in the century when Repton promoted conservatories attached to houses in such a manner that they became features from within. At first they were conceived of only for large country seats: Doneraile, Co. Cork, had a very splendid one that included some stained-glass panes and an elaborate tiled floor. One of the best in Ireland, though detached from the house, is at Ballyfin, Co. Leix, where the recurrent Coote crest and coat of arms appear over the door. Lord Meath's great conservatory at Kilruddery was topped by a cupola and dome, while Carriglea, Co. Waterford, had a fine example whose high-pitched roof and great Gothic windows made it resemble a small cathedral. In 1853 when James Kearney Aylward and his bride returned home to Shankill Castle, Co. Kilkenny, after their honeymoon in Paris and Florence, they made additions to the house that included a Gothic conservatory raised on an arcade like a Florentine loggia (p. 216). By 1865 even small houses were being designed with conservatories, sometimes with the only window of the drawing-room opening into them; and as good lines and simplicity went out of fashion so the conservatories became less pleasing.

Heraldry was a favourite Victorian pursuit, encouraged by the craze for heraldic bookplates, and frequently approached with the same disregard for historical truth as that betrayed by architects. Heraldic devices were often used in interior decoration, carved in wood or stone, worked in stained glass or even painted round the walls. At Donacomper, Co. Kildare, Alexander Richard Kirkpatrick (1813–91) renovated and enlarged his old family house. The interior decoration shows him to have been a heraldic enthusiast and a man of taste. The staircase newels are in the shape of large timber swans, so carved as to seem to be swimming downwards, and worthy of one of Ludwig's Bavarian castles. Round the cupola over the staircase-gallery a dozen cut-down oil portraits are interspersed with no less than forty-eight different coats of arms in inverted escutcheons. The finest room is the library, which has a panelled ceiling and beautifully carved bookcases standing against a mellowed Victorian wallpaper (p. 175). The house is now the residence of Mr J. Bruce Bredin, and excellently maintained.

Stained-glass windows were another favourite feature, not only because they produced a churchy effect and limited the amount of light admitted (considered a distinct advantage) but also because they were discreetly colourful. Many were inserted in old houses, and some of the best have heraldic themes, such as that on the staircase at Markree Castle, Co. Sligo. Mr Cooper had engaged Ulster King of Arms to trace his genealogy and received an extensive – if dubious – pedigree, stretching far beyond his settler ancestor, Cornet Edward Cooper, to one Sir William Cooper of the time of Henry VIII, and still further to one Sir Brian Cooper in the reign of King John. These two knights and the armoured and sworded Cooper of Queen Elizabeth's day, along with their three respective sovereigns, are depicted in the panels of the gloriously pompous and richly colourful window, between alternate panels showing the family tree.

Among several other Victorian additions, Castle Durrow, Co. Kilkenny, also acquired a fine stained-glass window on its main staircase. This shows the arms confirmed to Captain Thomas Flower in 1681 with scenes illustrating stages in the Life of Man – infant, schoolboy, lover, soldier, old age, second childhood – as well as Fame, Truth and Justice. The hall too was given stained-glass windows and these show incidents from Shakespeare's plays.

The conservatory, Shankill Castle, parish of Shankill, Co. Kilkenny

Right: window of a terrace-house, Mayor's Walk, Waterford

The invention of plate glass enabled the Victorians to put large panes in their window-sashes. For some reason they decided that glazing bars spoiled the view (although they draped their windows first with lace and then with heavy velvet or chenille, through whose layers they had to burrow in order to look out at all), and often ruined the façade of an old house by removing its glazing bars and inserting plate-glass sashes. Sad examples of such treatment are Beauparc, Co. Meath, Seafield, Co. Dublin and Hazlewood, Co. Sligo. In houses for which they were designed, however, the plate-glass windows looked well; an example is the late nineteenth-century terrace-house in Mayor's Walk, Waterford.

St Michael's, 83 Merrion Road, Dublin (originally Mount St Michael's, Ailesbury Road), is an interesting example of a superior mid-Victorian suburban house. It was built in 1860 for his own residence by Michael Meade, a Dublin builder who, in 1866, built St Patrick's Catholic Church in Monkstown. It remained with the Meades until 1906 when it was bought as a town residence by Sir Ernest Cochrane, Bart., the mineral-water manufacturer, who sold it in 1913 to Mr George N. Jacob, the biscuit king. Such substantial houses, so common in the suburbs of London and provincial English towns like Birmingham where new fortunes were being made in great numbers, were relatively rare in Ireland, where in any case there was always a selection of good Georgian houses on the market. The Florentine water-tower of St Michael's is derived from that on Queen Victoria's Osborne, which inspired a veritable rash of mini-Osbornes throughout England. Such towers proved rather popular in Ireland, and are to be found on many Victorian houses, not only on big suburban ones like St Michael's or on country-seats such as Straffan House, Co. Kildare, but also on suburban villas and seaside hotels. Except for its oak-panelled hall, the interior of St Michael's is now mainly a reproduction of the Georgian style, installed by Sir Ernest Cochrane. There is no conservatory, but the garden has a delightful octagonal summer-house with coloured glass windows and a conical roof.

A desire to emulate the rich man in his castle accounts for the pair of semi-detached castles overlooking the sea at Killiney, Co. Dublin, which were built

Semi-detached castles,
Killiney, Co. Dublin

Left: the former Mount
St Michael's, Dublin,
now St Michaels',
83 Merrion Road

about 1860. Their site was most convenient, for they economically served the dual purposes of a residence near the capital (to which speedy access was available by train) and a seaside house. Since the eighteenth century it had been fashionable for the landowning families of Co. Waterford – the Musgraves, Smyths, Usshers and Odells – who lived around the Blackwater, to have a secondary house on the near-by coast for summer visits. By the latter half of the nineteenth century the idea of a seaside house had taken general hold, and resort villas were rapidly developed in such places as Ballybunion, Co. Kerry, Milltown and Kilkee, Co. Clare, Glengariff, Co. Cork, and along the coasts north and south of Dublin. As a building speculation in 1869–70 Hugh Andrews had a block of four seaside houses built at a new watering-place, Chichester-by-the-Sea, on Belfast Lough. Designed by the architect T. Hevey, they were intended for letting during the season.

Though with the slow financial recovery of the 1860s, a few moneyed and intrepid landlords did venture to build country houses, agrarian agitation was once more rearing its head in the form of the Tenants' League and other groups pressing for land reforms. The Irish Republican Brotherhood, or the Fenian movement, had been founded simultaneously in Dublin and New York in 1858, and received great support from Irish emigrants in America. While Thomas Davis's Young Ireland movement promulgated the idea of Irish Nationalism by peaceful means, the Fenians believed this impossible. Not surprisingly, their converts were mainly among the working class: labourers, small farmers, clerks and artisans. Their militant agitation culminated in the Fenian Rising of 1867 which did nothing to tranquillize landowners in rural areas, merely awakening remembrances of the Whiteboys and 1798, not to mention the blood-letting of the seventeenth century which, due to the long memories of the Irish, had not yet been forgotten.

It was on the eve of the Fenian Rising that William Pery, 3rd Earl of Limerick, decided to build a great castle on his lands in the west of that county. A superb site was chosen at Dromore, on a hill-top overlooking the Shannon and dominating the surrounding countryside. The Perys were one of the few great landowning families who did not already possess a grand seat on their Irish estates: they had been very much absentees, living in England, and hitherto a house in Limerick city had sufficed them. The 3rd Earl (1840–96) was a scholarly young man, President of the Architectural Society in London. To design his new house he selected the Society's Vice-President, Edward William Godwin (1833–86), a native of Bristol, who had moved to London in 1865. There he met the famous actress, Ellen Terry, who left her husband to live with him as his mistress for some years. They moved in a circle of artists and aesthetes, which included the painter Whistler, for whom Godwin built a London house, and Oscar Wilde, for whom he did some interior decorating. Wilde expressed the opinion that Godwin was one of the most artistic spirits of the day. Unlike many of his contemporaries Godwin did understand the essential nature of the architectural sources on which he drew, instead of merely adapting their obvious characteristics. Before designing Dromore, he had already toured in Ireland and done work of minor importance in Co. Kerry, where a considerable number of country houses were built in the 1860s and 1870s. In England he had used both Venetian-Gothic and French-Gothic, but for the Earl of Limerick he decided to create a house inspired by Celtic sources. He studied and surveyed several ancient Irish castles, tower-houses and ecclesiastical edifices, including the Rock of Cashel, and his sketchbooks[1] contain accurate and interesting drawings of many Irish medieval buildings.

Dromore's walls were built 6 feet thick and with a batter, like the strongest early Irish fortresses. No doubt the unsettled state of the country and the Fenian threat provided ample justification for building a real stronghold. Moreover, the Earls of Limerick were not among the popular landlords, and had good reason to feel the need of a defensible place when they decided to live out in the wilds. The *Building News* of 29 March 1867 confirms this, writing, 'the corridors are kept on the outer side of the building and all the entrances are well guarded, so that in the event of the country being disturbed the inmates of Dromore Castle might not only feel secure themselves but be able to give real shelter to others.' This was indeed a repetition of the situation in Ireland in the sixteenth and seventeenth centuries, very different from the conditions that pertained in neighbouring England.

In his design Godwin incorporated many attractive features from early Irish castles – stepped crenellations, tall chimney-stacks, corbelled-out machicolations, loopholes, trefoil windows, wall-walks along the battlements of the courtyard and a round tower like that rising above Cormac's Chapel on the Rock of Cashel. The arrangement of a main castle with a detached banqueting-hall was inspired by Askeaton, a few miles away. Although the interior stonework and marble columns are of high quality, the whole large complex took only two years to complete. Godwin, who had sketched the castle by moonlight, declared that its silhouette enchanted him. Today, though the interior has been dismantled and the great walls stand almost like an ancient ruin, the wonderful silhouette still enchants. Lord Limerick, too, was delighted with the result, despite some problems such as the terrible damp which nothing would eliminate, and which caused the project for decorating the walls with painted scenes to be abandoned, though Godwin did design furniture for the house. Godwin was so discouraged by the losing battle against the damp that he warned all architects against building in Ireland. Dromore's term as a residence was brief, a mere eighty years. After the First World War the Earl of Limerick's family ceased to live there, and it was later sold to the McMahons, Limerick merchants, who remained there until 1950. Subsequently the interior was demolished and materials such as mantelpieces and doors were sold.

Window of the gate-lodge, Glenstal, parish of Abington, Co. Limerick

Door between two of the
reception-rooms,
Glenstal

Left: silhouette of
Dromore Castle, parish
of Kildimo, Co.
Limerick

Whereas Dromore was amazingly completed in two years, the building of Glenstal in the same county dragged on for forty-five years. It was designed by William Bardwell in 1837 for the Barrington family, and though the round keep was finished in 1839, the main body of the house was not completed until 1875. Since 1927 it has been a Benedictine Abbey and school. It is an enormous pile, approached by a carriage entrance in the form of an English medieval keep-gatehouse. The stonework throughout is remarkable: the front door is flanked by figures of Edward I and Queen Eleanor, sculpted by a stonemason from Cappamore. Amusingly the Queen holds a scroll on which is inscribed the Irish welcome, *Cead mile failte*. Between the two main reception-rooms is a very elaborately carved stone doorway, copied from the Romanesque one in Killaloe Cathedral. All the bedroom doorways are in the manner of Irish Romanesque church doorways, and features such as the massive capitals have been copied from Romanesque ecclesiastical buildings like Clonmacnoise, and abound throughout the house. Most of this stone-carving was done by local masons from Newport. The oak-shelved library, which has a blue ceiling studded with gold stars, is an octagonal room, whose octagonal central fireplace has mirrored panels between the columns. The staircase, balusters and gallery-rail are in dark oak, elaborately carved with Celtic motifs, leaves and animals, and were the work of trainees of a wood-carving school. They bear the inscription 'Carved by M. Minahan, P. Downer and others of the Ahane class, 1888.' The small cut-stone gate-lodge on the main road is a curiosity. It has a mask sculpted above the doorway, but its strangest feature is the window placed across one of the front corners and behind a column with masks on its capital.

Brittas House, Co. Leix, was designed by McCurdie in 1869 just after the Fenian Rising, and reflects the desire of its owner, General Francis Plunkett Dunne, for a stronghold. It is faced in punched sandstone with chiselled limestone dressings and has a solid, rather forbidding castle-like aspect. Rather surprisingly, it was estimated to cost only £7,000.

Since the beginning of the century architects had not confined themselves to one form of revivalism, and as time went on the sources used became increasingly eclectic, inspiration being drawn from diverse and often obscure regional styles. Sir Charles Lanyon's Scots Baronial has already been mentioned, as well as the Early Gothic and Tudor Revival, but there was even Scots-Baronial-Tudor and,

Figure of Queen Eleanor
flanking the door,
Glenstal

Staircase-hall,
Cahermoyle, parish of
Rathronan, Co. Limerick

Right: the Great Hall,
Gurteen-le-Poer, parish
of Kilsheelan, Co.
Waterford

Door, No. 53 Leeson
Park, Dublin

still more ambiguous, the 'Italian villa' style. While serious historicism is evident in much Victorian ecclesiastical architecture, it is rare in the domestic field, which remained far less inhibited in its expression. Some of the amalgamated revival styles defy classification, though grandiloquent epithets such as 'Franco-Venetian-Gothic', 'High-Venetian-Renaissance', 'Flemish-Renaissance', and even 'Saxon' and 'Early Christian' were glibly employed in advertisements describing houses. 'American-Romanesque' was even used in 1899 to describe the style of a Belfast church.[2]

Hybrids of this kind were freely built to mammoth proportions in the Rhineland, where their very size lent them a strange aura of quality, and on a lesser scale in the south of France (where an imaginative writer coined for them the label *style Sarah Bernhardt*), but they were infinitely less successful when built on an economy budget in Ireland. In the Belfast suburb of Malone Road there is a house of this genre, originally called Clanwilliam House, now called Danesfort and the headquarters of the Electricity Board. It was built in 1864 for Samuel Barbour by the architect W. J. Barre. Some of its ancestry certainly lies along the Loire, for over an arcaded Italianate *porte-cochère* it has a tower with an extremely high-pitched mansard; this whole unit is attached to a plump two-storey villa.

Cahermoyle House, Co. Limerick, built for Edward O'Brien in 1871, is a case where the architect used an assortment of elements with unexpected result. It has a long, open arcade like one side of a cloister, and the general attempt to reproduce traditional Romanesque/Gothic has produced instead a curiously Moorish aspect. Inside the theme persists. The saloon rises two storeys in height: an arcade with Connemara marble columns supports an upper arcade round the staircase-gallery, all of whose chunky marble columns have bizarre carved-stone capitals. These depict, among other subjects, a spaniel, a horse and jockey, a man fishing, a man shooting, vegetables, flowers and weeds, and the stairway itself ends in the carving of an owl. The reception-rooms have extravagant polychrome mantelpieces made especially for the house: their base is black Ennis limestone, and the marble composition includes Cork red, Mitchelstown brown porphyry, Connemara green and Kilkenny black.

Revivals went on apace. Curvilinear gables were resurrected by the architect of the Presbyterian manse at Portrush, Co. Antrim, built with funds raised in America

in 1850. Gurteen-le-Poer, Co. Waterford, combines fancy gables with plain triangular ones on the garden front. As at Glenstal, work here was spread over a long period. Though it was begun in the 1830s, only the stables were completed by 1837,[3] and subsequent activities were interrupted both by the Famine and the death of the owner, so that the whole was not completed until 1866.[4] The interior is more seriously Gothic. The Great Hall, which rises the full height of the house, has an almost cathedral effect. On the upper floor Gothic arches at either end of the gallery give access to the wings. As at Ballyfin, the family crest is used as a continuous motif, even to adorning both gate-lodges. The house now belongs to Count Edmond de la Poer, a grandson of the 1st Count for whom it was built.

Dunore House, Aldergrove, Co. Antrim, is nothing less than Neo-Egyptian, built of granite and with its pediment terminating in a miniature obelisk. The highly elaborate door-surround is composed of four terms with busts of ancient Pharaohs, complete with scarab breastplates.

On the edge of the town of Youghal, Co. Cork, a perfectly plain house, now called South Abbey House, was distinguished from its neighbours by being given a marvellous Moorish portico and door-surround.

Fancy door-surrounds were much in vogue in the growing suburbs of Dublin, and many a red-brick Victorian house boasts an elaborate and extraordinary door and surround, such as that on a semi-detached house, No. 53 Leeson Park, the ancestry of whose design is definitely mixed but owes at least something to Irish Romanesque, as demonstrated by the heavy chevron decoration.

Ardmulchan, on the banks of the Boyne in Co. Meath, is a substantial brick house of hybrid style, built about 1870 by Scottish workmen of Scottish materials. Other hybrid houses may be found scattered through the country, such as Cahernane House, Co. Kerry, now a hotel, built in 1877 on the shores of the Lower Lake of Killarney, or Classiebawn, on a particularly beautiful site above the sea in Co. Sligo, and now the property of Earl Mountbatten. Whatever else they lacked, the Irish Victorians had an unerring eye when choosing positions for their houses. Tinode House, Co. Wicklow, designed by W. F. Caldbeck of Dublin and built in 1864 of granite, is in a commanding situation near Blessington, and was at the time considered very handsome. In fact it was ill-proportioned and wholly lacking in

Ardmulchan, parish of Ardmulchan, Co. Meath

Portico, South Abbey House, Youghal, Co. Cork

221

architectural merit: over the front door polished red marble pillars supported a heavily moulded and particularly graceless hood. Another true hybrid is Runkerry House, Co. Antrim, now an old people's home, which combines a number of obvious details from various sources. Built of variegated sandstone for the 1st Lord MacNaghten by the architect Close in 1883, its interior arrangement is wildly inconvenient.

Henry Chappell of Newtownards was responsible for the extensive alterations and additions made in 1875–76 at Killynether House, Co. Down, for the 5th Marquess of Londonderry, who declared himself absolutely satisfied with the result, which was alleged to be 'elegant and commodious'. While its elegance may be in doubt, for it combines haphazard Gothic and Tudor elements and has minarets on its many slender turrets, it was certainly commodious. The basement contained kitchen, scullery, pantries, servants' hall and bedrooms, cellars and a lift; on the ground floor were the drawing-room, dining-room, library, agent's room, two sitting-rooms, housekeeper's room, butler's pantry, store-room, cleaning-room, men-servants' room and water-closet. The first floor had nine bedrooms, all with dressing-rooms, a bathroom, linen-closet and water-closets. The water-supply came from a well sunk in trap-rock half a mile away and was conveyed in pipes to a cistern cut in a hillside at a level sufficient to ensure pressure. The interior plumbing was called 'very complete and comprising all the most recent suggestions and practical improvements in sanitary science'.[5]

In the last decades of the century one of the most prolific builders of country seats in Ireland was James Franklin Fuller, born in Kerry in 1835. He was also architect to the Church of Ireland, for which he built several churches. Among his country houses were Harristoun House, Co. Kildare, Ballyburly House, Co. Offaly, Mount Falcon, Co. Mayo, and Baronston House, Co. Westmeath; but he is best known for the imposing Ashford Castle, Co. Mayo, which he built in 1870 for the beer magnate Lord Ardilaun, for whom he also designed St Anne's near Dublin. Ashford, now a hotel, has recently been enlarged, but Fuller's successful castle-style mansion, incorporating not only an old tower-house but also a house in the French château style, is still intact.

Another successful house in the castle manner is Humewood, Co. Wicklow, built between 1867 and 1869 for W. W. F. Hume Dick. It was designed by an English architect, William White, an individualist, an inventor and an eccentric. The builder, Albert Kimberley of Banbury, was also English, and so eager was he to get the contract that he rashly made a tender for £13,560, White having been told that £15,000 was the ceiling price. When Mr Hume Dick received a bill for £25,000 they all went to law – the case dragged on for five years and was won by Kimberley, but White's reputation was ruined in the process. Neither he nor Kimberley skimped their work at Humewood. The massive walls are of local dark granite cut in irregular blocks. White was especially skilful in achieving a composition with triangular forms, and the stepped gables, chimneys and spires form a remarkable pattern of levels gradually mounting towards the great centre tower. White himself wrote, 'for exterior effect our attention must be directed to the sky outline before expending it upon minutiae, and this is of the greatest consequence in an undulating and picturesque country.' At Humewood he achieved a most impressive outline, different though in its way hardly inferior to Godwin's Dromore. There is a basement, and having been instructed to build a house capable of defence in case of need, White provided it with small barred windows. Though the skyline

is so romantic, the unrelieved dark stone is forbidding, and today the long garden front presents a cheerless aspect. The entrance front is more agreeable, and the clock-tower above the gateway to the stable-yard is one of the most attractive elements of the whole complex. In the illustration it is seen from the carriage entrance at the front of the house, and shows clearly White's clever juxtaposition of different forms. Humewood Castle has passed by descent to its present owner, Mrs Hume-Weygand.

In 1871 the 4th Marquess of Ely decided to rebuild his ancestral home, Loftus Hall near the end of the Hook Peninsula in Co. Wexford. Parts of the old house (which had been renowned for its haunted tapestry-room) were retained and joined to the new one, which has a depressingly nondescript exterior, with an impressive display of plate-glass windows and a balustrade round the cornice. The interior contains some magnificent Victorian workmanship, such as the multi-coloured tiled floor of the large entrance-hall which leads to the panelled staircase-hall. This latter is the most handsome room in the house, with an elaborate parquet floor and a stair of oak panelled in mahogany whose balusters are executed in fine carving and marquetry. Its gallery is carried on beautifully carved columns, whose capitals are decorated with masks. The drawing-room has a very pretty Victorian white marble mantelpiece with a brilliantly coloured floral enamel surround to the grate. The house is now a Rosmenian Convent, and the Sisters have clothed the nakedness of the *putti* in the centre plaque by slapping on plaster knickers.

The Glebe Loans Act gave great encouragement to the building of residences for the Church of Ireland clergy in the 1870s following Disestablishment. Good examples of this phase of building are the Glebe House, Burnfoot, Co. Derry, and the Parsonage, Ardara, Co. Donegal, both built in 1875 and designed by William M'Elwee, a Derry architect. The Burnfoot Glebe was for the incumbent of the parishes of Burt and Inch and had a suitably sober if not dreary exterior. The ground floor had a drawing-room and dining-room on either side of the hall, with a study, kitchen, scullery and pantry behind. There were front and back stairs, and on what

Above left: the stable entrance seen from the carriage entrance, Humewood Castle, parish of Kiltegan, Co. Wicklow

Above: the staircase, Loftus Hall, parish of Hook, Co. Wexford, and below: detail of Victorian mantelpiece: the naked putti have been clothed

the architect called the 'Chamber Floor' were four bedrooms, a linen-closet, a water-closet and two servants' rooms, the one on the back passage being intended for a boy or man-servant. No bathroom was included. Round the stable-yard were set a cart-house, byre and stable, with space for manure and ashes, and two water-closets. Alexander M'Elwee, a member of the architect's family, was the builder, Henry M'Indoe the painter and Messrs M'Laughlin and M'Cullagh the plumbers, all of Derry. The whole thing, exclusive of the architect's commission and an intended conservatory, cost £940, paid for partly by a grant from the Commissioners of Public Works under the Glebe Loans Act.

Ardara Parsonage had an identical floor-plan with a different exterior. Both houses were of rubble masonry from local stone, finished in lime or Portland cement, roughcast and roofed with Bangor slates.

Some Victorian houses had gate-lodges in keeping with their own style, or even miniatures of the house itself. Castle Leslie, Co. Monaghan, the work of Lanyon and Lynn, is in the Scots-Baronial tradition, with crow-stepped gables, and its semi-detached gate-lodge is in the same manner. The gate-lodge of Humewood, by contrast, is not in the style of the castle but more like what the Victorians conceived as a model cottage, with latticed bow-fronted windows. The gate-lodge of The Aske is earlier and typical of those of the substantial houses built round Bray, Co. Wicklow in the 1860s, mostly for prosperous Dublin merchants who commuted to the city by train. It is sturdy and cosy and so contrived as to give a prosperous and pleasing appearance at the entrance to the avenue.

When landlords and architects undertook housing improvements for tenants and workers, they now did so with a degree of earnest high-mindedness. In 1875 some cottages designed by E. Townsend, a civil engineer, for the Board of Works in Mayo and Galway were particularly praised for 'having the advantage of three bedrooms which prevents the evil of the different sexes sleeping in one room which only too often occurs in country places'.[6] These cottages, of rubble masonry, with a concrete-floored living-room and a yard containing an ashpit, water-closet and piggery, cost £120 to put up.

That the building of adequate houses for the poor was not always entirely altruistic was evinced by some of the remarks made by Joseph Maguire, architect and civil engineer, on 18 March 1867 when he lectured to an Evening Scientific Meeting at the Royal Dublin Society. His subject was 'Healthy Dwellings for Labourers, Artizans, and the Middle Classes and Improved Structural Arrangements'. If the bedrooms front the east,' he observed, 'there is the advantage that the first rays of sun may remind the industrious labourer and artizan of the duties of the day.' He then admonished his listeners to 'improve the dwellings of the labouring classes and afford them the means of greater cleanliness, health and comfort in their own homes; to extend education and thus raise the social and moral habits of these most valuable members of the community are among the first duties, and ought to be among the truest pleasures of every enterprising man.'[7]

The 1861 Census of Ireland shows there was indeed not just scope but dire need for such improvements on a vast scale. It returned a total of 579,042 mud cabins, of which 89,374 had only one room and yet were occupied by 1,079,062 families – an average of over two families to each one-roomed cabin. The remaining 489,000 mud cabins, which had two or more rooms, were occupied by 553,496 families – just over one family per cabin, indicating that the worst overcrowding was at the very poorest level. Five was the average content per family at this time, so each

single-room cabin housed an average of eleven persons; and since the Census showed a number with only one occupant others must have been full to bursting.

The shortage of houses was partly due to the abandonment and unroofing of cabins during the Famine and subsequent years when evictions for non-payment of rent were rife. Of the total population of just under four and a half million, three and a half million were living in mud cabins, of whom one million were in the single-room variety. A Sligo medical officer wrote of the homes of the poor in the 1860s as 'planted anywhere, regardless of situation or soil, the low walls, the black half rotten thatch, the want of any proper flue or window, the clay floor which becomes soaked with the pig's food or more dangerous filth, and the adjacent manure heap are all highly promotive of disease: for the want of a backdoor thorough airing can never be effected'. He described the prototype of these hovels, the home of a small farmer, tenant to a nobleman, as being about twelve feet wide and twenty-four feet long, and inhabited by the sick farmer, his wife, four daughters, one son, three cows, two calves, a horse, two pigs and poultry. The pigs dwelt beneath the beds, the people in them, and the poultry in the rafters above. This miserable family, as the doctor pointed out, thus enjoyed the constant company and prospect of bacon, beef and chicken, which they seldom or never tasted.

The living conditions of the city poor were just as deplorable, Dublin being the worst. The old mansions in the Liberties, once the homes of rich merchants, had become dilapidated tenement dwellings, each house accommodating as many as fifteen families. When the windows broke they were seldom reglazed, merely stuffed with sacking or patched with paper. In the overcrowded rooms the wretched inhabitants huddled together on rough beds surrounded by lines of damp clothes, coal, coke or wood and a few cooking-pots. Corridors and stairs were usually cluttered with rusty pans, oyster shells, rags, piles of ashes and the occasional dead cat. Contemporary descriptions of these conditions are nauseating. In 1861 Dublin's population was just over a quarter of a million, with an average of eleven individuals per house. While the city's average density over all was 71 persons per acre, in the old parishes like St Nicholas's it rose to 195 persons per acre: there, in narrow lanes and alleys, lived over forty thousand Dubliners, averaging 3·49 persons per room and 2·71 per bed.

There were some Societies, such as the Dublin Building Association, which promoted the building of small houses, but they reached only the upper strata of the working classes, such as might even contemplate borrowing a small sum to

The gate-lodge, The Aske, near Bray, Co. Wicklow

Left: the gate-lodge, Humewood Castle, Co. Wicklow

225

purchase a house. In 1867 the Industrial Tenements Company put up a building in Meath Street containing 124 rooms, including lavatories and communal drying-rooms, the whole being designed to have the appearance of a group of commodious houses. Though other such blocks of working-class flats, such as those financed by the Iveagh Trust, had been built by the end of the century, these ventures were all too few. Blayney Terrace at Castleblayney, Co. Monaghan, is a rare example of such flats in the provinces. Built of red brick in 1879, it consists of twenty units, four flats to each entrance, two on the ground floor and two above. These were advanced dwellings for their time, and still look neat and smart after nearly a century in use. There is also a red-brick lodge for a superintendant, and in the neatly terraced garden, which separates the flats from the main road, stands a monument, surmounted by a Celtic Cross, to Cadwallader Davis, 12th Lord Blayney, who died in 1874, and whose family's munificence can be contemplated by the inhabitants.

Joseph Maguire, when architect to the Dublin Building Association, offered twelve designs for 'improved dwellings for labourers, artizans and the middle classes', among which were:

	DENOMINATION	ACCOMMODATION	HEIGHT	AREA
			feet	*square feet*
1	Labourer's Dwelling	Living-Room	8	144
		Bed-room	8	144
		Scullery	7	24
2	Labourer's Double Cottage	Living-Room	8	88
		Bed-room	8	$93\frac{1}{2}$
		2nd Bed-room	8	30
		Scullery	7	24
12	A Pair of Farm Labourer's Cottages	Living-room	8	120
		Bed-room	8	120
		2nd Bed-room	8	$68\frac{1}{4}$
		Scullery	8	$68\frac{1}{4}$
5	Dwelling for the Middle Class	Parlor	10	121
		Bed-room	9	99
		2nd Bed-room	9	120
		3rd Bed-room	9	45
		Kitchen	9	121
6	Dwelling for the Middle Class	Parlor	11	168
		Drawing-room	11	232
		Bed-room	11	182
		2nd Bed-room	11	$184\frac{1}{2}$
		3rd Bed-room	11	$104\frac{1}{2}$
		Kitchen	8	138
		Servants' room	7	48

Three-bedroomed houses with two reception-rooms, such as those Maguire recommended, were going up in large numbers in the suburbs of Dublin during the 1860s and 1870s. The high cost of land in the more fashionable districts was forcing people out to the new suburbs, north and south of the city. Many families

Blayney Terrace,
Castleblayney, Co.
Monaghan

(such as those of civil servants) now had annual incomes of between £100 and £150 and required a respectable house of moderate size at a moderate price. Such small suburban houses, as well as the more substantial ones on the fringes of smart southern Dublin continued to follow a vaguely Georgian style: such streets of tall, stuccoed and painted houses with columned porticoes as were then going up in Belgravia and Pimlico and which are so representative of Victorian London, were never built in Ireland. Even in Belfast – never a great eighteenth-century city – the Georgian tradition died slowly, though by 1878 architects like William Batt were putting up gabled terraces such as that in College Gardens. The fronts of these houses were broken by bay and square windows and decorated with bands of polychrome brick; the doors had hood-mouldings and carved bosses and the window-sashes, of course, were filled with plate glass. Belfast's biggest new houses were the prosperous villas still to be seen along the Malone Road, most of which went up between 1870 and 1890. The Belfast Gas Works Company was one of the first to operate in Great Britain or Ireland, being founded by the Marquess of Donegall in 1821. The first gas street-lighting functioned there in September 1823, and a month later Dublin followed suit. However it was not until the 1860s that gas came into general use in private houses in the better parts of the cities.

The 3rd Earl of Clancarty was a good, improving and resident landlord. In 1866 he was awarded the Gold Medal of the Royal Agricultural Society of Ireland for his four labourers' cottages at Deer Park, Ballinasloe, Co. Galway. The committee reported these to be:

> well-built cottages with a good deal of accommodation, having a very convenient form of step ladder or cheap stair, 8 ins. in head and 8 in rise, which gives sufficient width for the foot to allow the ladder to be sheeted at the back. The four cottages are in a row, with back doors which open out of a small scullery taken off the bedroom on the ground floor; altogether they are a well constructed, good and reasonable lot of cottages which merit the prize. . . .[8]

The total outlay on the row was £278 17s 7d, or about £70 for each. £22 12s 10d of the total sum went on the four sets of offices, each of which included a piggery and privy, both with doors and floored with Malbay flags. Though the privies had seats (costing 2s 6d each) they were mere pits encased in brickwork. The front doors of the cottages opened into the kitchen (12 by 10 feet), from which rose the stair, the remainder of the ground floor being occupied by a bedroom (6 by 8 feet) and the scullery (3 by 3½ feet). The attic had two bedrooms, one 12 by 10 feet, the other 12 by 6 feet.

When the Duke of Leinster was improving his tenants' dwellings in 1871, four types of house were built: small cottages for labourers and small farmhouses (both of one storey), pairs of two-storey semi-detached cottages and free-standing two-storey double-fronted farmhouses. All had sensible foundations, the floor-level being kept at least six inches above the ground, and roofs of slate. The larger farmhouses were quite superior dwellings, externally close descendants of the smaller gentry Georgian box, though their interior lay-out was quite different. The kitchen (12½ by 14 feet) was on one side of the minute entrance-hall (4 by 3½ feet) and 'the room' (11 by 14 feet) on the other. Behind 'the room', and communicating with the kitchen by a corridor, was the dairy (14 by 8 feet). These ground-floor rooms were 9 feet high. Upstairs were three bedrooms, to one of which was attached a closet. The water-closet was outside the house in a spacious yard, which also had a piggery, manure-pit, cattle-shed and fowl-house over a pig-house.

The smaller one-storey farmhouse was equally sturdily constructed with 21-inch-thick walls and hammer-dressed stone quoins. Here the front door opened directly into the kitchen (14 by 12½ feet) which occupied the entire centre of the house and off which led a small store-room and three small bedrooms.

On the ground floor the semi-detached cottage had only a kitchen (12 by 11½ feet) and one small bedroom, whose window was to the front in the left-hand cottage

Back of Victorian terrace-houses in Cobh

and to the back in the right-hand cottage, since one cottage had the front and the other the back half of the centre bay. Upstairs the main bedroom (12 by 14 feet) was reached directly by the stair from the kitchen, and off it was a small bedroom, with the same window-plan as on the ground-floor.

The line of cottages near St Canice's Cathedral in Kilkenny is of the improved type built in the nineteenth century, often with three rooms but otherwise not much different to those in The Coole at Newcastle West of at least two hundred years before. Indeed they continued to be built, even by Local Authorities, into the twentieth century. Trinity Square, Waterford, built by the Corporation in 1914–16 consists of two rows of cottages of this kind, without any indoor plumbing.

Queenstown, Co. Cork (now Cobh) was a busy port in the second half of the nineteenth century, handling among other things much of the emigrant traffic to America. This accounts for its rapid growth in the 1860s when officers of the Royal Navy, master mariners, harbour and custom officials as well as sailors on regular pay, all required decent accommodation. Barrack Street was built at this time. It consists of twenty-three houses, known as the Pack of Cards, which must be one of the most picturesque terraces of this date in Europe (p. 176). Built up a steep hill and with frilly bargeboards on their gables and little projecting bow-fronted windows to their first-floor parlours, each house is painted a different colour, which enhances their novel appearance, already set off by the lofty steeple of the Catholic Cathedral and the waters of Cork Harbour. Rows of similar, if less pretty, terraces were put up along the streets nearer the quays: a view of the backs of some of these shows their little yards and outside water-closets.

Michael Davitt founded the Irish Land League in 1879 in order to provide a nation-wide organization and platform for agrarian agitation, and Charles Stewart Parnell was its first President. It combined all degrees of nationalists from moderate Home Rulers to extreme Republicanists. Its principal aim was to provide systematic resistance to landlords, to prevent evictions, reduce rents and ultimately transform the tenant farmers into small freeholders. The immediate result was the so-called Land War of 1879–82, during which was successfully introduced the scheme of ostracism called 'boycotting', which gained its name from Captain Boycott, a Co. Mayo land-agent towards whom the League had reason to feel hostile. In such an atmosphere country house building naturally came to a virtual standstill, and some landlords left Ireland forever. Of those who remained, some took up a career to supplement their reduced incomes from property, and the favourite professions were, as hitherto, the Army, Navy and Colonial Service. When these gentlemen returned to Ireland – either temporarily or permanently – the much-improved modes of transport enabled them to bring far more substantial souvenirs than the Nankin dinner-services brought by the East India Company's employees a century before. Sir Henry Arthur Blake, KCMG, from Co. Galway, started his career as a cadet in the Royal Irish Constabulary, rose to be sub-inspector, then a magistrate, and subsequently Governor successively of the Bahamas, Newfoundland, Jamaica and Hong Kong. When he came back to Myrtle Grove (which he called 'Ralegh's House') he brought with him the gates of the city of Kemtein, which he erected in the old city walls of Youghal which ran through his garden. After his death the Kemtein elders wrote to his widow assuring her of their good behaviour and requesting the return of their gates. These she duly dispatched to China, from whence the grateful elders sent back a replica as a gift from the Municipality. These, complete with their Chinese inscription, now grace the garden at Myrtle Grove.

The Chinese gates, Myrtle
Grove, Youghal, Co.
Cork

Right: the Chinese
mantelpiece, Drishane,
parish of Castlehaven,
Co. Cork

Colonel T. C. F. Somerville, eldest son of the owner of Drishane, Co. Cork, was
aide-de-camp to General Cameron in China from 1885 to 1889. On his return to
Drishane he brought a black marble mantelpiece, made in China, complete with
carved dragons, Chinese characters and the Somerville arms, crest and motto
executed by a Chinese craftsman. This was installed in the Georgian drawing-room,
where it keeps company with the eighteenth-century portrait of Mary Morris and a
host of miniatures. The Colonel's sister Edith, the author, added another exotic
touch to Drishane by erecting a front door surround brought from Ceylon.

Despite the defeat of Parnell, the land troubles abated by the end of the century,
and at the time of Queen Victoria's death there seemed a genuine prospect that
Home Rule for Ireland might be achieved by peaceful means. The situation was not,
however, stable enough to encourage country house building in any quantity,
particularly as there were plenty of properties available vacated by emigrant and
ruined landlords. The businessmen took heart and suburban building thrived,
particularly on the edges of the cities of Dublin and Belfast, and to a lesser degree on
the northern approaches of Limerick. Many of these houses incorporated designs
popularized in England by William Morris – Art Nouveau, stained-glass and
verandas – and in consequence have a distinctly English appearance. At the same
time, too, were built many villas such as that at Rushbrooke, convenient to Cork
city by rail but in a rural setting and with a fine view across the Harbour. Indeed,
Cork Harbour is a microcosm of Irish domestic building, and the visitor who takes
time to travel by boat can pick out, dotted above its shores, many landmarks that
chart much of the chequered course of the history of Ireland's houses. Above the
trees is the massive Monkstown Castle, built for a groat before Cromwell came to

Ireland; near Glanmire a bevy of Georgian seats, including the elegant Lotas of Ducart and Hargrave and the solid Neo-Classical Dunkettle; on its lovely island is Fota, altered by Morrison, just masking from view the old tower-house of Belvelly; high on a distant cliff gleams the white façade of Ringabella House, facing across the mouth of the Harbour to the crescent of Regency coast-guard cottages at Roche's Point; and on Great Island are the steeply rising Victorian terraces of Cobh and the Edwardian villas of Rushbrooke.

Possibly the last great country house to be built in Ireland before the First World War is Hollybrook near Skibbereen, which looks like an English Edwardian house, of the kind showing the influence of Norman Shaw and Edward Lutyens. Completed in 1903 for Colonel Anthony H. Morgan and his wife, it was designed by R. S. Balfour, a Scots architect, who brought foremen and workmen with him from Scotland. The drawing-room is quite a surprise, being entirely panelled in marquetry which was made for a house in Cape Cod by Miss Jane Morgan, the Colonel's aunt, and brought back from America for installation at Hollybrook. Miss Morgan's craftsmanship stands up to scrutiny, even though the stern texts in the inlay like 'Go to the ant, thou sluggard' are a trifle dismaying. The room has a central chimney with two fireplaces. The house is now the residence of Madam O'Donovan, a niece of Mrs A. H. Morgan.

Since the beginning of this century most Irish domestic building has been rather dreary and quite devoid of any national characteristic, save perhaps for the inventive carpenter who carved shamrocks on the bargeboards of the gabled hoods on the little terrace-houses in Roscrea, Co. Tipperary. Even since Independence in 1922 no specifically Irish styles have evolved. Perhaps the tale might have been different had not the declining population left so many beautiful old houses throughout the country looking for buyers, and so many large mansions available for administrative and institutional use. None the less, the fact that so many of these mansions did become convents, religious houses or schools has saved them from almost certain destruction, and in the vast majority of cases the nuns and clerics in charge are most attentive to their maintenance and preservation, for which the future will owe them a deep debt of gratitude. Perhaps in years to come – and not too far distant – enthusiastic Irish architects, disenchanted with merely emulating English or American ideas, will create exciting new buildings, worthy heirs to those of the past.

Hollybrook House, parish of Abbeystrowry, Co. Cork

Left: Edwardian villa, Rushbrooke, Co. Cork

Shamrock bargeboards, Roscrea, Co. Tipperary

Acknowledgments

All the photographs were taken expressly for this book by George Mott, with the following exceptions:

Illustrations on pages 54, 80, 81, 108 (right), 112, 116, 120, 149, 164, 167 (left), 143 and 217 (right) were taken for this book by the Hon. Guy Strutt, to whom we are also grateful for his kindness in reading the text and making many helpful comments; the illustration on page 214 (right) was taken for us by Mr Edward McParland.

The illustrations on pages 65 (above) and 73 are by the Government of Northern Ireland Archaeological Survey and are reproduced by courtesy of the Northern Ireland Ministry of Finance. Illustrations on pages 79 (below) and 212 were kindly supplied from their photographic library by the Northern Ireland Tourist Board, Belfast. Illustrations on page 107 (left and right) by the Green Studios, Dublin, and page 179 (right) are reproduced by courtesy of Mr N. W. English of Athlone. The illustration on page 93 (left), an old photograph, was kindly supplied by Sister M. Mercy, the Presentation Convent, Castle Durrow. The illustration on page 23 was kindly loaned by Lord Muskerry. The illustrations on pages 17 and 69 are reproduced by courtesy of the Trustees of the British Museum, London. The illustration on page 25 (right) is by the National Monuments Branch, Dublin, and is reproduced by courtesy of the Commissioners of Public Works in Ireland. The National Trust, Committee for Northern Ireland, supplied the illustration on page 79 (below). The illustration on page 36 is reproduced by courtesy of the National Gallery of Ireland. The illustration on page 90 is by Mr Howard Konikoff and was kindly loaned by Mr John Griffith of Shannongrove. The maps are by David Eccles.

The plans and drawings were made specially for this book by Mark Berman, to whom we are most grateful.

We must also express our appreciation to Bord Failte Eireann (the Irish Tourist Board) and the Tourist Board of Northern Ireland for their assistance. For useful suggestions in the course of our work we are grateful to many people, particularly Mr Edward McParland, Mr N. W. English and Mr Noel Ross. We also owe a considerable debt to the pioneers in the study of Irish domestic architecture, especially the Hon. Desmond Guinness, Dr Maurice Craig, the Knight of Glin and the late Harold Leask. We wish to thank the Keeper of MSS, Trinity College Library, for allowing us to use and quote from the Beaufort diaries.

Lastly, but most of all, we are extremely indebted to all the gracious, hospitable and patient people, from the castle to the cottage, who opened their doors to us or gave us the freedom of their grounds, and without whose co-operation the book would not have been possible. They are too numerous to mention individually by name but we hope that collectively they will accept our most sincere thanks.

Adams, C. L., *Castles of Ireland*, London 1904.

Brett, C. E. B., *Buildings of Belfast 1700–1914*, London 1967.

Craig, Maurice, *Dublin 1660–1860*, London and Dublin 1952, paperback 1969.

Craig, Maurice, and the Knight of Glin, *Ireland Observed*, Cork 1970.

Curran, C. P., *Dublin Decorative Plasterwork of the Seventeenth and Eighteenth Centuries*, London and New York 1967.

FitzGerald, Desmond, 'Nathaniel Clements and Some Eighteenth Century Irish Houses', *Apollo Magazine*, London, Oct. 1966.

Guinness, Desmond, and Ryan, William, *Irish Houses and Castles*, London and New York 1971.

Leask, Harold G., *Irish Castles*, Dundalk 1941, 3rd edition 1951. Chester Springs, Pa. 1948.

MacLysaght, Edward, *Irish Life in the Seventeenth Century*, Cork 1939, 3rd. edition, Shannon 1969.

MacNamara, T. F., 'The Architecture of Cork 1700–1900', in *Yearbook of The Royal Institute of Architects of Ireland*, Dublin 1960.

Milton, Thomas, *A Collection of select views from the different seats of the Nobility and Gentry . . . in Ireland*, London 1783–93.

Morris, Francis O., *A Series of Picturesque views of seats of the Noblemen and Gentlemen of England and Ireland*, 6 vols, London 1866–80.

Muschenheim, W., *The Elements of the Art of Architecture*, London 1956, New York 1964.

O Danachair, Caoimhin (Danaher, Kevin), 'The Bothain Scoir', in *North Munster Studies*, ed. Eticnne Rynne, Limerick 1967.

Sadleir, T. U., and Dickinson, P. L., *Georgian Mansions in Ireland*, Dublin 1915.

Stalley, R. A., *Architecture and Sculpture in Ireland 1150–1350*, Dublin 1971.

Summerson, John, *Architecture in Britain*, London 1953, 5th edition 1963, paperback 1970, Baltimore 1963.

The Georgian Society Records of Eighteenth Century Domestic Architecture in Ireland, 5 vols, Dublin 1909–13.

PERIODICALS

Journal of the Royal Society of Antiquaries of Ireland
The Irish Ancestor, Dublin 1969–
Irish Georgian Society, Quarterly Bulletins, Dublin 1958–
Country Life

Notes on the text

CHAPTER 1

1 *Guide to the National Monuments of Ireland* by Peter Harbison (Dublin 1970).

2 *A History of the Town and County of Wexford* ed. by W. Hore (London 1900–11).

3 *The Antiquities of Ireland* by F. Grose (London 1791–97).

4 *De Rebus in Hibernia Gestio* (Antwerp 1584).

5 Pacata Hibernica (1586), quoted in 'Notes on Askeaton, Co. Limerick' by T.J. Westropp, *Journal of the Royal Society of Antiquaries of Ireland*, vol. 33.

6 Engraving by P. Sandby, RA, published 1779.

7 F. Grose, op. cit.

8 *Survivors of the Armada* by Evelyn Hardy (London 1966), pp. 37 et seq.

9 *The Treasures of the Armada* by Robert Stenuit (London 1972).

10 Evelyn Hardy, op. cit.

11 Peter Harbison, op. cit.

12 Ibid.

13 Letter patent of 8 November 1310, quoted by E.M. Jope and W.A. Seaby, *Ulster Journal of Archaeology*, vol. 22, pp. 115–18, 1955.

14 A statute of the reign of Henry VI, *The Statutes at Large passed in the Parliaments held in Ireland from the third year of Edward the Second AD 1310 . . .*, ed. by Francis Vesey (Dublin 1765).

15 'The Mint, Carlingford' by H.G. Leask, *Co. Louth Archaeological Journal*, vol. 11, pp. 305–8.

16 Ordnance Survey, quoted in *Irish Castles* by H.G. Leask. The Civil Survey of Co. Tipperary 1654, lists 315 castles in addition to stone houses with bawns. This contrasts with 250 listed by the Ordnance Survey of Co. Tipperary. As most of the 315 were specified as 'wanting repayre' or as a 'stumpe of a castle', 'the walls only standing', an 'old broken down castle' etc., it is likely that their disappearance is accounted for by extensive quarrying.

17 'A Discourse of Ireland (1620)' appearing in *Illustrations of Irish History and Topography Mainly of the Seventeenth Century* by C. Litton Falkiner (London 1904).

18 'Old Castles Around Cork Harbour' by J.C., *Journal of the Cork Historical and Archaeological Society*, vol. 21, July–September 1915.

19 *Alumni Dubliniensis*, ed. G.D. Burtchaell and T.U. Sadleir (Dublin 1935).

20 Calendar of Cork Administration Bonds, Public Record Office, Dublin.

21 *The Antient and Present State of the County and City of Cork* by Charles Smith (Dublin 1750).

22 *The History of the County and City of Cork* by Charles B. Gibson (London 1861).

23 Journal of the Rev. D.A. Beaufort. Library of Trinity College, Dublin, MSS. 4026–33.

24 *Tipperary's Families, being Hearth Money Records for 1665–7* by Thomas Laffan (1911).

25 'On Irish Half Timbered Houses' by W. Frazer, *Journal of the Royal Society of Antiquaries of Ireland*, vol. 21, pp. 367 et seq., 1891.

26 *A History of Dublin* by Walter Harris (Dublin 1766).

27 Rev. D.A. Beaufort, op. cit.

28 *The Civil Survey AD 1654–6* vol. 6, Appendix, 'Kilkenny City and Liberties', ed. Robert Simington (Dublin 1942).

29 John Rothe's will, quoted in *The History and Antiquities of Kilkenny* by William Healy (Kilkenny 1893).

30 These extendable tables were a considerable refinement on the usual 'table boords'.

31 *The Council Book of the Corporation of the City of Cork*, Appendix A, ed. Richard Caulfield (1876).

32 *The Irish Ancestor*, 1970, No. 2, and 1972, No. 1.

33 'Shee's Almshouse, Kilkenny' by J.G. Robertson, *Journal of the Royal Society of Antiquaries of Ireland*, vol. 23, pp. 235–6, 1892

34 Rev. D.A. Beaufort, op. cit.

35 Ibid.

CHAPTER 2

1 *A History of Bandon* by George Bennett (Cork 1869).

2 *The Life and Letters of the Great Earl of Cork* by Dorothea Townshend (London 1904).

3 *A Topographical Dictionary of Ireland* by Samuel Lewis (London 1837).

4 T.J. Westropp, *Journal of the Royal Society of Antiquaries of Ireland*, vol. 34, p. 425.

5 'Ralegh's House at Youghal' by Goddard H. Orpen, *Journal of the Royal Society of Antiquaries of Ireland*, vol. 33, pp. 349 et seq.

6 Ibid.

7 Ibid.

8 'Report of the Commissioners of James I to Enquire into the State of Munster' quoted in *An Anglo Irish Miscellany* by Maurice Denham Jephson (Dublin 1964).

9 *A Census of Ireland, circa 1659 with supplementary material from the Poll Money Ordinances 1660–1661*, ed. Seamas Pender (Dublin 1939).

10 *Philosophical Survey* by Dr Campbell (1775).

11 *A Census of Ireland*, op. cit.

12 Dr Campbell, op. cit.

13 Journal of the Rev. D.A. Beaufort, Library of Trinity College, Dublin, MSS. 4026–33.

14 *Researches in the South of Ireland* by Thomas Crofton Croker (London 1824).

15 'Kilmallock, Co. Limerick' by the Rev. James Dowd, *Journal of the Royal Society of Antiquaries of Ireland*, 9th Series, 1889–90.

16 *Handbook to Galway, Connemara and the Irish Highlands*, illustrated by T. Mahony (London 1854).

17 *Ireland Observed* by Maurice Craig and the Knight of Glin (Cork 1970).

18 *The Civil Survey 1654–6, Co. Waterford*, ed. Robert Simington (Dublin 1931).

19 Charles Alcock to Sir John Percival, 18 April 1663, Egmont MSS, vol. 21.

20 Originals are in Lambeth Palace Library, London.

21 In *An Historical Account of the Plantation of Ulster* by George Hill (Belfast 1877).

22 'Fortification to Architecture in the North of Ireland, 1570–1700' by E.M. Jope, *Ulster Journal of Archaeology*, 3rd Series, vol. 23, 1960.

23 *Ancient Monuments of Northern Ireland, Vol. 2: Not in State Care*, HM Stationery Office (Belfast 1969). Round angled turrets are also cited at Dunluce, Co. Antrim, Mountcastle, Co. Tyrone and Monea, Co. Fermanagh.

24 George Hill, op. cit.

25 *Two Centuries of Life in Co. Down* by John Stevenson (Belfast 1920).

26 'New Light on Jigginstown' by Maurice Craig, *Ulster Journal of Archaeology*, 1972. (Pearce's drawing is at Chatsworth.)

27 Hearth Money Roll for Co. Dublin, 1664. MS. in Society of Genealogists, London.

28 *The Civil Survey 1654–6, Co. Tipperary*, ed. Robert Simington (Dublin 1931).

29 The portrait, now in the possession of Anne, Lady Inchiquin, was illustrated in 'Irish Portraits 1660–1860', *Catalogue* to the exhibition by Anne Crookshank and the Knight of Glin (London 1969).

30 'Lemenagh Castle', *Journal of the Royal Society of Antiquaries of Ireland*, 5th Series, vol. 10, p. 403.

31 Lismore Papers, 16 February 1634, vol. IX, p. 72.

32 'Kinsale in 1641–2' by J.F. Fuller, *Journal of the Cork Historical and Archaeological Society*, vol. 13.

33 Ibid.

34 Inventory of the estate of Thomas Ronaine of the City of Cork, Alderman, taken 5 June 1641, printed in *Journal of the Royal Society of Antiquaries of Ireland*, 2nd Series, vol. 1, p. 75.

35 Egmont MSS.

36 Egmont MSS.

37 Commission of Grace, Cork Roll 3, 13 June, 1 James II, inrolled 28 June 1685; abstracted in the *Report of the Commissioners of the Public Records of Ireland*.

38 *Cork Remembrancer* by Francis H. Tuckey (Cork 1827).

39 'The Old Castles around Cork Harbour' by J.C., *Journal of the Royal Society of Antiquaries of Ireland*, 2nd series, vol. 20, pp. 58–9, 1915.

40 Letters Patent of 15 Charles II (20 September 1639), quoted in 'Everard's Castle, now Burntcourt Castle, near Cahir, Co. Tipperary' by the Rev. John Everard, *Journal of the Royal Society of Antiquaries of Ireland*, vol. 37, 1907.

41 Limerick and Clare Depositions for Losses in the Rebellion of 1641. MS. in Trinity College, Dublin.

42 *The Antient and Present State of the City and County of Cork* by Charles Smith (Dublin 1750).

43 Journal of the Rev. D.A. Beaufort, Library of Trinity College, Dublin MSS. 4026–33.

44 Ibid.

45 The oil painting by James O'Connor, 1819, now at Westport House, Co. Mayo.

46 Rev. D.A. Beaufort, op. cit.

47 Hearth Money Roll of Co. Donegal. MS. 538 in Genealogical Office, Dublin Castle.
48 *Tipperary's Families, being the Hearth Money Records for 1665–6–7* by Thomas Laffan (1911).
49 Samuel Lewis, op. cit.
50 'A description of the County of Westmeath' by Sir Henry Piers, 1682, printed in vol. 1 of *Collectanea de Rebus Hibernicis* by Charles Vallance (Dublin 1770–1804).
51 'Athlone in the seventeenth century' by the Rev. Professor Stokes, *Journal of the Royal Society of Antiquaries of Ireland*, 5th Series, vol. 1, part 1, 1890.

CHAPTER 3

1 Act, 24 September 1657, cited in Firth and Rait, *Acts*, vol. 2, 1255.
2 Letter from John Desminieres to Sir John Percival, 3 June 1684. Egmont MSS., vol. 42.
3 *Calendars of the Antient Records of Dublin*, vol. 4, p. 298.
4 Letter from John Desminieres to Sir John Percival, 3 June 1684. Egmont MSS., vol. 42.
5 Cited in 'On Irish Half Timbered Houses' by W. Frazer, *Journal of the Royal Society of Antiquaries of Ireland*, vol. 21, p. 367 et seq., 1891.
6 e.g. the Desminieres family, Peter Wybrants, will proved 1639, and Cornelius Van Winghen of Dublin, tailor, will proved 1674.
7 e.g. Abraham Vanhoegaerden of Limerick, merchant, will proved 1665, and Allart Clasen Vanwycke of Dundalk, will proved 1639.
8 *Dublin 1660–1860* by Maurice Craig (Dublin 1969). Page 86 gives a drawing of a house in Marrowbone Lane, 1703.
9 *Account of Houses, Hearths and People – Dublin*, made by J. South, 10 January 1695. British Museum, Add. MS. 18022.
10 Hearth Money Roll, Co. Dublin, 1664. Typescript transcript in Society of Genealogists, London.
11 *Irish Houses and Castles* by Desmond Guinness and William Ryan (London 1971).
12 Ibid.
13 'Rathbeale Hall, Co. Dublin' by John Cornforth, in *Country Life*, 24 August 1972.
14 Desmond Guinness and William Ryan, op. cit.
15 There was a family of this surname at Eyrecourt. The *Limerick Chronicle* of 23 September 1815 has an obituary of a Martin of Eyrecourt.
16 *History of Donaghcloney* by the Rev. E.D. Atkinson (Dublin 1898), appendix VI.
17 Ibid., p. 26.
18 Print of Ballintober as it was at the end of the seventeenth century, now in Kinsale Museum.
19 Rev. D.A. Beaufort, op. cit.
20 Reproduced in the *Ulster Journal of Archaeology*, vol. 23, 1960.
21 'Ancient Churches of Ballingarry parish' by Henry Molony, *Journal of the Royal Society of Antiquaries of Ireland*, 5th Series, vol. 15, 1905.
22 Ibid.
23 'The Family of Odell' by Brian de Breffny, *The Irish Ancestor*, vol. 1, No. 2, 1969, and vol. III, No. 1, 1970.
24 Egmont MSS., vol. 23.
25 Egmont MSS., vol. 26
26 Egmont MSS., vol. 28

27 Egmont MSS., vol. 28.
28 Egmont MSS., vol. 23.
29 Egmont MSS., vol. 32.
30 Egmont MSS., vol. 39.
31 Ibid.
32 Ibid.
33 Egmont MSS., vol. 40.
34 Egmont MSS., vol. 41
35 *Historical and Topographical Notes on Buttevant, etc.* by Col. J.C. Grove-White (Cork 1911–13), p. 329. The author erroneously inferred that this was the house as built by Kenn under the agreement of 1670.
36 British Museum, Add. MS. 6948, 16/17. Inventory of Sir John Percival, taken 31 May 1686.
37 Ibid.
38 Egmont MSS., vol. 44.
39 Hearth Money Roll, Co. Donegal. MS. 538 in Genealogical Office, Dublin Castle.
40 *A Topographical Dictionary of Ireland* by Samuel Lewis (London 1837).
41 *Historye of the World* by Sir Walter Ralegh, 1614. Book 1, Chap. 5, Section 5.
42 *Historic Doubts on the Life and Reign of King Richard III* by Horace Walpole (Dublin 1768). He cited the Old Countess having danced with Richard III in evidence that he did not have a crooked back.
43 *The Complete Peerage* by G.E. Cokayne (London 1910–40).
44 Indenture dated 21 July 30th Eliz., Sir Walter Ralegh to Sir John Clever of London, reserving the rights of the 'Ladie Cattelyn old Countess Dowager of Desmond Widdowe', quoted in *Vissicitudes of Families* by Sir Bernard Burke, vol. 2, p. 293 (London 1888).
45 His first wife was alive in 1505, cf. indenture in the Kildare Papers, British Museum, cited in *Dromana* by Terese Muir Mackenzie (Dublin, n.d.).
46 *Observations made on a tour in Ireland, 1681* by Thomas Dineley, National Library of Ireland MS. 392.
47 *The History and Antiquities of the Diocese of Ossory* by the Rev. William Carrigan (Dublin 1905).
48 *The Pooles of Mayfield and other Irish Families* by Rosemary ffolliott (Dublin 1957).
49 *Ireland. Its Scenery, Character, etc.* by Samuel Carter Hall and Mrs (Anna Maria) Hall (London 1841–43).
50 *The Civil Survey of Co. Meath, 1654–6*, ed. Robert Simington (Dublin 1940).
51 Will of William Conyngham, cited in *An Ulster House and the People who Lived in it* by Mina Lenox-Conyngham (Dundalk 1946).
52 *Ulster Journal of Archaeology*, 3rd Series, vol. 1, pp. 81–3.
53 Registry of Deeds, Dublin, 6–1–1332.
54 'Scanlan of the Barony of Upper Connelo' by Brian de Breffny and Alicia E. Evers, *The Irish Ancestor*, vol. IV, No. 2, 1972 (which includes a photograph of the front of the house).

CHAPTER 4

1 'The Burgh or Ville of Youghal' by M.J. Buckley, *Journal of the Royal Society of Antiquaries of Ireland*, vol. 33, 1903.
2 Registry of Deeds, Dublin, 36–127–21789.
3 Registry of Deeds, Dublin, 63–171–43078.
4 Entry of 21 October 1787 in Journal of Rev.

D.A. Beaufort, MS. Library of Trinity College, Dublin.
5 *Ireland Observed* by Maurice Craig and the Knight of Glin (Cork 1970).
6 Ibid.
7 'William Kidwell, Sculptor, *c.* 1664–1736, and some contemporary mason-sculptors in Ireland' by Homan Potterton, Appendix A, *Bulletin of the Irish Georgian Society*, July–December 1972.
8 Registry of Deeds, Dublin, 21–106–10903.
9 Calendar of the wills proved in the Prerogative Court, Ireland, Public Record Office, Dublin.
10 Registry of Deeds, Dublin, 83–127–57901.
11 *Irish Houses and Castles* by Desmond Guinness and William Ryan (London 1971).
12 *Historical and Topographical Notes on Buttevant, etc.* by Col. J.C. Grove-White, vol. 3 (Cork 1913).
13 Desmond Guinness and William Ryan, op. cit.
14 National Library of Ireland MSS. 11,453, 11,455, 11,469, *passim*.
15 *Three Hundred Years in Inishowen* by Amy Isabel Young (Belfast 1929).
16 Registry of Deeds, Dublin, 30–534–19360.
17 Desmond Guinness and William Ryan, op. cit.
18 The designs are at Elton Hall, Peterborough, England.
19 Desmond Guinness and William Ryan, op. cit.
20 Ibid.
21 The designs are at Elton Hall, Peterborough, England.
22 Illustrated in Desmond Guinness and William Ryan, op. cit.
23 Ibid.
24 Registry of Deeds, Dublin, 81–34–55980.
25 Maurice Craig and the Knight of Glin, op. cit.
26 Swanzy MSS., MS. S/10, Library of the Representative Church Body, Dublin.
27 Desmond Guinness and William Ryan, op. cit.
28 Maurice Craig and the Knight of Glin, op. cit.
29 National Library of Ireland MS. 10,139.
30 Calendar of the wills proved in the Prerogative Court, Ireland, Public Record Office, Dublin.
31 Ibid.
32 Illustrated in *Illustrated Glossary of Architecture 850–1830* by John Harris and Jill Lever (London 1966).
33 'Some Country Houses near Athlone' by N.W. English, *The Irish Ancestor*, vol. v, No. 1, 1973.
34 *The Georgian Society Records*, vol. v, p. 105 (London 1913).
35 'Curraghmore, Co. Waterford' by Mark Girouard, *Country Life*, vol. CXXXIII, pp. 256 et seq., 308 et seq., 368 et seq. (London 1963).
36 *The Whole Works of Sir James Ware Concerning Ireland* revised and improved by Walter Harris, vol. 1 (Dublin 1764).
37 'The Noblest Quay in Europe – the City of Waterford' by Mark Girouard, *Country Life*, vol. CXL (London 1966).
38 Registry of Deeds, Dublin, 89–126–62436.
39 Registry of Deeds, Dublin, 139–80–93094.
40 Index to the Dublin Grant Book, Public Record Office, Dublin.
41 *The Antient and Present State of the City and County of Cork* by Charles Smith (Dublin 1756).

42 Rev. D. A. Beaufort, op. cit.

43 *An Introduction to the Abercorn Letters*, ed. John H. Gebbie, pp. 42–3 (Omagh 1972).

44 Ibid.

45 Hazlewood Papers, quoted in *Historical and Topographical Notes on Buttevant, etc.* by Col. J. C. Grove-White, vol. 2 (Cork 1913).

46 *Reflections and Resolutions proper for the gentlemen of Ireland* by Samuel Madden (Dublin 1738).

47 *Two Centuries of Life in County Down* by John Stevenson (Belfast 1920).

CHAPTER 5

1 *Pococke's Tour in Ireland in 1752*, ed. G. T. Stokes, with an introduction and notes (Dublin 1891).

2 'On Irish Half Timbered Houses' by W. Frazer, *Journal of the Royal Society of Antiquaries of Ireland*, vol. 21, 1891.

3 A deed cited in *Dublin Decorative Plasterwork in the 17th and 18th Centuries*, by C. P. Curran (London 1967).

4 'Nathaniel Clements and Some 18th Century Irish Houses' by Desmond Fitzgerald, *Apollo*, October 1966.

5 Registry of Deeds, Dublin, 138–306–93295.

6 Registry of Deeds, Dublin, 156–201–104284.

7 *History of Crosshaven* by Dairmuid O Murchadha (Cork 1967).

8 'Francis Bindon, His Life and Works' by the Knight of Glin, *Bulletin of the Irish Georgian Society*, vol. 10, Nos. 2 and 3, April–September 1967.

9 Registry of Deeds, Dublin, 549–471–364708.

10 Registry of Deeds, Dublin, 103–553–72522.

11 Journal of the Rev. D. A. Beaufort, MS. in Library of Trinity College, Dublin.

12 Faulkner's *Dublin Journal*, 1 July 1758; *Dublin Hibernian Journal*, 24 February 1772.

13 *Dublin Hibernian Journal*, 4 October 1771.

14 Rev. D. A. Beaufort, op. cit.

15 *The Irish Tourist . . .*, by A. Atkinson (Dublin 1815).

16 *A Statistical Account or Parochial Survey of Ireland* by William Shaw Mason, vol. 3 'Parish of Shrule' by Rev. John Graham (Dublin 1819). *The Beauties of Ireland* by J. N. Brewer, vol. 2, p. 278 (Dublin 1826). *The Parliamentary Gazetteer of Ireland*, part 2, p. 358, 1844.

17 *Ireland Observed* by Maurice Craig and the Knight of Glin (Cork 1970).

18 *Irish Houses and Castles* by Desmond Guinness and William Ryan (London 1971).

19 *A Topographical Dictionary of Ireland* by Samuel Lewis (London 1837).

20 'A Baroque Palladian in Ireland: the Architecture of Davis Ducart' by the Knight of Glin, *Country Life*, vol. CXLIII, p. 735 et seq. (London 1967).

21 *An Introduction to the Abercorn Letters*, ed. John H. Gebbie, p. 301 (Omagh 1972).

22 *Bulletin of the Irish Georgian Society*, vol. 4, No. 2, p. 26, June 1961.

23 *Historic Buildings, Groups of Buildings, Areas of Architectural Importance in North Antrim* prepared by W. D. Girvan for the Ulster Architectural Heritage Society (Belfast 1971–72).

24 'The Oldest Registers of Ballingarry Co. Limerick', *The Irish Ancestor* vol. II, No. 1, 1970, and 'Entries from Sampson Cox's Family Bible', *The Irish Ancestor*, vol. V, No. 1, 1973.

25 Vestry books of Ballingarry parish, with list of churchwardens.

26 *A Tour in Ireland with general observations on the present state of that Kingdom, made in the years 1776, 1777 and 1778 and brought down to the end of 1779* by Arthur Young (London 1780).

27 MS. memoranda by Elizabeth Freeman of Nenagh and Ballinware written 1777–86, now in the custody of Miss S. Waller, Prior Park, Co. Tipperary.

28 Ibid.

29 *The Life of James Gandon Esq.*, prepared for publication by T. J. Mulvaney (Dublin 1846).

CHAPTER 6

1 *Headfort & Robert Adam* – drawings from the collection of Mrs Paul Mellon by John Harris, RIBA, 1973.

2 The plans are in the National Library of Ireland.

3 *Irish Houses and Castles* by Desmond Guinness and William Ryan (London 1971).

4 The plans are in the National Library of Ireland and the designs for the ceiling in the Metropolitan Museum, New York.

5 *Historical and Topographical Notes on Buttevant, etc.* by Col. J. C. Grove-White (Cork 1911–13).

6 'An 18th Century Abduction' by Rosemary ffolliott, *The Irish Ancestor*, vol. I, No. 2, 1969.

7 Journal of Rev. D. A. Beaufort, MS. in Library of Trinity College, Dublin.

8 Obituary notice.

9 *Mrs Montague 'Queen of the Blues', her letters and friendships from 1762–1800*, ed. Reginald Blunt (London 1923).

10 British Museum, Additional MS. 11, 7222.

CHAPTER 7

1 *Historical and Topographical Notes on Buttevant, etc.* by Col. J. C. Grove-White, vol. 1, pp. 285–6 (Cork 1911–13).

2 *The Antient and Present State of the County and City of Cork* by Charles Smith (Dublin 1756).

3 Col. J. C. Grove-White, op. cit., vol. 3, p. 46.

4 *Ireland. Its Scenery, Character etc.* by Samuel Carter Hall and Mrs (Anna Maria) Hall (London 1841–43).

CHAPTER 8

1 Godwin's sketchbooks are in the Victoria and Albert Museum, London.

2 *The Belfast Newsletter*, 13 January 1899.

3 *A Topographical Dictionary of Ireland* by Samuel Lewis (London 1837).

4 *Journal of the Royal Society of Antiquaries of Ireland*, vol. 39, p. 271.

5 *The Irish Builder*, 15 August 1876.

6 Ibid., 25 September 1875.

7 Fully reported in ibid., 1 April 1867.

8 Report of the Council of the Royal Agricultural Society of Ireland for 1866.

Glossary

AMBRY A storage recess in a wall.

ARCADE A series of arches carried on piers or columns.

ARCHITRAVE The moulded frame of door or window.

ASHLAR Squared cut stone laid in regular courses with fine joint.

ASTRAGAL A narrow convex moulding, often decorated with a bead.

BALUSTER A small pillar or column supporting a rail or coping, particularly of staircases.

BARBICAN An external defence to protect the entrance to a castle.

BARGEBOARDS Boards set on the slope of a gable to shield the projecting roof timbers from the weather.

BAROQUE An architectural style that flourished in Italy, Austria and Germany, and which was deliberate'y aimed at involving the spectator physically as well as emotionally by its manipulation of mass, space and silhouette.

BARTIZAN A turret corbelled out from an external wall.

BATTER The inward slope of a wall face.

BREAKFRONT A shallow projection, usually in the centre of a façade and always rising the full height of the building.

BELLCOTE A turret intended for a bell or bells.

BLIND ARCADE Arches used decoratively against a wall.

BRESSUMMER A massive beam, usually carrying a projecting superstructure.

BUCRANIUM A decorative motif of the head or skull of an ox.

CAGE-WORK A framework of timber. In seventeenth-century Ireland it was used to describe a house made of lath and plaster.

CANTILEVER A structural member that projects beyond the line of support, used particularly of staircases.

CAPITAL The topmost part of a column or pilaster: its decoration varies with the orders.

CHAIR RAIL The capping of a dado (q.v.).

CLOACINA A privy.

COFFER A recessed decorative panel in a ceiling.

COMPOSITE One of the Roman orders, and the most elaborate of all orders with the most variations. Its capital combines Ionic volutes (q.v.) with the Corinthian foliate bell.

CONSOLE A scrolled bracket.

CORBEL A supporting projection on a wall face, usually of stone, sometimes carved or moulded.

CORNICE A moulded projection which terminates the part to which it is attached.

CORONA Part of a cornice, with a broad vertical face and usually of considerable projection.

COVE, COVING A large, concave moulding, especially that between a ceiling and its cornice.

CRENELLATE To build an indented parapet or battlement.

CROW-STEPPED GABLE One with stepped sides.

CUPOLA A small domed roof; also the interior of a dome.

CURTAIN-WALL The outer wall of a fortress linking flanking towers and gatehouse.

DADO The lower part of a room wall, when faced or coloured differently from the upper part.

DENTIL One of a series of small rectangular blocks projecting from the lower part of a cornice.

DIOCLETIAN WINDOW A semicircular window divided by two upright mullions in such a way that the centre portion is larger than those at the sides.

DORIC One of the Greek orders, characterized by the triglyphs and metopes (q.v.) in its frieze and the mutules (q.v.) under its corona (q.v.). The column has a fluted shaft and no base.

DORMER A small upright window set in a projection from a sloping roof.

ECHELON Parallel formation.

ENTABLATURE In the classical orders the assembly of architrave (q.v.), frieze and cornice (q.v.) supported by a column, or the same on a wall without the column.

FILLET A flat, narrow band, separating two mouldings, or between flutes of a column.

FINIAL An ornament topping a gable, roof, pediment, pier, etc.

FLUTING Decorative effect formed by vertical grooves.

FRONTISPIECE The chief façade, or chief bay, of a building.

GARDEROBE A medieval privy in the walls of a castle.

GARGOYLE A spout, carved as a grotesque human or animal head, projecting from a wall to shed rainwater.

GIBBS (IAN) SURROUND Door or window with a triple keystoned head under a cornice and with blocks of stone at the jambs. Much favoured by the English architect James Gibbs (1682–1754).

HOOD-MOULDING A projecting moulding over a door or window to shed rainwater, usually ending in an outward bend away from the aperture.

IONIC One of the Greek orders, characterized by the volutes (q.v.) of its capitals and the dentils (q.v.) in its cornice (q.v.).

JAMBS The side posts of a doorway, window, etc., especially the stone sides of a fireplace.

KEYSTONE A large wedge-shaped block at the centre of the arch, locking the whole together; also used decoratively on the heads of doors and windows.

LUNETTE A semicircular window, not divided on Diocletian principles.

MACHICOLATION A projecting parapet high on a castle wall and borne on corbels (q.v.), with openings in its floor through which objects or liquid could be dropped on an enemy.

MANSARD A roof with two contiguous slopes, the lower of which is the steeper.

MARBLEIZE To paint in imitation of marble.

MEDALLION A round or oval plaque with carved or painted decoration.

METOPE The square space between the grooved triglyphs in a Doric freize.

MULLION An upright dividing a window into lights.

MUTULE A projecting bracket under corona (q.v.) on a cornice of the Doric order.

NEWEL Either the principal post at the angles of a square staircase carrying the handrail, or the central pillar of a winding stair.

NICHE An arched, semicircular recess in a wall.

OCULUS A small round or oval window.

OGEE-SHAPED A form where the upper part is concave and the lower convex.

PAVILION An ornamental building often attached by wings or walls to the main house; also a summer-house in a garden.

PEDIMENT A low-pitched triangular gable, often placed on the centre of a façade.

PILASTER A rectangular column set against a wall and only projecting slightly from it.

PORTICO A roofed projection (or recess) forming an entrance.

QUOIN Stones – usually decorated or otherwise emphasized – applied to the external angles of a building.

REEDING Decorative effect formed by parallel convex mouldings placed together, usually on a column.

RISER The vertical member between the treads of a stair.

ROCOCO An eighteenth-century form of decoration, characterized by free and fanciful forms, normally without any set symmetrical appearance.

ROMANESQUE A style of building, based on round-headed arches, that preceded Gothic, and was current in the eleventh and twelfth centuries. In Ireland genuine examples only survive in ecclesiastical buildings.

RUSTICATION Stones, usually with a roughened surface, emphasized by deeply recessed joints.

SALOON A lofty reception-room, normally occupying two storeys of the house.

SCAGIOLA Plasterwork of Italian origin intended to simulate stone.

STRING One of the sloping members carrying the ends of the treads and risers of a staircase.

STRING-COURSE A narrow course of stone set horizontally along the external wall of a building.

TAENIA The uppermost fillet (q.v.) on a Doric architrave (q.v.) dividing it from the frieze.

TRIGLYPH Triple groove on Doric frieze.

TUSCAN One of the Roman orders, and a simplified form of Doric. It is very plain and massive.

TYMPANUM The space between the enclosing mouldings of a pediment (q.v.).

VENETIAN WINDOW A tripartite window, with its centre portion arched and wider than the two side openings whose heads are flat.

VESTIBULE A hall between the entrance door and the main body of the house.

VOLUTES The spiral scrolls characteristic of capitals on the columns of the Ionic, Corinthian and Composite orders.

WAINSCOT Panelling in timber.

WALL POST A timber member resting on a corbel (q.v.), and forming part of the truss carrying a hammer-beam roof.

Index

Page numbers in italics indicate illustrations

ABBEVILLE, Co. Dublin 168
Abbeyleix, Co. Leix 124, 178
Abercorn, Earl of 143; 8th Earl of 163; 1st Marquess of 163, 165
Achmet, Dr *see* Joyce, Patrick
Adam, Robert 143, 153–4, 160
Adare, Co. Limerick 178–9; Manor 194
Adderley, Thomas 125
Aldborough, Earl of 178, 181
Aldworth, Richard 91
Alcock, Charles 40
Alexander, Mrs Cecil Frances 211
Allen, Sir Timothy 112; Mr and Mrs William 113
Allenton, Co. Dublin 112, *113*
All Hallows College *see* Drumcondra House
Altamont, Lord 159; *see also* Sligo, Marquess of
Andrews, Hugh 217
Annesbrook, Co. Meath 189–90, *190*
Annesgrove, Co. Cork 84
Anson, Clodagh 183
Arbuthnot, Commander Bernard 35
Archdeacon, John 45–6
Archer, Rose 27
Ardara, Co. Donegal, Parsonage 223–4
Ardbraccan, Co. Meath 86, 102, 106, *159–60*
Ardglass, Co. Down 17
Ardilaun, Lord 222
Ardmulchan, Co. Meath 221
Ardress House, Co. Armagh 155
Armagh, Co. Armagh *104*, 205, *206*, 208
Arthur, Benedict 98, 132; John 98
Ashbrook, Viscounts 94
Ashe, Thomas 132
Ashford Castle, Co. Mayo 222
Ashgrove, Co. Limerick 84
Ash Hill, Co. Limerick 160, 187
Ashley Park, Co. Tipperary 202
Askeaton, Co. Limerick *14*, 15, *126*, 218
Assolas, Co. Cork 75, 92
Athenry, Co. Galway 123
Athlone, Co. Westmeath 56, 123
Athy, Co. Kildare *110*
Atkinson (family) 202; Dr 174; Mr 141
Avondale, Co. Wicklow 160
Aylward, James Kearney 215

BALFOUR, Blaney Townley 163; R.S. 231
Ballea, Co. Cork 48
Ballina, Co. Mayo 179
Ballinaha, Co. Limerick 80–1, 173
Ballingarry, Co. Limerick 37, 64, 65, 66, 80, 172–3
Ballinrobe, Co. Mayo 179
Ballintaylor, Co. Waterford 77
Ballintober, Co. Cork 63
Ballintober Abbey, Co. Mayo 12
Ballintober, Co. Roscommon 12
Ballitore, Co. Kildare 183
Ballyandrew, Co. Cork 202
Ballyboy, Co. Tipperary 48
Ballybunion, Co. Kerry 222
Ballyburly House, Co. Offaly 222
Ballycastle, Co. Derry 41
Ballyclogh, Co. Clare 74
Ballydonellan, Co. Galway *137*, 141
Ballyduff, Co. Cork 117

Ballyfin, Co. Leix *187–8*, 205, 215, 221
Ballygalley Castle, Co. Antrim *41*
Ballygiblin, Co. Cork 199
Ballygrenan *see* Castle Park
Ballyhaise, Co. Cavan *100*, 101
Ballyin, Co. Waterford 183, *184*
Ballykealy, Co Carlow *199*
Ballyknockane, Co. Limerick 81, *173*, 205, *206*
Ballylee *see* Thoor Ballylee
Ballylinch House, Co. Kilkenny 138
Ballymacward, Co. Donegal 71–3
Ballymascanlan, Co. Louth 161, *162*
Ballynacarriga Castle, Co. Cork *16*
Ballynarooga, Co. Limerick 161
Ballynatray, Co. Waterford *165*, 166
Ballynlina, Co. Cork 116
Ballynoe, Co. Limerick 141, 147, *148*
Ballysaggartmore, Co. Waterford *194*
Ballyscullion, Co. Derry 167–8
Ballyshannon, Co. Donegal 71
Ballysteen, Co. Limerick 114
Balmoral, Scotland 212
Banagher, Co. Offaly *125*
Bandonbridge (Bandon), Co. Cork 32
Bangor, Co. Down 119
Bangor, Lord *see* Ward, Bernard
Bantry, and Earl of 141
Bantry House, Co. Cork 103, 138, 141
Barbavilla, Co. Westmeath 84, 100
Barbor, John 70
Barbour, Samuel 220
Bardwell, William 219
Baronscourt, Co. Tyrone 163, *164*, 178
Baronston House, Co. Westmeath 227
Barre, W. J. 220
Barrett, John 62
Barrington, Sir Jonah 181; Lady 181
Bathe, Nicholas 26
Batt, William 227
Bealdurogy, Co. Limerick 172, 202
Bearforest, Co. Cork *189*
Beaufort, Rev. D. A. 24, 37, 53, 64, 88, 113, 124, 138, 148, 156, 161, 164, 166, 180, 191, 193; Mrs D. A. 101, 109, 137; Miss 194
Beaulieu, Co. Louth *60*–1, 107
Beauparc, Co. Meath 130, 216
Bective, Earl of 154
Belfast, Co. Antrim 40, 124, 180, 208, 227; Castle 212; Clanwilliam Ho. (Danesfort) 220
Bellamont Forest, Co. Cavan 97, 130, 133, 146
Belline, Co. Kilkenny *121*, 174, *177*
Bellingham, Sir William 205
Bellinter, Co. Meath 86, *106*, 107
Belmore, Lord 163; Earls of 163
Belvedere, Countess of 209
Belvelly Castle, Co. Cork *22*, *49*
Benduff, Co. Cork 75
Beresford, Rt. Hon. John 169; Lady 72; Sir Marcus 107
Berwick Hall, Co. Down 80, 114
Bessborough, Earl of 192
Bessborough, Co. Kilkenny 133
Bessbrook, Co. Armagh 84, 209
Bettesworth, Richard 64

Bindon, Francis 126, 129, 135
Birr, Co. Offaly 208
Black, Squadron-Leader R. B. 192
Blackrock Castle, Co. Cork 194
Blackrock *see* Bantry House
Blake, Lady 229; Sir Henry Arthur 34, 229; Mrs 137
Blakeney, Lord 117
Blayney, 12th Lord 220
Bonnetstown, Co. Kilkenny *85*, 107, *108*
Bossi 102, 181, 186
Bourke, Lady Anne 136; Mrs 92
Bourneville, England 209
Bowen, Elizabeth 91
Bowen's Court, Co. Cork 91
Boyce, John 205
Boycott, Captain 229
Boyle, Lady Juliana 138; Michael, Archb. of Armagh 47; Richard, 1st Earl of Cork 32–4, 183
Boyle, Co. Roscommon, Abbey 7; King House *88*, 100
Bracegirdle, Rev. George 114
Brandon, Lord 102
Bray, Co. Wicklow *214*, 225
Brazier-Creagh, Capt. W. J. 191
Bredin, J. Bruce 215
Breffny 15, 31
Bristol, Earl of *see* Derry, Earl Bishop of
Brittas, Co. Leix 219
Brooke, Sir Basil 44–5; Sir Henry 45
Browne, Sir George 137; Bishop Jemmett 112–14; John 101; Robert 144
Browne's Hill, Co. Carlow *144–5*
Bruce, Henry 168; Mr 126
Bulkeley, Archdeacon William 42, 59; Archbishop 42
Buncrana, Co. Donegal 94
Bunratty Castle, Co. Clare 12
Burke (family) 31, 193; Edmund 117
Burlington, Lord 89, 141
Burn, William 198
Burncourt, Co. Tipperary 47, 48, 51, *76*
Burnfoot, Co. Derry, Glebe House 223
Burton Hall, Co. Cork 62, 66, *69*, 70–1, 73
Bury, John 90; William 90, 96
Bushfield, Co. Kildare 84
Bushmount, Co. Kerry 202, *203*
Bute, Earl of 145
Butler (family) 11, 43, 54, 155
Byrne (family) 59

CADAMSTOWN, Co. Offaly *185*
Caherdorgan North, Co. Kerry 8
Cahermoyle House, Co. Limerick *220*
Cahernane House, Co. Kerry 221
Cahernarry, Co. Limerick 66
Cahir Park, Co. Tipperary 201, *203*
Caldbeck, W. F. 221
Caledon, Co. Tyrone 208
Cameron, General 230
Campbell, Colen 141, 143; Dr 133; Dr 217
Candler (family) 74
Cane, Alderman Robert 205
Cappoquin, Co. Waterford *126*
Carew, Sir George 34; Lord 95
Carlingford, Co. Louth 18, 19, 123
Carlow, Lord *see* Portarlington, Earl of
Carnelly, Co. Clare 133, 147

Carrick, 1st Earl of 137; 2nd Earl of 155
Carrickfergus, Co. Antrim 17, 40–1, 124; Castle 8
Carrickmacross, Co. Monaghan 179
Carrick-on-Suir, Co. Tipperary 24–5, 42, 54
Carriglea, Co. Waterford 189, *199*, 201, 215
Carton, Co. Kildare 96, 101
Cashel, Co. Tipperary 25, 96, 218; Archbishop's Palace 55, 97
Cassels, Richard *see* Castle, Richard
Cassye, Ann 37
Castle Bellingham, Co. Louth *204*, 205
Castle Bernard, Co. Offaly 194
Castleblayney, Co. Monaghan 226, 227
Castle Carbery, Co. Kildare 130
Castlecoole, Co. Fermanagh 163
Castlecore, Co. Longford 141, *142*
Castle Durrow, Lord *see* Flower, William
Castle Durrow, Co. Leix 92, *93*, 215
Castle Garde, Co. Limerick 194
Castle Hacket, Co. Galway 137
Castlehaven, Co. Cork 172
Castle Hyde, Co. Cork *192*, 193
Castle Leslie, Co. Monaghan 224
Castlemartyr, Co. Cork 161
Castle Morres, Co. Kilkenny 133
Castle Park, Co. Limerick 133, *135*, 136
Castle, Richard 101–2, 105–6, 108, 119, 127, 129–30, 133, 141, 156, 160
Castleroche, Co. Louth 11, 12
Castle Saffron, Co. Cork 191–2
Castletown, Co. Carlow 174, *196*, 197
Castletown, Co. Kildare 95, 112
Castletown, Co. Limerick 51
Castletown Conyers, Co. Limerick 66, 75, *78*, 79
Castletown Cox, Co. Kilkenny 143
Castletown McEnery *see* Castletown Conyers
Castle Upton, Co. Antrim 160, 168
Castleward, Co. Down 144, 150
Catherine's Grove *see* Rathbeale Hall
Caulfeild (family) 161
Caulfield, Sir Toby 41
Celbridge, Co. Kildare 90, *91*
Chambers, Sir William 143, 150, 153, 155, 160, 168
Chancellor's House, Co. Kerry 8
Chapelizod, Co. Dublin 59
Chappell, Henry 222
Charlemont, Earl of 143
Charlemont, Co. Tyrone 41
Charles I 42, 48, 53
Charles II 48, 57
Charleville, Earl of 186
Charleville, Co. Cork 148
Charleville Forest, Co. Offaly 186
Chearnley, Anthony 76; family 51
Chichester, Sir Arthur 41
Chichester-by-the-Sea, Co. Antrim 217
Clanbrassil, Earl of 123
Clancarty, 2nd Earl of 199; 3rd Earl of 227
Clara Castle, Co. Kilkenny 19, *20*, 21
Classiebawn, Co. Sligo 221
Clements, Nathaniel 129–32
Clermont, Co. Wicklow 100
Cléry, Desirée 77; Mr 77

Cloghan, Co. Offaly 205, *206*
Clogheen, Co. Cork 115–17
Cloghprior, Co. Tipperary 149
Clonakilty, Co. Cork 208
Cloncurry, 2nd Baron 188
Clondermot, Co. Derry 41
Clonfert, Co. Galway, Cathedral 7
Clonmacnoise, Co. Offaly 7, 219
Clonmannan, Co. Wicklow 100
Clonmell, Lady 181
Clontarf, Co. Dublin 59
Close, Mr 222
Cloyne, Co. Cork 52
Cobden, Thomas 199
Cobh, Co. Cork *176*, 228, 229, 231
Cochrane, Sir Ernest 216
Cockburn, Messrs 214
Cockerell, Sir Charles 190
Coghill, Sir John 97; Marmaduke 97
Coleraine, Co. Derry 179
Colganstown, Co. Dublin 130, 132
Colley (family) 130; Mary 130
Comerford (family) 74; Richard 94
Congreve (family) 160
Connor (family) 59
Connolly (family) 146; Thomas 95; Mr 185; William 95
Conyers, Charles 78
Conyngham, 1st Marquess 160; 1st Earl 160; 2nd Baron 160; 3rd Baron 160; William 78
Cook, Allan 123
Cookstown, Co. Tyrone 123
Coolbanagher Church, Co. Leix 169
Coole, Co. Galway 137
Cooley, Thomas 151, 156, 163, 168
Cooper, Sir Brian 215; Edward 215; Lt.-Cmdr Edward F.P. 186; Col. Edward H. 186; Edward Joshua 186; John 45; Joshua 185–6; Sir William 215
Coote (family) 215; Anne 133; Sir Charles Henry 187; Chidley 187; Sir Ralph 188; Thomas 97
Coppinger, Sir Walter 39
Coppinger's Court, Co. Cork 39, *67*
Cork, Earl of *see* Boyle, Richard
Cork city 56, 180, 209; Skiddy's Almshouses *89*
Cornell, Mr and Mrs P.A. 201
Cornforth, John 60
Court Devenish, Co. Westmeath 56
Courthorpe (family) 24; Peter 22; Sir Peter 22
Courtney, Sir William 35
Cox, Hugh 148; Sir Richard 70, *91*; Sampson 147; William 141, 147
Coyne, Cathiline 37
Craigdun Castle, Co. Antrim 212
Crawley (Crowley), Benjamin 92
Creagh, Dr John 191; Rev. John B. 202
Creagh Castle, Co. Cork 19, 21, *191*
Croker, Thomas Crofton 37
Cromwell, Oliver 48, 57, 75
Crossguns, Co. Meath *117*
Crosshaven House, Co. Cork *133*
Cullenstown, Co. Wexford 157
Cullinane, Catherine 16
Cuninghame, General Robert 156
Curraghmore, Co. Waterford 72, 107, *108*, 112, *122*

Dalloway, John 41
Dalway's Bawn, Co. Antrim 41
Daly (family) 136–7; Denis 136–7; James 137
Damer, John 87; Joseph 87
Danesfort, Co. Antrim 220
Darby, Jonathan 146
Darnley, Earl of 145
Daunt (family) 24
Davis, Thomas 217
Davitt, Michael 229
Dawes, Howard 98
Deane, Sir Robert Tilson 165
de Arcourt, Daviso *see* Ducart, Davis
de Burgh (Burgho) *see* Burke
de Cogan (family) 12
de Cuellar, Captain 15
Deer Park, Ballinasloe, Co. Galway 227
de Gree, Peter 159
de Jarnac, Comte 197
Delacour, Robert 189
de Lacy (family) 66
Delaford, Co. Dublin 202
Delahoyd, Andrew 98
Delaney, Mrs. 132, 144
de la Poer, Count Edmund 221
Delmege, Christopher 136
de Moleyns (family) *see* Mullins
de Montmorency (family) *see* Morres
de Mortone, Geoffrey 17
Denny, Sir Edward 32
Derry, Earl Bishop of 164, 106–8, 177
Derry, Co. Derry 40, 179
Derryhivenny Castle, Co. Galway *52*, 53
Derrymore, Co. Armagh 178
Desminieres, John 58
Desmond, 7th Earl of 14, 72; 16th Earl of 31, 72; Eleanor, Countess of 73; Katherine, Old Countess of 72
de Verdon, Nicholas 11; Roesia 11
Devonsher, Abraham 143; Abraham J. N. 143; John N. 143
Devonshire, Duke of 183
Dick, W. W. F. Hume 222
Dineley, Thomas 74
Dingle, Co. Kerry 124
Dinis Island, Killarney, Co. Kerry 202
Dobbin, Leonard 208
Doddington, Edward 41
Doe Castle, Co. Donegal 15
Dominick, Elizabeth 129
Donacomper, Co. Kildare *175*, 215
Donaghcloney, Co. Down 62
Donagheady, Co. Tyrone, Glebe Ho. 114
Donamon Castle, Co. Galway 12, *160–1*
Donegal Castle *44*, *50*, 54
Donegall, Earl of 94, 227; Marquess of 211, 227; 5th Earl of 180
Donellan, Anne 137; John 137; Malachy 137
Doneraile, 1st Visct 91; 7th Visct 91; Viscts 181
Doneraile Court, Co. Cork 91, *94*, 180, 191, 215
Dooley, Mr and Mrs J. J. 113
Downer, P. 219
Downhill, Co. Derry 166–8
Downpatrick, Co. Down 17, 123
Doyle (family) 59
Drishane, Co. Cork *104*, 172, *230*
Drogheda, Earl of 146
Drogheda, Co. Louth *26*, 87, 126, *127*, 146
Dromahaire, Co. Leitrim 15; Castle 15
Dromana, Co. Waterford 72–3, 123, *158*, 190–1
Dromoland Castle, Co. Clare 45, 193–4
Dromore Castle, Co. Limerick 217–18, *219*
Dromore Cross, Co. Cork 191
Droumada, Co. Cork 52
Drumcondra House, Co. Dublin *96–7*
Drumsna, Co. Leitrim 179
Dubhan, Saint 10
Dublin city, 17, 26, 56–9, 95, 125, 127–9, 180–2, 209, 225–7; Aldborough Ho. 180; Blessington Ho. 180; the Carbry 26; No. 20 Dominick St *128*, 129; Ely Place *207*; Hume St *207*; Henrietta St 89, 97; Kildare Ho. *see* Leinster Ho.; No. 53 Leeson Pk *220*, 221; Leinster Ho. *2*, 101, 128; Merrion Sq. *180*, 181–2, 202, 205, *207*; Mountjoy Ho. 89; Mountjoy Sq. *207*; Mount St Michael's, No. 83 Merrion Rd 216, *217*; North St George's St *207*; Phoenix Pk 129; Rotunda 127–8; Rossmore Ho. 180; No. 86 Stephen's Green 129; Tyrone Ho. 101; Upper Pembroke St *207*
Ducart, Davis 142–3, 155, 192, 231
Dufour of Paris 201
Duleek, Co. Meath 190
Dundalk, Co. Louth 123
Dundrum, Co. Down 9
Dungannon, Lord 58
Dungannon, Co. Tyrone 88, 130
Dungar *see* Frenchpark
Dungiven, Co. Derry 41
Dunkettle, Co. Cork 231
Dunluce Castle, Co. Antrim 15
Dunmoe, Co. Meath 12, *13*
Dunmore, Co. Kilkenny 62
Dunne, General Francis P. 219
Dunore House, Aldergrove, Co. Antrim 221
Dunsandle, Co. Galway 137
Dunscombe (family) 170

Echlin, Michael 119
Echlinville, Co. Down 64
Edgeworth, Maria 174; Richard Lovell 174
Edgeworthstown, Co. Longford 174
Elgee, Charles 123; William 123
Elizabeth I 25
Elmvale 84
Ely, 4th Marquess of 223
Emo Park, Co. Leix *122*, 169, 187
Emsworth, Co. Dublin *168*
Ennis, Co. Clare 124
Enniskillen, Co. Fermanagh 40, 179
Ensor, George 151, 155; John 151
Esker, Co. Leix 118, *119*
Este, Bishop Charles 109–10
Eustace (family) 31; Robert 26
Everard, Sir Richard 48; Lady 48
Eyrecourt, Co. Galway 61, presbytery *61*

Fanningstown, Co. Kilkenny 177
Fermoy, Lords 143
Fiddown, Co. Kilkenny *81*
Finglas, Co. Dublin 59
FitzGerald (family) 15, 23, 29, 31, 72, 195; Gerald 72–3; Katherine 72–3; Margaret 51; Richard 110
Fitzmaurice (family) 66; Anne 165; James 34
Fitzpatrick, Joanna 43–4; John 44
Fitzwilliam 128
Florence Court, Co. Fermanagh 131
Flower, Capt. Thomas 215; Col. William 92–3, 119
Foley, P. 183
Folliot, Henry, 1st Baron 71; Major John 71; Col. John 71; 2nd Baron 71
Fortwilliam, Co. Limerick 202
Fota, Co. Cork 193, 202, *204*, 231
Francini 15, 108, 112–13, 154, 191
Francklin, Richard 73
French, Arthur 105–6; Dominick 105; John 105; Magdalene 105
Frenchpark, Co. Roscommon 84, 105
Fuller, James Franklin 222

Gabbett, Dorothea 136
Galilei, Alessandro 95, 97, 102, 141
Galway, Co. Galway 29, 37, *38*; Lynch's Castle 29
Gandon, James 150, 168–9, 178, 187
Gandy, Joseph Michael 199
Garbally, Co. Galway 199
Gardiner, Luke 89, 127–9
Garretstown, Co. Cork 84
Gernon, Luke 21, 23
George IV 160, 166, 190
Gibbingsgrove, Co. Cork 205
Gibbs, James 141
Gill Hall, Co. Down 72–3, *73*
Glengall, 1st Earl of 202
Glengariff, Co. Cork 217
Glenstal, Co. Limerick *218–19*, 221
Glenwilliam, Co. Limerick *174*
Glin, 25th Knight of 195
Glin Castle, Co. Limerick 195
Gloster, Co. Offaly 98, *99*, 100, 146
Godfrey, Col. John 55, 76
Godwin, Edward William 218
Goodwin, Francis 200
Goold, Anastasia 45–6; Thomas 45
Gore, Rev. Francis 92; Ralph 74
Gore-Booth (family) 200; Constance 200; Eva 200; Sir Robert 200
Gorges, Hamilton 5
Gort, 2nd Viscount 193
Gracehill, Co. Antrim 178
Graham, Rev. John 142
Graiguenamanagh, Co. Kilkenny 213
Granagh (Granny) Castle, Co. Kilkenny *11*
Grand Canal, Co. Dublin, Twelfth Lock *139*, 185
Grandison, Earl of 123
Grantstown, Co. Leix 11, *13*
Greenhouse, Co. Carlow *174*
Gregory, Lady 137; Robert 137
Griffith, John 90
Grogan, Catherine (Lady Barrington) 181
Gubbins, Blakeney 116; Joseph 117; Mrs Joseph 116
Guinness, Hon. Desmond 16; Richard 131
Gurteen-le-Poer, Co. Waterford 205, *220*, 221

Haggardstown, Co. Louth 202
Halfpenny, William 110, 119
Hamilton, Archibald 212; Rev. James 195; Sir James 42
Handcock, Robert 107
Harberton, Lord 130
Hare Hill, Co. Cork 84
Hargrave, Abraham 151, 192, 231
Harman, Rev. Cutts 141
Harmony Hall, Co. Westmeath 84, *206*, 208
Harris, Cholmeley 187
Harristoun House, Co. Kildare 222
Hart (family) 15
Hartland, Lord 209
Hawkins, Alderman 72; John 72
Hawkins-Magill, Robert 145
Hayes, Sir Henry Browne 166, 177; William 133
Hayman (family) 33
Hazlewood, Co. Sligo *101*, 216
Head (family) 202
Headborough, Co. Waterford *201*
Headfort, Marquess of 154
Headfort House, Co. Meath 154
Hely, Simon 37
Hely-Hutchinson, John 98
Hennessy, Sir John Pope 34
Henn (family) 84
Henry II 8
Henry VII 29
Henry, Hugh 131
Herbert, Dorothea 171; Henry A. 198; Rev. Nicholas 171, Mr 202
Hermitage, Co. Cork 202
Hermitage, Kilcullen, Co. Kildare 202, *203*
Hervey, Frederick Augustus *see* Derry, Earl Bishop of
Hevey, T. 217
Hillsborough, Co. Down 179
Hodder (family) 48
Hodnet, Edmund 22
Holden's Hill, Co. Down 62
Hollybrook, Co. Cork *231*
Hollybrook, Co. Sligo 71
Holywood, Co. Down 42
Howth, Lord 59
Howth, Co. Dublin 59
Hume-Weygand, Mrs 223
Humewood Castle, Co. Wicklow 222, *223*, 224, *225*
Humphreys, William 100
Huncks, Col. 47
Hurly, Symon 37
Hussey, Thomas 142
Huston, John 189
Hutchinson, Emanuel 141; Hugh 141; Margaret 147; Samuel 141
Hyde, John 142

Ikerrin, 8th Viscount *see* Carrick, Earl of
Inchiquin, Lord 47, 64
Ightermurragh, Co. Cork 48, 51, *52*
Ingoldsby, Henry 96
Innishannon, Co. Cork *124*
Ivory, Thomas 151, 156

Jacob, George N. 216
James I 39, 41, 53, 72
James II 71, 81, 83, 190
Jephson, Sir John 64
Jerpoint, Co. Kilkenny 7
Jigginstown, Co. Kildare 42
Johnston, Francis 151, 160, 163, 185–7; John 208; Peyton 142; Richard 151, 156, 163
Johnstown Castle, Co. Wexford 197
Jones, Inigo 141; Sir Theophilus 59; William 33
Joyce, Patrick 135, 181
Joymount, Co. Antrim 41

Kanturk Castle, Co. Cork *38*, 48, 53
Kauffmann, Angelica 154, 166
Kearney (family) 84
Kearny, Patrick 37
Keily, Arthur 194; John 193–4
Kelly (family) 59
Kenn, Benjamin 69; William 66, 69
Kent, William 145
Kenure Park, Co. Dublin 129
Kerry, 20th Lord 66, 147
Kilbline, Co. Kilkenny *74*
Kilbolane Castle, Co. Cork 12
Kilclief Castle, Co. Down 12
Kilcranathan, Co. Cork 115
Kilcrump *see* Mount Odell
Kilcullen, Co. Kildare *203*
Kildare, Earl of 26, 101, 127–8
Kildrought House, Co. Kildare 90, *91*
Kilkee, Co. Clare 217
Kilkenny city 56, 126, *179*, 229; Bishop's Palace *109*, 110; Castle 197; Rothe Ho. *27*; Shee's Almshouse *28*
Killaloe Cathedral, Co. Clare 219
Killashee, Co. Kildare 213
Killiney, Co. Dublin 193, 216, *217*
Killooney, Lord 59
Killowen, Co. Derry 41
Killyleagh, Co. Down 42, *212*
Killymoon, Co. Tyrone 193
Killynether House, Co. Down 222
Kilmainham, Co. Dublin, Royal Hospital 71
Kilmalkedar, Co. Kerry *8*
Kilmallock, 2nd Viscount 62; 4th Viscount 62
Kilmallock, Co. Limerick 15, *36*, 37
Kilruddery, Co. Wicklow *140*, 197–8, 205, 215
Kilshannig, Co. Cork 143
Kiltarton, Baron *see* Gort, 2nd Viscount
Kimberley, Albert 222
King (family) 88, 125; Sir Henry 88, 97
Kingston, 1st Earl of 88; 4th Baron 110, 125
Kingston College, Mitchelstown, Co. Cork *124*, 125
Kinsale, Co. Cork 124; Southwell Almshouses 78
Kirkistown, Co. Down 41
Kirkpatrick, Alexander Richard 215
Knight, Henry 116; James 115–17
Knockgraffon, Co. Tipperary 55, 76; Rectory 114, *170*, 171
Knox, Daphne 108
Kyle, Henry 198

Landsdown, Co. Tipperary 149, *150*, 172
Langley, Batty 146
Lanyon, Sir Charles 42, 198, 212, 219
Lanyon and Lynn, Messrs 212, 214, 224
Laughlin, Henry A. 192
Laugier, Abbé 153
Laurelhill House, Co. Armagh 198
Lawless, Valentine *see* Cloncurry, 2nd Baron
Leamaneh Castle, Co. Clare 11, *44*, 45
Leap, Co. Offaly 146, *147*
Lecky, John James 199
Ledred, Bishop 109
Ledwithstown, Co. Longford *107*
Leeson, Lady Anne 131; Joseph *see* Milltown, Earl of
Le Gros, Raymond 10, 165
Leicester (family) 45
Leinster, Duke of 228
Leixlip, Co. Kildare 146
Le Poer (family) 11; Catherine 107
Leslie, James 132; James F. 132; Bishop Robert 54
Leslie Hill, Co. Antrim 132
Lestrange (family) 205
Lett, Thomas 93–4
Leuventhen 84
Levitstown Mill, Co. Kildare 183, *184*
Limavady, Co. Derry 124
Limerick, 3rd Earl of 217
Limerick city 29, 56, 78, 80, 126, 136, 180
Lisanoure, Co. Antrim 145
Liscarrol, Co. Cork 66
Lisheenanoran, Co. Galway *118*
Lisle, Lord 115
Lismore, 1st Lord 192
Lismore, Co. Waterford 183
Lisnabin, Co. Westmeath *195*, 197
Lissadell, Co. Sligo *200*
Llandaff, 2nd Earl of 197
Lloyd (family) 98, 146; Trevor 98
Lodge, Co. Tipperary 114, *115*
Lodge Park, Co. Kildare *131*
Loftus, Archbishop 38; Lady Dorothy 59
Loftus Hall, Co. Wexford 84, *223*
Londonderry, 5th Marquess of 222
Londonderry city *see* Derry
Lota, Co. Cork 143, 147, 231
Lotabeg, Co. Cork 192, 231
Lough Cutra, Co. Galway 193
Lough Fea, Co. Monaghan 197, *198*
Loughmoe, Co. Tipperary *43*, 44
Loughrea, Co. Galway 179
Love, John 191
Lovett, Christopher 98; Sir Jonathan 146; Susanna 146
Lucan, Co. Dublin 59, 185; Lucan Ho. 155
Lunham, Col. 48
Lurgan, Co. Armagh, Brownlow Ho. 198
Lutrel, John 26; Joan 26
Luttrell, Thomas 59
Luttrelstown, Co. Dublin 59
Lutyens, Edward 231
Lynch (family) 29
Lynn, Henry 212
Lyons House, Co. Kildare 144, *188*
Lysaght, John 115–16; William 115–17, 149

McCalmont, Maj. Victor 155; Hon. Lady 155
McCarthy (family) 15, 31, 48; Charles 48; Donough 38; Florence 75
McClure, Sir Robert 123
McCurdie, J. P. 214, 219
McDarby 174
McDonnell, Charles 133; Sorley Boy 15
McEnery, Simon 66
M'Elwee, Alexander 224; William 223
McMahon (family) 218; Red Mary 12, 45; Sir Tirlogh 45
MacNaghten, 1st Lord 222
McNeill, Sir John Benjamin 199, 200
MacSweeney (family) 15
Macartney, Lord 145
Macosquin, Co. Derry 41
Madden, Samuel 118
Magenis (family) 62
Maghera, Co. Derry 124; Glebe Ho. 27
Magherafelt, Co. Derry 41, 179
Magill, John 72; Sir John 72
Maguire, Joseph 224, 226
Mahon, John 102; Nicholas 102, 105; Thomas 102
Malahide, Co. Dublin 54, 202; Casino 202, *203*
Malcolmson 209
Mallow, Co. Cork 124; Castle *34*, 35, 41, 64
Marino, Co. Dublin 143
Markievicz, Countess 200
Markree, Co. Sligo 185, *186*, 215
Marshall, Robert 129
Martin 61; Elizabeth 194
Maryborough, Co. Leix 31
Maryborough, Douglas, Co. Cork *204*, 205
Massareene, Lord 58
Massy (family) 174; George 174
Mathew, Archbishop David 197; Francis *see* Llandaff; George 197; Father Theobald 197
Mathews, Samuel 108–9
Maunsell, Richard 136; William 136
Maxwell, Bishop Henry 160
Meade, Michael 215; Col. William 62
Meath, Earl of 197, 215
Meenogahane, Co. Kerry 83
Mellifont Abbey, Co. Louth 26
Mellon, Paul 154
Mellon, Co. Limerick *171*, 172
Merrion, Co. Dublin 202
Merry, Commdr and Mrs Douglas 143
Milltown, 1st Earl of 101
Milltown, Co. Clare 185
Milltown, Co. Dublin 217
Minahan, M. 219
Mitchell, Mary Brodrick 165
Mitchelstown, Co. Cork *124*, 125, 194
Moate, Co. Westmeath 179
Monaghan town 124, 208

Monatrea, Co. Waterford 201
Monkstown Castle, Co. Cork 45, 46, 47–8, 230
Montagu, Mrs Elizabeth 178
Moone mill, Co. Kildare 183
Moone, Co. Kildare 132
Moore (family) 213; Andrew 92; Jane 90
Moore Abbey, Co. Kildare 146
Morgan, Anthony H. 231; Jane 231
Morgans, Co. Limerick 80, 114
Morough, William 185
Morres (family) 155, 193
William 75, 230
Morris, Fortunatus 75; Mary 230; William 75, 230
Morrison, John 125, 151, 169; Sir Richard 151, 169–71, 173, 187–9, 193, 197–8, 205, 231; William Vitruvius 193, 205
Mosse, Dr 127
Mountbatten, Earl 221
Mount Congreve, Co. Waterford 160
Mount Desart, Co. Cork 170
Mount Falcon, Co. Mayo 222
Mount Ievers, Co. Clare 90–1
Mountjoy, 2nd Lord 182
Mount Juliet, Co. Kilkenny 84, 138, 154–5
Mount Kennedy, Co. Wicklow 156
Mount Long, Co. Cork 46, 47
Mount Long, Co. Limerick 80
Mount Odell, Co. Waterford 77
Mount Oliver, Co. Louth see Mount Pleasant
Mount Ophaley (Mount Ophelia), Athy, Co. Kildare 110
Mount Pelier, Co. Dublin 141
Mount Pleasant, Co. Limerick 80
Mount Pleasant, Co. Louth 200
Mount Stuart, Co. Waterford 123
Mount Temple, Co. Sligo 157, 202
Mount Uniacke, Co. Cork 84
Movanagher, Co. Derry 41
Movilla Castle, Co. Galway 105
Moyvanine, Co. Limerick 75, 76, 77
Muckross House, Co. Kerry 198, 202
Mullins (family) 193
Murray, Mrs E.A.S. 173
Musgrave (family) 217
Muskerry, Lord 23; 1st Baron 165
Mussenden Temple, Co. Derry 167–8
Myrtle Grove, Youghal, Co. Cork 33–4, 229–30, 230

Nash, John 193, 201
Neale, J.P. 187
Nenagh, Co. Tipperary 9
Newberry Hall, Co. Kildare 130–1
Newbridge, Co. Dublin 129
Newburgh, Arthur 100; Brockhill 100; Col. Thomas 100; William Perrott 100
Newcastle, Co. Longford 141
Newcastle West, Co. Limerick 15, 35, 37, 229
Newenham, John 143
New Geneva, Co. Waterford 178
Newhall, Co. Clare 78, 133, 134, 135
Newman, Misses 48
Newport, Co. Mayo 200, 201
New Ross, Co. Wexford 56
Newry, Co. Down 40
Newtown (Ballynoe), Co. Cork 117
Newtown Pery, Limerick 180
Norreys, Sir Thomas 33–5

Oak Park, Co. Kerry 213
O'Brien (family) 78; Conor 45; Edward 220; Sir Edward 193; John 90; Red Mary 12, 45
O'Bryen, Helena 76
O'Byrne (family) 42
O'Carroll (family) 146
O'Casey, Sean 137
O'Connor (family) 12; Cathal Crowdeag 12; Rory 8
Odell (family) 217; Catherine 201; Charles 64, 66, 77–8; Frances 173; John 64, 66, 78, 147, 172, 198; John FitzCharles 161; Thomas 172; Col. William 172–3

Odellville, Co. Limerick 161, 162
O'Donel (family) 200
O'Donnell (family) 15; Hugh Roe 44
O'Donovan, Madam 231
O'Grady, Hon. Waller 194
O'Hurley (family) 16; Randal 16
Oldbawn, Co. Dublin 42, 59
Old Conna House, Co. Wicklow 214
Oldcourt, Co. Cork 202
Oliver, Philip 92
O'Madden, Daniel 52–3
Omagh, Co. Tyrone 179
O'More (family) 31
O'Neill (family) 31; Hugh see Tyrone, Earl of
Oranmore, Co. Galway 137
Ormond, Earl of 25
Ormonde, Duke of 25, 40, 54, 57–9, 62; Marquess of 197
Ormsby, Edward 135
O'Rorke (family) 31
O'Rorke's hall, Co. Leitrim, 15
Orrery, Earl of 14, 66
Osborne, Sir John 40; Nicholas 40; Patrick 143, 155; Sir Richard 39, 77; Sir Thomas 40
O'Shee (family) 28
O'Sullivan (family) 31
O'Sullivan Bere, Sir Owen 55
Oswald, Bishop John 54
O'Toole (family) 42
Ott, Theresia Pauline 191
Otway, James 149
Oughterard, Co. Galway 178

Pain, George Richard 193–4; James 193–4
Pakenham-Mahon, Mrs 102
Palladio, Andrea 84, 96–7, 130
Pallas, Co. Limerick 64, 66
Palmer, Francis 129
Palmerstown, Co. Dublin 59
Parker, William 150
Parnell, Charles Stewart 160, 229, 230
Parsons, Laurence see Rosse, Earl of; Sir Laurence 34, 208; Sir William 58
Parsonstown see Birr
Pearce, Sir Edward Lovett 42, 88–9, 95–8, 119, 127, 129–30, 133, 141, 146
Percival (family) 62; Sir John 40, 58, 66, 70, 71; Sir Philip 45, 69, 70; Philip 45
Perrot, Sir John 36
Pery, William see Limerick, 3rd Earl of
Peters 144
Peter Stott Martin House, Co. Antrim see Craigdun Castle
Philips, Noblet 143
Philipstown, Co. Offaly 31
Phillips, Richard 59; Sir Thomas 41
Phoenix Lodge, Co. Dublin 59, 129
Pierse (family) 83
Pike, Mary 166
Pilkington, William 131
Piranesi, 153
Playfair, William 198
Plunkett, Oliver 60; Thomas 47; Sir Walter 59, 60
Pococke, Bishop Richard 109, 123
Pole, William Wellesley 187
Pomeroy, Arthur see Harberton, Lord
Portarlington, Co. Leix 111, 125
Portarlington, Earl of 150, 168–9, 189; 2nd Earl of 187
Porthall, Co. Donegal 112
Portlaw, Co. Waterford 209
Portrush, Co. Antrim 220
Portumna Castle, Co. Galway 53, 54, 136–7, 140, 191
Power (family) 31; Alexander 39, 40; Richard 39
Powerscourt, Co. Wicklow 101, 107
Powerscourt, 1st Viscount 101
Preston (family) 106; John 106
Priestley, Michael 112
Prince Regent see George IV
Prior Park, Co. Tipperary 149
Pugin, Augustus Welby 205

Purcell, Richard 43; Theobald 43–4; Thomas 43
Purdon, Capt. Denis J.D. 195; Edward 195

Queenstown see Cobh

Raford, Co. Galway 133, 136
Ralegh, Sir Walter 22, 32–3, 72
Randalstown, Co. Antrim 205
Raphoe, Co. Donegal, Bishop's Palace 54
Rathbeale Hall, Co. Dublin 59, 60, 84, 131
Rathfarnham Castle, Co. Dublin 38, 59, 129
Rathfryland, Co. Down 72
Rathkeale, Co. Limerick 173
Rathmore, Co. Galway 136
Raven, Thomas 41
Red House, Youghal, Co. Cork 84, 87
Reenadisert, Co. Cork 55
Reeves, Mrs 150
Reid, Dr Thomas 209
Repton, Humphry 190, 201–2
Richard III 72
Richardson, Edward 63
Rich Hill, Co. Armagh 62–4, 65
Rickman, Thomas 197
Ringabella House, Co. Cork 231
Riverstown, Co. Cork 68, 112, 113
Roberts, John 108
Robertson, William 197
Robinson, John 92; Richard 131
Roch, George 11
Roche, Edmond-Edward 143; Stephen 77; William 28
Rochfort (family) 209
Rogers, Christopher 143; George 143; Noblet 143; Robert 143
Rokeby, Co. Louth 178
Rorke, Edward 11
Roscrea, Co. Tipperary 231; Damer Ho. 84, 87
Rose, George 80; Henry 80; Thomas 80
Rosse, 1st Earl of 142; 2nd Earl of 208
Rossmore, Lord see Cuninghame, Robert
Rossmore Park, Co. Monaghan 198
Rothe, John 27–8; Peter 27–8
Rothery, George 90; Isaac 90–1; John 90–1; Joseph 91; Nathaniel 90; Thomas 90; William 90
Rudd, John 93–4
Runkerry House, Co. Antrim 222
Rushbrooke, Co. Cork 101, 230, 231
Russborough, Co. Wicklow 131, 133
Ryan (family) 74; Mrs 118; Thady 94

St Anne's, Raheny, Co. Dublin 222
St Brendan's House, Co. Kerry 8
St Cleran's, Co. Galway 189
St George, Ussher 129
St Leger (family) 91; Elizabeth 91
Sabatier, John 110
Sandes, Maurice FitzGerald 213
Sandymount, Co. Dublin 202
Santry, Co. Dublin 59
Sarsfield (family) 28
Saunders Grove, Co. Wicklow 100
Scanlan, Capt. Michael 173
Schuyler, Cornelia 143
Scott, Sir Gilbert 211, 213
Seafield, Co. Dublin 98, 99, 132, 216
Shanahan, Michael 166–7
Shanid, Co. Limerick 9
Shankill Castle, Co. Kilkenny 195, 196, 197, 215, 216
Shannon, Earl of 70
Shannongrove, Co. Limerick 85, 90–1, 96, 172
Shaw, Bernard 47–8; Bernard Robert 48; George Bernard 48; James 41; Norman 231
Shee, Marcus 28; Sir Richard 28
Sheephouse, Co. Meath 77
Shelswell-White, Mrs Clodagh 141
Shirley (family) 197; Evelyn John 197; Major J.E. 198
Shortall, Thomas 74

Shrewsbury, 1st Earl of 76
Singleton, Henry 87
Skiddy, Clement 89
Slane, Co. Meath 178
Slane Castle, Co. Meath 160, 186, 190
Sligo, 1st Marquess of 156; 10th Marquess 159
Sligo town 126
Smith, Charles 51, 136, 191; Henry 190; Nicholas 135–6; Rebecca 136; Thomas 69, 70–1
Smith-Barry, John 193
Smyth (family) 52, 217; Beverley 52; Elizabeth 166; Grice 165–6; Rev. Percy 201; Percy 52
Soane, Sir John 164, 178, 199
Somerville, Brig. Desmond 172; Edith 172, 230; Thomas 172; Col. Thomas C.F. 230
Southwell, Robert 66, 78
Spenser, Edmund 91
Speranza see Wilde, Lady
Spring (family) 24
Springfield Castle, Co. Limerick 8, 22–3, 165
Springhill, Co. Derry 78, 79
Stamer, George 133
Stanley, Sir Thomas 40
Stapleton, Michael 155–6, 181
Stephens, Sir John 59
Stewart (family) 198; George 163; William 123
Strabane, Co. Tyrone 143
Straffan House, Co. Kildare 216
Strafford, Earl of 42
Strancally Castle, Co. Waterford 193–4
Strokestown, Co. Roscommon 102, 209
Strokestown House, Co. Roscommon 102, 105, 106
Stupinigi, Italy 142
Summer Grove, Co. Leix 111, 112
Supple, Edmond 51
Supple's Court, Co. Cork see Droumada
Swanlingbar, Co. Cavan 124
Swift (family) 62; Godwin 62; Dean Jonathan 62, 127; Thomas 62
Swiftsheath, Co. Kilkenny 62, 63
'Swiss Cottage', Cahir Park, Co. Tipperary 201, 203
Synge, J.M. 137

Talbot, John 59; Sir John 76
Talbot Castle, Trim, Co. Meath 76, 195
Tallow, Co. Waterford 205
Tara, Co. Meath 116, 117
Templeton, Lord 154
The Aske, Co. Dublin 224, 225
The Grove, Co. Limerick 172, 173
The Hook, Co. Wexford 10, 11, 165
The Neale, Co. Galway 137
The Turret, Ballingarry, Co. Limerick 64, 65, 66, 78, 172
Thomastown, Co. Tipperary 197, 204, 205
Thomastown Castle, Co. Tipperary 196, 205
Thompson, Hugh 194
Thoor Ballylee, Co. Galway 24
Tichbourne, Sir Henry 60
Tickincor, Co. Waterford 39, 40, 77
Tinode House, Co. Wicklow 221
Tobin, Catherine 48
Toler-Aylward, Maj. H.J. 197
Townley Hall, Co. Louth 163, 186
Townsend, E. 224
Trabolgan, Co. Cork 143
Tralee, Co. Kerry 32, 124, 208, 213
Trim Castle, Co. Meath 8, 9
Truell, Holt 100
Trumbull, Frank 94
Tuck, Isaac 93–4
Tuckey, Francis H. 48
Tullamore, Lord 90
Tullamore, Co. Offaly 179
Tully, Mrs 144
Tyrone, Earl of 40; Earls of 159; Lord 72

Tyrrellspass, Co. Westmeath 209

Uniacke (family) 84
Upper Dromore House, Co. Cork 165
Ussher (family) 217

Vanbrugh, Sir John 96, 108, 141
Vaughan, George 94; Capt. Henry 94; John 112
Ventry, Lords 193
Verdon, William 28
Vereker, Col. Charles see Gort, 2nd Visct.
Vernon, Col. Edward 59
Vernon Mount, Co. Cork 166, 167
Vesey, Agmondisham 155; Thomas 124, 178
Victoria, Queen 230
Vierpyl 95
Villiers, Edward 73; Sir William 15
Villiers-Stuart, Henry 190, 205
Villierstown, Co. Waterford 123, 204, 205
Vincent, Thomas 59
Von Feinagle, Professor 181

Waller, George 149; Sir Hardress 51; Sally 149
Walsh, John 177; Peter 177
Walterstown, Co. Meath 205
Ward, Bernard 144–5; 150; Lady Anne 145, 150
Wardhouse, Co. Leitrim 117, 118
Wardtown see Ballymacward
Waring, William 62
Waringstown, Co. Down 62
Waringstown Ho. 62
Waterford city 56, 126, 155, 206, 216, 229; Bishop's Palace 110
Waterford, Marquess of 209; Louisa, Marchioness of 159
Waterston, Co. Westmeath 107
Weir, Mr 124
Wellington, Duke of 195
Wentworth, Thomas see Strafford, Earl of
West, Robert 111, 129, 154–5
West Johnnea, Co. Cork 115
Westport, Co. Mayo 124, 156, 159
Westport House, Co. Mayo 101, 156
Westropp, Grace 171; John 171; Rose 171; T.J. 33
Whaley, Caroline 187; Richard Chapell 129
Whelan, Mr and Mrs Barrie 111
Whetcombe, Tristram 46–7
Whistler, James McNeill 218
White, Richard 141; William 222
Whitechurch, Co. Waterford 113
White House, Co. Antrim 41
White-Spunner, Col. 150
Whyte, Gerard 90
Winckelmann, Johann Joachim 153
Wilde, Oscar 123, 218; Lady 123
William III 58, 81, 83, 114, 190
Williamstown, Co. Kildare 130
Wingfield, Richard see Powerscourt, Visct.
Wolfe, Father 29
Woodstock, Co. Kilkenny 133
Wood Village, Lisheenanoran, Co. Galway 118, 120
Woodward (family) 149
Woolstenholme, Edward 131
Worlledge Sybil 174
Wrixon (family) 92
Wrixon-Becher (family) 92; Sir William 199
Wyatt, James 106, 156, 159–60, 163, 186
Wynne, Lucy 171; Owen 101

Yarner, Abraham 100
Yeates, Benedict Arthur 132; Samuel 132
Yeats, William Butler 24, 137
Youghal, Co. Cork 32–4, 84, 87, 229, 230; South Abbey House 221
Young, Arthur 149

Zucchi, Antonio 159